THE COMPLETE IDIOT'S GUIDE® TO

200-300-400 Calorie Meals

by Heidi Reichenberger McIndoo, MS, RD, LDN, and Ed Jackson

ALPHA

A member of Penguin Group (USA) Inc.

ALPHA BOOKS

Published by Penguin Group (USA) Inc.

Penguin Group (USA) Inc., 375 Hudson Street, New York, New York 10014, USA • Penguin Group (Canada), 90 Eglinton Avenue East, Suite 700, Toronto, Ontario M4P 2Y3, Canada (a division of Pearson Penguin Canada Inc.) • Penguin Books Ltd., 80 Strand, London WC2R 0RL, England • Penguin Ireland, 25 St. Stephen's Green, Dublin 2, Ireland (a division of Penguin Books Ltd.) • Penguin Group (Australia), 250 Camberwell Road, Camberwell, Victoria 3124, Australia (a division of Pearson Australia Group Pty. Ltd.) • Penguin Books India Pvt. Ltd., 11 Community Centre, Panchsheel Park, New Delhi—110 017, India • Penguin Group (NZ), 67 Apollo Drive, Rosedale, North Shore, Auckland 1311, New Zealand (a division of Pearson New Zealand Ltd.) • Penguin Books (South Africa) (Pty.) Ltd., 24 Sturdee Avenue, Rosebank, Johannesburg 2196, South Africa • Penguin Books Ltd., Registered Offices: 80 Strand, London WC2R 0RL, England

International Standard Book Number: 978-1-61564-186-4
Library of Congress Catalog Card Number: 2012930858

14 13 12   8 7 6 5 4 3 2 1

Interpretation of the printing code: The rightmost number of the first series of numbers is the year of the book's printing; the rightmost number of the second series of numbers is the number of the book's printing. For example, a printing code of 12-1 shows that the first printing occurred in 2012.

Printed in the United States of America

Note: This publication contains the opinions and ideas of its authors. It is intended to provide helpful and informative material on the subject matter covered. It is sold with the understanding that the authors and publisher are not engaged in rendering professional services in the book. If the reader requires personal assistance or advice, a competent professional should be consulted.

The authors and publisher specifically disclaim any responsibility for any liability, loss, or risk, personal or otherwise, which is incurred as a consequence, directly or indirectly, of the use and application of any of the contents of this book.

Most Alpha books are available at special quantity discounts for bulk purchases for sales promotions, premiums, fund-raising, or educational use. Special books, or book excerpts, can also be created to fit specific needs. For details, write: Special Markets, Alpha Books, 375 Hudson Street, New York, NY 10014.

Publisher: *Marie Butler-Knight*
Associate Publisher: *Mike Sanders*
Executive Managing Editor: *Billy Fields*
Executive Acquisitions Editor: *Lori Cates Hand*
Senior Development Editor: *Christy Wagner*
Senior Production Editor: *Kayla Dugger*

Copy Editor: *Amy Lepore*
Cover Designer: *Kurt Owens*
Book Designers: *William Thomas, Rebecca Batchelor*
Indexer: *Johnna VanHoose Dinse*
Layout: *Ayanna Lacey*
Senior Proofreader: *Laura Caddell*

To the three people I enjoy cooking for and with the most: Sean, Laila, and Colin. And to my mom, for her tireless support. —Heidi

To Cicely, my best fan. —Ed

Contents

Introduction

Over the years, countless diets have promised quick and lasting weight loss. Those wishing to whittle down their waistlines have been told to cut out carbs, cut out fat, eat only cabbage soup, eat only one meal a day, ... the list goes on and on.

Most of these diets are unhealthy, requiring elimination of an entire food group or food type, which could lead to missing out on essential nutrients. Some encourage very low calorie intakes—a setup for failure because they slow down your metabolism, training your body to survive on fewer calories and making weight loss even more difficult. Very-low-calorie diets also aren't practical in the long term because they leave you feeling frequently hungry and result in overeating and bingeing—again, a setup for failure.

So is there a method to lose weight successfully—and keep it off? Yes! And it doesn't require making drastic changes that are difficult to maintain, cutting out your favorite foods, or subsisting on only steamed veggies and tofu. In fact, including your favorite foods is one of the tricks to losing weight and keeping it off!

To lose pounds, and not find them again and again, you need to adopt new eating habits that you can live with. That means finding ways to fit your favorite foods, even if they're less than healthy, into your eating plan. It means gradually making small changes in your habits instead of overhauling everything all at once.

Successful weight loss requires cutting your calorie intake enough to lose 1 to 2 pounds a week but not so much that you're depriving your body of necessary energy and nutrients. And finally, to shed pounds and keep them off, you need to have an arsenal of delicious, nutritious, and moderate-in-calorie meals and snacks to enjoy throughout the day.

Luckily for you, all of these concepts are explained in the following pages to get you well on your way to a healthier weight.

To help you out a bit when you're selecting recipes to try, we've organized the recipes in each chapter by calorie content. The lowest-calorie recipes are in the beginning of the chapter, and the calorie level increases as you go toward the end of the chapter.

How This Book Is Organized

This book is divided into five parts:

Part 1, Nutrition Know-How, gives you the basics of healthy eating, including the nutrients your body requires and tips for figuring out your calorie needs. We explain how to create a balanced meal and what kitchen staples you should always have on hand to make doing so easier. Lastly, we give you 2 weeks of menus for three different calorie levels.

Part 2, Unbeatable Breakfasts, gives you a variety of delicious and nutritious ways you can start your day while still sticking to your healthy eating plan. You'll find recipes for egg lovers, pancake fanatics, and much more.

When it's time for your lunch break, flip through the chapters in **Part 3, Luscious Lunches,** to find a bevy of energizing lunch ideas. You'll find warming soups, chilled salads, and countless sandwiches and wraps.

Part 4, Delicious Dinners, offers no shortage of meals when the dinner bell rings. You'll find recipes for meat lovers and vegetarians, from entrées, to one-dish dinners, to side dishes, plus belly-warming stews and soups you can cook in your slow cooker.

Part 5, Sassy Snacks, is where to turn when you're looking for something to satisfy your midday hunger. You'll also find yummy drinks and snacks for when you're on the run.

At the back of the book, we've included a glossary of helpful terms plus a list of further resources you can use to learn more about enjoying low-calorie cooking.

Extras

You'll notice sidebars of extra information scattered throughout the chapters. Here's what to look for:

DEFINITION

The worlds of nutrition and cooking are considered sciences. And like most sciences, every now and then you run across a word you may not recognize or just aren't quite sure what it means. These sidebars explain what those words mean.

CULINARY KNOW-HOW

These sidebars teach you some of the little tips and tricks chefs know and use to help make cooking easier, safer, and more efficient.

TASTY TIDBIT

In these sidebars, you'll find little nuggets of nutrition or cooking knowledge to give you a better understanding of why certain ingredients, cooking methods, or other techniques are used.

MAKE IT A MEAL

These sidebars let you know what other recipes or foods can be paired with a recipe to round out the meal.

Acknowledgments

Although only two names appear on the front of this book, you certainly wouldn't be holding it in your hands now without a lot of behind-the-scenes help.

We'd like to thank Marilyn Allen for believing we were the right people to bring this book to life. And we'd like to thank Lori Cates Hand and Christy Wagner for answering all our questions along the way and guiding us in the right direction to make this the best book it could be.

From Heidi:

I would also like to thank Sean for all his support and encouragement with this and any and all projects I get myself into; Laila and Colin for sharing Mommy with the computer more than they'd like to; my mom, Sandy Swadley, for all her extra help with whatever needed to be done; and Gretchen, Mia, and Lauren DeMore for hosting extra play dates.

And I would like to thank the tireless recipe testers who donated their time and palates (and those of their unsuspecting families) to ensure each and every recipe was as yummy as it was healthy: Ali Corton, Gretchen DeMore, Diane Desautelle, Michelle Feudo, Deb Goeschel, Lauren Knight, Sally Kuzemchak, Gail MacCleverty, Kirsten Marafioti, Fatima Mavrikis, Sharon Shearman, Sandy Swadley, and Jo Willingham. Thank you.

From Ed:

I would like to thank all those who took the time to test recipes as well: Amanda Moore, Andy Dixon, Ann Schauffler, Anne Engelhart, Barbara Bools, Barbara Strell, Becky Sue Epstein, Beth Gould, Beth Guertin, Betsy and Walter Leutz, Bonnie Jackson, Branko Gerovac, Brenda Deutsch, Brenda Dziadzio, Bryan Stroup,

Caroline Walters, Cas Groblewski, Cheryl Meadow, Chloe Durant, Cicely Hall, Cristina Burwell, Cynthia Revelle, Dave and Diane Abe, Debbie DeBotton, Doug Durant, Ellie Baker, Fran Sullivan, Fred Johnson, Gordon Hardy, Hanna Pink, Harriet Peterson, Heather Craig, Howie and Beth Bernstein, Jane Spickett, Janet Farnsworth, Jean Foster, Jen Vogelzang, Jenny Marshall, Joellen Masters, Julie Bentley, Karen Longeteig, Kevin McCarthy, Lauren Franzblau, Leslie Griffin, Linda Degnen, Lisa Caldwell, Lydia Swan, Maggie Herzig, Marilyn Falkowski, Meg Muckenhoupt, Melinda Saris, Molly Dunn-Hardy, Paula Grace O'Connell, Peter Holton, Rachel Hyde, Rachel LeBlanc, Rob Hardy, Robin Steele, Sally Cassells, Sandy Stone, Stan Griffith, Susan Weycher, Theresa Condict, and Zoe Meadow.

Special Thanks to the Technical Reviewer

The Complete Idiot's Guide to 200-300-400 Calorie Meals was reviewed by an expert who double-checked the accuracy of what you'll learn here, to help us ensure that this book gives you everything you need to know about cooking delicious, nutritious meals that fall within your calorie restrictions. Special thanks are extended to Densie Webb, PhD, RD.

Trademarks

Nutrition Know-How

It's tough to open a magazine or webpage, or turn on the television or radio, without being told about the latest and greatest way to lose weight. Unfortunately, the majority of these are fad diets that don't work as promised, are unhealthy, or both!

The reality behind losing excess weight and keeping it off is just a bit of science— balancing what you take in with what you burn off. The chapters in Part 1 help you figure out how many calories your body needs as well as how to turn those numbers into real food so you know what and how much you should be eating.

Then, to make it even easier, we offer three 2-week meal plans of differing calorie levels to help get you started with your new balanced, healthy eating plan. These meal plans feature some of the hundreds of delicious recipes in Parts 2 through 5 to make eating healthy a breeze.

Nutrition 101

In This Chapter

- Carbohydrates: your body's fuel
- Filling protein, fat, and fiber
- Knowing your nutritional needs
- What not to do while dieting

One of the keys to successful and lasting weight loss is understanding what you're eating and why you're eating it. When you realize the role different foods play in reaching your weight-loss goals, you can make the appropriate choices—and changes—in your eating habits. If your goal is to lose weight by watching your calories, you need to learn how many calories and other nutrients are in the foods you eat. Armed with that information, you'll begin to look at food differently, and you'll begin to eat a healthier diet.

In this chapter, we go over some of the basics of nutrition, including how many calories you need in a day, so you can make better and more nourishing food choices.

Getting Your Major Nutrients

You've probably heard the terms *protein*, *carbohydrates*, and *fats* bantered about. Usually it's in the context of someone telling you *not* to eat this one or to *only* eat that one. In reality, all three play vital roles in keeping you strong and healthy, and you need all of them. Yes, even fats.

Essential Protein

Protein is essential to life. It forms the main part of your body's building blocks that create muscles, tissue, cells, hormones, and more. When you're trying to lose weight, protein plays another crucial role: because your body digests it slowly, protein keeps you feeling fuller longer. That means eating protein regularly throughout the day can help keep the hungries at bay and prevent you from feeling hungry or deprived.

Aim for roughly 20 percent of your daily calories to come from protein. Another way to look at it is that just under $\frac{1}{4}$ of each meal and snack should be protein, if possible. Protein-rich foods include meats, fish, poultry, tofu, dairy, nuts and nut butters, and eggs.

Energizing Carbs

Carbohydrates are basically the opposite of protein. They're still essential, but they're used more immediately and aren't body builders like protein is. Because carbs are used quicker, they're digested quicker as well. So after you eat carbs (by themselves), you'll find yourself feeling hungry again soon after. And unfortunately, it's a vicious cycle—you eat carbs, get hungry, eat more carbs, get hungry, ... you get the idea.

But carbs aren't all bad. They do provide energy for your body. They're the fuel your body's engine runs on. So do consume carbs, but only eat them alone if you're looking for a quick, short burst of energy. Otherwise, be sure to pair them with protein and healthy fats. Carbohydrate-rich foods include fruits and grains such as bread, cereal, pasta, and rice.

CULINARY KNOW-HOW

As often as you can, and preferably half the time, choose whole-grain products such as whole-wheat pasta, whole-wheat brown rice, and 100 percent whole-grain breads and cereals. Whole grains contain more fiber and other nutrients than processed grains.

Healthy Fats

There *is* a role for fat in a healthy eating plan, even if you're trying to lose weight. Fatty foods are a great source of the fat-soluble vitamins A, D, E, and K.

When it comes to weight loss, fat's role is similar to protein's. Fat is digested slowly and, therefore, helps you feel fuller longer after a meal.

The most important factor to keep in mind when it comes to fats is to choose the healthy kinds of fats most often. Healthy fats are called *unsaturated fats*. Healthy fats are found in fatty fish like salmon, nuts and nut butters, canola and olive oils, avocados, and more.

The bad fats, saturated fats, increase your risk of developing heart disease. Saturated fats are found primarily in animal-based foods such as meat and dairy foods. To minimize the negative effects these foods have, choose lean meats and low-fat dairy products as much as possible, and only use butter and higher-fat meats and dairy foods sparingly.

A Look at the Mini Nutrients

Protein, carbs, and fats—the big three—are the most important when it comes to weight loss, but other nutrients play a role as well.

If you're making changes in your eating habits that you expect to follow long term—which should be your goal if you want to lose weight and keep it off—it's important to ensure you're meeting your body's vitamin and mineral needs as well.

In fact, some vitamins and minerals play a role in weight regulation. Calcium and vitamin D are two that work together. Both have well-known roles in ensuring strong bones. But research has shown that women who consume enough of both of these nutrients tend to weigh less than women who are lacking in these nutrients.

Another mineral to be aware of is sodium. Although it's much maligned, our bodies do actually need some to function properly, but our needs are closer to 1,500 milligrams a day than the 4,000 milligrams or more that most Americans consume in a day. Excess sodium intake can increase your risk of developing high blood pressure and having a stroke. As long as you're healthy, a good goal is no more than 2,400 milligrams a day. One simple step to lowering your sodium intake if it's high is to limit your intake of processed foods and eat more whole foods—something we help make easier for you with the yummy recipes in this book.

 TASTY TIDBIT

To learn more about your body's nutritional requirements, go to cdc.gov/nutrition/everyone/basics/vitamins.

Filling Fiber

Fiber probably plays the biggest role in weight loss. It's another one of those nutrients that helps you feel fuller longer. And the more foods you can eat that will keep you full and prevent the munchies when you're trying to eat less and lose weight, the better!

Fiber is also beneficial for keeping your digestive system running smoothly, preventing sometimes uncomfortable gastrointestinal problems. Eating adequate fiber can also help keep cholesterol levels in check, lowering your risk of heart disease.

Fiber is plentiful in fruits, vegetables, and grains. Aim for about 25 to 30 grams fiber each day.

Wonderful Water

Any book about healthy eating and weight loss must include water. Water is necessary for fiber to do its job correctly, so whenever you start eating more fiber, you should up your water intake, too. Water helps transport nutrients around the body, aids in proper digestion, and helps rid the body of waste. Research has also shown that drinking adequate water regularly can help with weight loss.

There are a variety of ways to calculate fluid needs—not just water, but also fluids from watery fruits and veggies, milk, soups, and 100 percent fruit and vegetable juices—but they all say roughly the same thing. You need about 8 (8-ounce) cups of fluids per day. Not all that fluid has to be from water, but because it is calorie, sugar, fat, and sodium free, unlike the other sources, we'd recommend the majority actually be water.

How Many Calories Do You Need?

Before you get any crazy ideas about losing weight as fast as you can, keep in mind losing 1 or 2 pounds a week is usually the most you should lose. Often the first week or two after making changes to your eating habits, you'll lose a bit more weight right off the bat, but after that a slow, steady pace is best. This helps prevent muscle loss and encourages fat loss and also ensures you're making gradual changes that will be easier to maintain long term instead of drastic changes you'll have a hard time sticking with.

To get an idea of how many calories you should be eating each day to lose or maintain weight, you can use the Harris-Benedict formula:

For women:

> 655 + (4.35 × weight in pounds) + (4.7 × height in inches) – (4.7 × age in years) = base calorie needs

For men:

> 66 + (6.23 × weight in pounds) + (12.7 × height in inches) – (6.8 × age in years) = base calorie needs

Once you've figured out your base calorie needs, you need to factor in the amount of activity you do. Multiply the base calorie needs (X) by the following numbers based on how active you are on a daily basis:

> If you do little or no exercise: X × 1.2

> If you do light exercise or sports 1 to 3 days a week: X × 1.375

> If you do moderate exercise or sports 3 to 5 days a week: X × 1.55

> If you do hard exercise or sports 6 or 7 days a week: X × 1.725

The answer you get is approximately the number of calories your body needs each day to keep the status quo. If, however, your goal is to lose weight, you need to do a bit more math.

To lose 1 pound a week, you need to create a deficit of 500 calories. Basically, you need to either eat 500 calories fewer, burn 500 calories more, or better yet, do a combination of the two. Try cutting out 250 calories from your diet each day while at the same time bumping up your daily activity by 250 calories.

TASTY TIDBIT

Don't let lack of time keep you from exercising. A great goal is to be active at least 30 minutes a day, but if you don't have a 30-minute chunk at all the same time, divvy it up. Take a brisk 15-minute walk in the morning and another in the afternoon, for example.

If your current calorie intake is very high, you may be able to adjust your food and activity to produce a 2-pound-a-week weight loss. To do so, you must create a 1,000-calorie deficit. Again, that can mean eating less, exercising more, or a mix of the two.

Keep in mind, though, that you need at least 1,300 to 1,400 calories a day for your body to function properly and for you to get all the vitamins, minerals, and other nutrients you need. Going lower than that isn't healthy and won't help you lose weight faster.

To lose weight healthfully, the best bet for most people is to stick with the number of calories you get after subtracting 500 from your daily maintenance calorie needs.

Avoiding Fad Diets

You might be thinking this seems a bit complicated—wouldn't it be easier to just pick up a magazine and follow whatever diet of the week graces the cover? Well, yes and no.

The problem with those diets—one problem of many—is that they're fads. A fad is a short-lived craze, which is why there's a new fad diet every few weeks. Fad diets are almost always unbalanced, nutritionally speaking, and usually don't work, which is why they are short lived. Sure, you may lose a pound or two—or maybe even more. But typically, fad diets are either very difficult, if not impossible, to follow long term or cause you to lose a good deal of water at the beginning. Losing water drops off the pounds quickly at first, but the quick weight loss will cease. If you go back to your usual eating habits, you'll regain the weight you lost.

So on to the next easy diet, right? Wrong. Jumping from one quick-fix diet to the next can lead to yo-yo dieting. That means you continue to lose and gain weight over and over again.

Aside from disappointment and frustration, yo-yo dieting can wreak havoc on your *metabolism*. If you have a fast metabolism, you burn calories quickly. If it's slow, you burn calories slower, making weight loss more difficult. Yo-yo dieting can actually slow your metabolism. So for every fad diet you go on and off, with your weight going up and down, you're training your body to survive on fewer calories. If your body adapts to needing fewer calories (i.e., food) to lose weight, you'll need to eat even less. You're basically creating a situation where losing weight becomes increasingly more challenging.

DEFINITION

Metabolism is basically how fast your body takes the food you eat, breaks it down as fuel, and uses it for energy. A person with a fast metabolism burns the food they eat quickly, while it takes longer for a person with a slow metabolism to do so.

Losing weight and keeping it off in a healthful way may appear complicated at first. But remember, you're just learning what your body needs so you can choose the right foods in the right amounts to be healthy, feel satisfied, and lose weight safely. You won't need to count and add things every time you eat from now on. But doing this small bit of up-front work lets you know where you're starting from and helps you figure out how to get where you want to go. In a short time, your new way of eating will become second nature.

The Least You Need to Know

- Give your body the fuel it needs by making smart food and nutrition choices.
- Don't forget about vitamins and minerals. They're vitally important for good health.
- Skip the lose-weight-quick schemes. They'll get you nowhere and could do more harm than good.

Setting Yourself Up for Success

In This Chapter

- Taking a closer look at the food groups
- The importance of knowing when to eat what
- Saying "yes" to your favorite foods
- Prepping your kitchen and pantry

Just knowing how many calories you should be eating is sort of like having an ingredient list for a recipe but no directions—you might be able to piece something together, but chances are you'll miss a key step along the way.

In this chapter, you'll learn how to put foods together to meet your nutrient needs, maintain a healthy weight (or lose weight if you need to), and avoid that gnawing hunger so common with many diets.

Remember Your Food Groups

We used to have the four food groups, and although they've undergone many transformations over the years—more groups, fewer groups, etc.—the bottom line is that foods are grouped into categories. And for a good reason: their similar nutrition profiles. Each group shares a unique combination of nutrients, and we need to eat foods from each and every group to be healthy. It's all about balance.

Here are the basic food groups:

Proteins	Meat, chicken, fish, nuts, eggs, and tofu
Fruits	Fresh and dried fruits as well as 100 percent fruit juices
Vegetables	Raw and cooked veggies as well as 100 percent vegetable juices
Dairy	Milk, cheeses, yogurt
Grains	Breads, cereals, rice, and pasta

Within each food group, serving sizes are roughly the same. For example, in the grain group, a serving is about 1 ounce, which is about 1 slice of bread or $\frac{1}{2}$ cup rice or pasta. But when it comes to foods like cereals that weigh different amounts, serving sizes could range from $\frac{1}{2}$ cup to $1\frac{1}{2}$ cups. The same goes for all the food groups. Many resources are available to illustrate what's considered a serving, starting with the food's label. You can also go online for more serving size ideas.

TASTY TIDBIT

For more details about what foods belong in each group, what counts as a serving, and how many servings you need, go to: choosemyplate.gov/food-groups.

When you begin eating the recommended number of servings from each food group, you'll be on your way to healthier eating. Plus, choosing what to eat based on food groups is a simple way to ensure you're meeting your body's nutrient needs.

Figuring out serving sizes and portion sizes can be confusing. Keep in mind you aren't always limited to only one serving at a time. We're not saying you should disregard the serving sizes, but do look at all the foods you can choose from over the course of the day, and spread them out fairly evenly in a way that makes the most sense.

For example, let's look at the grain group. Say your requirements are 8 servings per day. You'll see that 1 slice of bread or a half of a hamburger roll each count as 1 serving. That doesn't mean you'll never have another sandwich again. Sure, you can go ahead and have 2 slices of bread on a sandwich or a top and bottom bun on that hamburger at lunch, but just realize you're using 2 of your 8 servings for the day, leaving yourself with 6 more to spread throughout the rest of the day's meals and snacks.

When to Eat What

Knowing what to eat is a big part of staying healthy, but another key factor is knowing *when* to eat. Starting the day with a huge breakfast and then not letting a crumb pass your lips the rest of the day is not going to help you get to the shape, size, and health level you desire. Neither will passing up meals all day and then gorging from dinner until bedtime.

It's important to spread out your meals and snacks throughout the day. Try to never go longer than 3 or 4 waking hours between meals or snacks. By having something to eat within an hour or two of waking and then eating something every 3 or 4 hours, you'll reap multiple benefits. You'll get your body's engine started by giving it the energy it needs (food) after your overnight "fast." Following that with a steady supply of food throughout the day prevents the highs and lows in energy, mood, appetite, and more you'd get with a fasting-and-bingeing cycle. When you go for long periods of time without eating, you feel tired and sluggish and begin to develop an intense hunger. That leads to overeating, which leads to feeling bloated and the desire to not eat for a while, and possibly some guilt, and … well, you can see how the cycle begins.

It helps to know your calorie needs, which you learned in Chapter 1. When you have that number, it's easier to see how you can spread out your calories throughout the day. For example, I usually divide my daily total by 4. I aim for roughly $\frac{1}{4}$ of my calories to come from breakfast, roughly $\frac{1}{4}$ from lunch, roughly $\frac{1}{4}$ from dinner, and the remaining $\frac{1}{4}$ to be divided up between my snacks. This way I have only one number to remember.

When you start to put together those meals and snacks, you learn how to spread out the food groups among them. Instead of having all your fruit at breakfast, your grains at lunch, and your meat at dinner, for example, try to choose one or two servings from as many groups as possible at each meal and snack.

 TASTY TIDBIT

To see what a healthy and balanced dinner (or breakfast or lunch) plate should hold, check out choosemyplate.gov.

To give you an idea of what this looks like, check out Chapter 3. There, we give you 2-week meal plans in three different calorie levels. Take advantage of these meal plans as you get started on this new, healthy way of eating. Feel free to follow the plans exactly or to mix and match meals and days to suit your needs and tastes. If you find a meal you're not crazy about, you can certainly replace it with any other similar-calorie meal in the book.

Fitting in Your Favorites

A common misconception about healthy eating and trying to lose weight is that favorite, albeit less-than-healthy foods, must be banned and never pass your lips again. That couldn't be further from the truth. While we're not suggesting you go hog-wild on a pint of your favorite premium ice cream or devour a big bag of chips or a giant pizza on a regular basis, you do need to find ways to fit in your favorites.

The changes you're making to your eating to lower your caloric intake should be considered permanent. One of the surest ways to sabotage those goals is to expect that you can live out the rest of your days without chocolate, french fries, or your other favorite "bad" foods.

Your first step is to stop thinking about foods as "good" or "bad," and instead think of them as foods to eat more of and foods to eat less of. You probably can figure out which foods go into which groups.

Next, you need to make a plan for how you're going to include the latter, the "eat less of" foods, into your eating plan. A successful plan usually includes both moderation in portion and frequency. So instead of a full-size candy bar or two a day, for example, how about a mini one a few days a week? Instead of half of a large pepperoni and sausage pizza several nights a week, how about two slices of a cheese/veggie-topped pizza one night a week, paired with a large, veggie-filled salad?

Planning Ahead

In this book, we give you an array of delicious, healthy meals and snacks, but you won't be able to enjoy any of them if you don't have the right ingredients. Organizing your grocery shopping and meal preparation is a great way to be able to enjoy all these nutritious meals whenever you want them. It takes a bit of time and planning up front, but it's actually a great time-saver in the long run.

By planning ahead, you can then make only one big trip to the supermarket each week. It means less time and money spent on multiple grocery runs for one or two items. Before you go, however, plan out your meals for the week. This can be as simple as deciding to make chicken and broccoli one night and fish and carrots another, as detailed as knowing that on Monday you'll cook sweet-and-sour chicken with brown rice and steamed broccoli, or something in between. The purpose here is to get an idea of the major ingredients you should have on hand and then stock them so you can cook nutritious, low-calorie dishes at every meal.

This might seem like just another task you don't have time for in your busy life, but the payoff is worth the investment. You'll never again experience that 5:30 "What are we going to have for dinner?" panic—which also means no last-minute runs through the drive-thru. You'll also have an array of healthy foods you can use to create delicious meals all week. Plus, shopping once a week enables you to buy and use more fresh produce and rely less on processed foods. That's a win all around!

When you've gotten your groceries home, take a few minutes to make the food easier and quicker to use later, when you're pressed for time and hungry. Wash and cut any produce that requires it, for example.

Making the food easy to use also applies to breakfasts and lunches, which you should prepare the day before whenever possible. Like dinner time, mornings are often busy and rushed. If you can have your ingredients measured, the eggs boiled, and so on, sitting down to a healthy breakfast will be that much simpler. Likewise, taking 5 minutes in the evening to pack your lunch for the next day means even less of a crunch in the morning, as well as less of a reliance on fast-food and vending-machine foods.

A Well-Stocked Kitchen

To make planning and preparing healthy meals a bit easier, it's a good idea to have a decent arsenal of basic ingredients on hand so that, come shopping time, all you need to worry about are the base ingredients recipes call for—the meats, veggies, etc.

Following is a list of staple items you should always have on hand. It's certainly not all-inclusive, but it should give you a good start. And of course, if we've included ingredients you just don't like, you don't have to stock them.

 TASTY TIDBIT

Having your pantry and fridge stocked with healthy staples gives you a jump-start on meal planning.

For your pantry:

Breads, grains, pastas:

- ❏ Whole-grain flake cereal
- ❏ Whole-grain English muffins
- ❏ Graham crackers
- ❏ Whole-wheat tortillas
- ❏ Whole-grain pasta in different shapes and sizes
- ❏ Oats, old-fashioned or quick-cooking
- ❏ Plain instant oatmeal packets

- ❏ Long-grain rice
- ❏ Brown rice
- ❏ Whole-grain bread
- ❏ Whole-grain crackers, regular or low-sodium
- ❏ Seasoned breadcrumbs
- ❏ Couscous
- ❏ Quinoa

Spices and seasonings:

- ❏ Cinnamon
- ❏ Nutmeg
- ❏ Ground ginger
- ❏ Black pepper
- ❏ Onion powder
- ❏ Garlic powder
- ❏ Minced onion

- ❏ Cayenne
- ❏ Crushed red pepper flakes
- ❏ Paprika
- ❏ Salt-free seasoning
- ❏ Garlic chile sauce or hot sauce
- ❏ Mustard

Baking:

- ❏ Brown sugar
- ❏ Granulated sugar
- ❏ Honey
- ❏ Chocolate syrup
- ❏ Semisweet chocolate chips
- ❏ Vanilla extract

- ❏ Peanut butter
- ❏ Cornstarch
- ❏ All-purpose flour
- ❏ Whole-wheat flour
- ❏ Whole-wheat pastry flour

Oils and dressings:

❑ Canola oil

❑ Olive oil

❑ Reduced-sodium soy sauce

❑ White vinegar

❑ Cider vinegar

❑ Nonstick cooking spray

Vegetables:

❑ Onions

❑ Potatoes

Canned goods:

❑ Canned tomatoes

❑ Canned beans, preferably low sodium

❑ Canned tuna, packed in water

❑ Canned (or boxed) low-sodium chicken, beef, and vegetable stock or broth

Dried fruits and nuts:

❑ Dried raisins, cranberries, cherries, and other fruits

❑ Various types of nuts

For your refrigerator:

❑ Skim or 1 percent milk

❑ Plain or vanilla yogurt

❑ Plain fat-free Greek yogurt

❑ Reduced-fat cheddar cheese

❑ Margarine spread or light butter spread

❑ Butter

❑ Reduced-fat sour cream

❑ Reduced-fat cream cheese

❑ Reduced-fat salad dressing

❑ Reduced-fat mayonnaise

❑ Large eggs

Freezer:

❑ Vegetables with no added sauces

❑ Fruit with no added sugar

❑ Whole-grain frozen waffles

Successful healthy eating and weight loss requires an understanding of the variety and amount of food you should be eating as well as how to spread your meals throughout the day. With that knowledge, along with working some of your favorite foods into your week, you'll rarely, if ever, find yourself wanting for food, which is the downfall of most "diets." Plus, you'll always have an array of healthy foods and ingredients at your fingertips when it's time for a quick bite or at mealtime.

The Least You Need to Know

- Choosing the right amount of food from each of the food groups helps you stick to a healthy eating plan.
- Eat throughout the day to keep hunger at bay.
- You can still fit in your favorite foods when lowering your calorie intake. Just be smart about the choices you make and you'll be fine.
- Stock a healthy pantry so you always have nutritious, healthful food at hand.

Meal Plans

In This Chapter

- Two-week meal plans for 1,300 calories a day
- Two-week meal plans for 1,550 calories a day
- Two-week meal plans for 1,800 calories a day

At this point, you may feel that eating healthfully is a bit overwhelming, and that's natural. Sometimes change seems hard at first, but in no time it'll be your new normal.

To help get you started, we give you three 2-week menu plans in this chapter. Simply pick the one closest to your calorie needs. Keep in mind, there are no hard-and-fast rules. If you don't have grapes one day, eat an apple instead. If you don't like broccoli, swap it out for carrots. The same goes for the meals; feel free to mix and match to suit your tastes, as long as the calories are roughly the same.

1,300-Calorie Meal Plan

If you're looking to get a quick jump-start on your weight loss or are on the petite side, this is the menu for you. The calories are low enough to promote weight loss but high enough to ensure you're meeting your nutrient needs.

Day 1

	Calories
Breakfast:	
1 serving Spinach and Potato Frittata (variation in Chapter 4)	
¾ cup skim milk	
1 medium apple	
Total breakfast calories:	*302*
Lunch:	
1 serving Crab-Topped Salad (recipe in Chapter 10)	
½ cup skim milk	
1 medium orange	
Total lunch calories:	*331*
Dinner:	
1 serving Layered Beef Stew (recipe in Chapter 18)	
1 cup skim milk	
1 cup garden salad (lettuce, tomato, cucumber, etc.)	
2 TB. reduced-fat dressing	
Total dinner calories:	*400*
Snack 1:	
1 serving Steamed Artichoke with Aioli (recipe in Chapter 20)	
Total snack 1 calories:	*144*
Snack 2:	
1 serving Chocolate Fondue (recipe in Chapter 22)	
Total snack 2 calories:	*139*
Total calories for day 1:	**1,316**

Day 2

	Calories
Breakfast:	
1 serving The Breakfast Club (recipe in Chapter 5)	
½ cup blueberries	
Total breakfast calories:	*303*
Lunch:	
1 serving Crunchy Tuna Pockets (recipe in Chapter 11)	
1 serving Vegetable Squash Soup (recipe in Chapter 9)	
½ cup seedless grapes	
Total lunch calories:	*312*
Dinner:	
1 serving Broiled Steak and Mushrooms (recipe in Chapter 14)	
1 medium baked potato	
1 TB. light sour cream	
½ cup skim milk	
Total dinner calories:	*398*
Snack 1:	
1 serving Sweet Bruschetta (recipe in Chapter 22)	
Total snack 1 calories:	*172*
Snack 2:	
3 low-sodium saltines	
1 TB. peanut butter	
Total snack 2 calories:	*130*
Total calories for day 2:	**1,315**

Day 3

	Calories
Breakfast:	
1 serving New England Breakfast Bowl (recipe in Chapter 6)	
Total breakfast calories:	287
Lunch:	
1 serving California Turkey Wraps (recipe in Chapter 12)	
1 cup melon cubes	
Total lunch calories:	317
Dinner:	
1 serving Southwestern Broiled Tilapia (recipe in Chapter 15)	
¾ cup brown rice	
½ cup skim milk	
1 cup garden salad (lettuce, tomato, cucumber, etc.)	
2 TB. reduced-fat dressing	
Total dinner calories:	428
Snack 1:	
¾ cup low-fat flavored yogurt (not fruit on the bottom)	
Total snack 1 calories:	170
Snack 2:	
1 serving Hot Ginger Tea (variation in Chapter 23)	
3 (2½-inch) square graham crackers	
Total snack 2 calories:	103
Total calories for day 3:	**1,305**

Day 4

	Calories
Breakfast:	
1¼ cups toasted oat cereal	
¾ cup skim milk	
1 medium banana	
Total breakfast calories:	*302*
Lunch:	
1 serving Delicata Squash Chili Bowl (recipe in Chapter 9)	
4 low-sodium saltines	
½ cup skim milk	
Total lunch calories:	*322*
Dinner:	
1 serving Chicken Picatta (recipe in Chapter 13)	
¾ cup whole-wheat spaghetti	
1 cup steamed broccoli	
1 tsp. margarine spread	
½ cup skim milk	
Total dinner calories:	*421*
Snack 1:	
¾ cup plain, nonfat yogurt	
½ cup blueberries	
Total snack 1 calories:	*117*
Snack 2:	
1 serving Pumpkin-Spiced Popcorn (recipe in Chapter 21)	
Total snack 2 calories:	*161*
Total calories for day 4:	**1,323**

Day 5

	Calories
Breakfast:	
1 serving Easy Soufflé (recipe in Chapter 7)	
½ cup blueberries	
1 cup skim milk	
Total breakfast calories:	*305*
Lunch:	
1 serving Cranberry and Walnut Chicken Salad (recipe in Chapter 10)	
1 medium apple	
Total lunch calories:	*333*
Dinner:	
1 serving Spaghetti Squash Marinara (recipe in Chapter 16)	
1 medium slice Italian bread	
1 cup garden salad (lettuce, tomato, cucumber, etc.)	
2 TB. reduced-fat dressing	
1 cup skim milk	
Total dinner calories:	*423*
Snack 1:	
1 cup carrot sticks	
2 TB. reduced-fat ranch dip/dressing	
Total snack 1 calories:	*133*
Snack 2:	
1 serving Silky Deviled Eggs (recipe in Chapter 19)	
Total snack 2 calories:	*108*
Total calories for day 5:	**1,302**

Day 6

	Calories

Breakfast:

1 serving Sunshine Smoothie (recipe in Chapter 8)

1 slice whole-wheat toast

1 tsp. margarine spread

Total breakfast calories: *301*

Lunch:

1 serving Quick Italian Beef Sandwich (variation in Chapter 11)

1 cup skim milk

$\frac{1}{2}$ cup strawberries

Total lunch calories: *321*

Dinner:

1 serving Jerk Shrimp (recipe in Chapter 15)

$\frac{1}{2}$ cup brown rice

$\frac{1}{2}$ cup skim milk

1 cup steamed green beans (fresh, frozen, or canned without added
  salt)

1 tsp. margarine spread

Total dinner calories: *384*

Snack 1:

1 serving Spicy Sweet Potato Chips (recipe in Chapter 21)

Total snack 1 calories: *71*

Snack 2:

1 Apple Cider Muffin (recipe in Chapter 6)

1 serving Ginger Spritzer (recipe in Chapter 23)

Total snack 2 calories: *196*

Total calories for day 6: **1,273**

Day 7

	Calories

Breakfast:

1 serving Scrambled Eggs and Turkey Bacon (variation in Chapter 4)

¾ cup 100 percent orange juice

1 slice whole-wheat toast

1 tsp. margarine spread

Total breakfast calories: *294*

Lunch:

1 serving Veggie Sandwich with Herb Mayo (recipe in Chapter 11)

½ cup skim milk

½ cup melon cubes

Total lunch calories: *325*

Dinner:

1 serving Mexican Meatloaf (recipe in Chapter 14)

½ cup corn

1½ cups garden salad (lettuce, tomato, cucumber, etc.)

2 TB. reduced-fat dressing

Total dinner calories: *390*

Snack 1:

4 medium strawberries

1 fat-free chocolate pudding cup

Total snack 1 calories: *140*

Snack 2:

½ cup low-fat, low-sodium cottage cheese

½ cup drained, crushed pineapple, packed in juice

Total snack 2 calories: *149*

Total calories for day 7:   **1,298**

Day 8

	Calories
Breakfast:	
1 serving Quinoa Porridge (recipe in Chapter 6)	
½ cup seedless grapes	
Total breakfast calories:	*295*
Lunch:	
1 serving Curry Chicken Salad (recipe in Chapter 10)	
1 small banana	
Total lunch calories:	*337*
Dinner:	
1 serving Coconut-Curried Chicken (recipe in Chapter 13)	
¾ cup brown rice	
¾ cup cooked carrots	
1 tsp. margarine spread	
Total dinner calories:	*410*
Snack 1:	
¾ cup plain, nonfat yogurt	
½ cup strawberries	
Total snack 1 calories:	*99*
Snack 2:	
1 serving Fiery Popcorn (recipe in Chapter 21)	
Total snack 2 calories:	*178*
Total calories for day 8:	**1,319**

Day 9

	Calories
Breakfast:	
1 serving Strawberry-Stuffed French Toast (recipe in Chapter 5)	
¾ cup skim milk	
Total breakfast calories:	*351*
Lunch:	
1 serving Lemongrass and Coconut Milk Soup with Chicken (recipe in Chapter 9)	
1 medium apple	
Total lunch calories:	*325*
Dinner:	
1 serving Braised Chicken with Apples and Sweet Potatoes (recipe in Chapter 18)	
1 cup garden salad (lettuce, tomato, cucumber, etc.)	
2 TB. reduced-fat dressing	
Total dinner calories:	*305*
Snack 1:	
1 cup baby carrots	
2 TB. reduced-fat ranch dip/dressing	
Total snack 1 calories:	*133*
Snack 2:	
1 serving Caramel Fondue (recipe in Chapter 22)	
Total snack 2 calories:	*137*
Total calories for day 9:	**1,251**

Day 10

	Calories
Breakfast:	
1 serving Fresh Melon Salad with Mint, Basil, and Pomegranate Dressing (recipe in Chapter 7)	
1 light multigrain English muffin	
1½ TB. peanut butter	
Total breakfast calories:	*310*
Lunch:	
1 Marinated Portobello Mushroom Burger (recipe in Chapter 11)	
1 cup skim milk	
½ medium cucumber	
1 TB. reduced-fat ranch dip/dressing	
Total lunch calories:	*312*
Dinner:	
1 serving Crispy Baked Cod (recipe in Chapter 15)	
1 cup steamed broccoli	
1 tsp. margarine spread	
¾ cup garden salad (lettuce, tomato, cucumber, etc.)	
1 TB. reduced-fat dressing	
Total dinner calories:	*353*
Snack 1:	
1 oz. low-sodium cheddar, sliced	
4 low-sodium whole-wheat crackers	
Total snack 1 calories:	*151*
Snack 2:	
1 serving Mango Power Smoothie (recipe in Chapter 8)	
Total snack 2 calories:	*175*
Total calories for day 10:	**1,301**

Day 11

	Calories
Breakfast:	
1 Morning Wake-Up Smoothie (recipe in Chapter 8)	
1 large hard-boiled egg	
1 tsp. margarine spread (to spread on egg)	
Total breakfast calories:	275
Lunch:	
1 serving Zesty Chicken Salad Wrap (recipe in Chapter 12)	
½ cup strawberries	
Total lunch calories:	353
Dinner:	
1 serving Smoky Stuffed Peppers (recipe in Chapter 14)	
1 cup skim milk	
1 cup garden salad (lettuce, tomato, cucumber, etc.)	
2 TB. reduced-fat dressing	
Total dinner calories:	383
Snack 1:	
2 (2½-inch) square graham crackers	
¾ cup skim milk	
1 TB. chocolate syrup	
Total snack 1 calories:	177
Snack 2:	
1 serving Velvety Edamame Hummus (recipe in Chapter 19)	
¾ cup baby carrots	
Total snack 2 calories:	152
Total calories for day 11:	**1,340**

Day 12

	Calories
Breakfast:	
1¼ cups wheat bran flakes cereal with raisins	
¾ cup skim milk	
Total breakfast calories:	*305*
Lunch:	
1 serving Asian-Style Chicken Soup (variation in Chapter 9)	
1 cup seedless grapes	
Total lunch calories:	*325*
Dinner:	
1 serving Chicken Satay with Zing (recipe in Chapter 13)	
½ cup brown rice	
1 cup steamed green beans	
1 tsp. margarine spread	
½ cup skim milk	
Total dinner calories:	*379*
Snack 1:	
1 Peanut Butter Banana Roll-Up (recipe in Chapter 21)	
Total snack 1 calories:	*192*
Snack 2:	
1 serving Limeade Spritzer (variation in Chapter 23)	
3 (2½-inch) square graham crackers	
Total snack 2 calories:	*107*
Total calories for day 12:	**1,308**

Day 13

	Calories
Breakfast:	
1 serving Steel-Cut Oatmeal (recipe in Chapter 6)	
1 cup 100 percent orange juice	
Total breakfast calories:	*313*
Lunch:	
1 serving Tuna in a Tomato (variation in Chapter 10)	
1 cup skim milk	
6 whole-grain crackers	
1 medium apple	
Total lunch calories:	*305*
Dinner:	
1 serving Vegetarian Chili (recipe in Chapter 17)	
1 cup garden salad (lettuce, tomato, cucumber, etc.)	
2 TB. reduced-fat dressing	
1 cup skim milk	
Total dinner calories:	*365*
Snack 1:	
3 low-sodium saltines	
1 TB. peanut butter	
Total snack 1 calories:	*130*
Snack 2:	
1 serving Pumpkin Custard (recipe in Chapter 22)	
Total snack 2 calories:	*177*
Total calories for day 13:	**1,290**

Day 14

	Calories

Breakfast:
1 serving Shirred Eggs (recipe in Chapter 4)
1 slice whole-wheat toast
1 tsp. margarine spread
Total breakfast calories: — 263

Lunch:
2 slices whole-grain bread
1 TB. peanut butter
1 tsp. all-fruit spread
1 cup melon cubes
Total lunch calories: — 322

Dinner:
1 serving Korean Wrap (recipe in Chapter 14)
1 small baked sweet potato
1 tsp. margarine spread
Total dinner calories: — 367

Snack 1:
1 serving Roasted Red Pepper Hummus (variation in Chapter 19)
Total snack 1 calories: — 177

Snack 2:
1 small banana dipped into 1 TB. hazelnut chocolate spread
Total snack 2 calories: — 175

Total calories for day 14: — 1,304

1,550-Calorie Meal Plan

If 1,300 calories a day isn't enough to keep your energy levels up, or you find you're losing more than 1 or 2 pounds a week, you may want to bump yourself up to 1,500 calories a day. You'll find yourself more satisfied while losing weight more healthfully.

Day 1

	Calories
Breakfast:	
1 serving All-in-One Egg Breakfast (recipe in Chapter 4)	
½ cup skim milk	
1 medium apple	
Total breakfast calories:	*335*
Lunch:	
1 serving California Crab Salad (recipe in Chapter 10)	
½ cup skim milk	
1 medium orange	
Total lunch calories:	*332*
Dinner:	
1 serving Layered Beef Stew (recipe in Chapter 18)	
1 cup skim milk	
1 cup garden salad (lettuce, tomato, cucumber, etc.)	
2 TB. reduced-fat dressing	
½ cup melon cubes	
Total dinner calories:	*427*
Snack 1:	
1 serving Loaded Potato (recipe in Chapter 20)	
Total snack 1 calories:	*194*
Snack 2:	
1 serving Angel Food Cake Trifle (recipe in Chapter 22)	
Total snack 2 calories:	*198*
Total calories for day 1:	**1,486**

Day 2

	Calories

Breakfast:

1 serving Comforting Couscous (recipe in Chapter 6)

Total breakfast calories: *359*

Lunch:

1 serving Pulled Chicken Sandwich (recipe in Chapter 11)

1 cup seedless grapes

Total lunch calories: *371*

Dinner:

1 serving Spicy Beef Satay (recipe in Chapter 14)

1 medium baked potato

1 TB. light sour cream

$\frac{1}{2}$ cup steamed green beans

$\frac{1}{2}$ tsp. margarine spread

Total dinner calories: *438*

Snack 1:

1 serving Sweet Bruschetta (recipe in Chapter 22)

Total snack 1 calories: *172*

Snack 2:

4 low-sodium saltines

$1\frac{1}{2}$ TB. peanut butter

Total snack 2 calories: *190*

Total calories for day 2:   **1,530**

Day 3

	Calories
Breakfast:	
1 serving New England Breakfast Bowl (recipe in Chapter 6)	
¾ cup 100 percent orange juice	
Total breakfast calories:	*370*
Lunch:	
1 Broiled Chicken Kabob Wrap (recipe in Chapter 12)	
1 cup melon cubes	
Total lunch calories:	*373*
Dinner:	
1 serving Southwestern Broiled Tilapia (recipe in Chapter 15)	
¾ cup brown rice	
½ cup skim milk	
1 cup garden salad (lettuce, tomato, cucumber, etc.)	
2 TB. reduced-fat dressing	
Total dinner calories:	*428*
Snack 1:	
¾ cup low-fat flavored yogurt	
Total snack 1 calories:	*170*
Snack 2:	
1 serving Mulled Cider (recipe in Chapter 23)	
2 (2½-inch) square graham crackers	
Total snack 2 calories:	*189*
Total calories for day 3:	**1,530**

Day 4

	Calories

Breakfast:

1½ cups toasted oat cereal

1 cup skim milk

1 medium banana

Total breakfast calories: 350

Lunch:

1 serving Delicata Squash Chili Bowl (recipe in Chapter 9)

5 low-sodium saltines

1 cup skim milk

Total lunch calories: 379

Dinner:

1 serving Chicken Picatta (recipe in Chapter 13)

¾ cup whole-wheat spaghetti

1 cup steamed broccoli

1 tsp. margarine spread

½ cup skim milk

Total dinner calories: 421

Snack 1:

¾ cup plain, nonfat yogurt

½ cup blueberries

Total snack 1 calories: 117

Snack 2:

1 Granola Bar (recipe in Chapter 21)

Total snack 2 calories: 278

Total calories for day 4: **1,545**

Day 5

	Calories
Breakfast:	
1 serving Hearty Canadian Breakfast (recipe in Chapter 4)	
½ cup fresh blueberries	
1 cup skim milk	
Total breakfast calories:	*351*
Lunch:	
1 serving Egg Salad–Stuffed Tomato (variation in Chapter 10)	
1 medium apple	
Total lunch calories:	*379*
Dinner:	
1 serving Spaghetti Squash Marinara (recipe in Chapter 16)	
1 medium slice Italian bread	
1 cup garden salad (lettuce, tomato, cucumber, etc.)	
2 TB. reduced-fat dressing	
1 cup skim milk	
Total dinner calories:	*423*
Snack 1:	
1 serving Fiery Popcorn (recipe in Chapter 21)	
Total snack 1 calories:	*178*
Snack 2:	
1 serving Baba Ganoush (recipe in Chapter 19)	
Total snack 2 calories:	*207*
Total calories for day 5:	**1,538**

Day 6

	Calories
Breakfast:	
1 serving Raspberry Cocoa Surprise Smoothie (recipe in Chapter 8)	
1 slice whole-wheat toast	
1 tsp. margarine spread	
Total breakfast calories:	*337*
Lunch:	
1 serving Old-Fashioned Chicken Salad Pita Pocket (recipe in Chapter 11)	
½ cup skim milk	
¾ cup strawberries	
Total lunch calories:	*412*
Dinner:	
1 serving Sautéed Scallops and Snap Peas (recipe in Chapter 15)	
½ cup brown rice	
1 cup skim milk	
Total dinner calories:	*359*
Snack 1:	
1 serving Bruschetta Caprese (recipe in Chapter 19)	
Total snack 1 calories:	*222*
Snack 2:	
1 Apple Cider Muffin (recipe in Chapter 6)	
1 serving Ginger Spritzer (recipe in Chapter 23)	
Total snack 2 calories:	*204*
Total calories for day 6:	**1,534**

Day 7

	Calories
Breakfast:	
1 serving Skillet Breakfast (recipe in Chapter 4)	
¾ cup 100 percent orange juice	
1 slice whole-wheat toast	
1 tsp. margarine spread	
Total breakfast calories:	*354*
Lunch:	
1 Veggie Sandwich with Herb Mayo (recipe in Chapter 11)	
1 cup skim milk	
½ cup melon cubes	
Total lunch calories:	*370*
Dinner:	
1 serving Mexican Meatloaf (recipe in Chapter 14)	
½ cup corn	
1 cup garden salad (lettuce, tomato, cucumber, etc.)	
2 TB. reduced-fat dressing	
½ cup skim milk	
Total dinner calories:	*422*
Snack 1:	
4 medium strawberries	
1 fat-free chocolate pudding cup	
Total snack 1 calories:	*140*
Snack 2:	
1 serving S'mores Trail Mix (recipe in Chapter 21)	
Total snack 2 calories:	*292*
Total calories for day 7:	**1,578**

Day 8

	Calories
Breakfast:	
1 Banana-Walnut Breakfast Bowl (variation in Chapter 6)	
Total breakfast calories:	*335*
Lunch:	
1 serving Avocado, Papaya, and Shrimp Salad (recipe in Chapter 10)	
1 small banana	
½ cup skim milk	
Total lunch calories:	*396*
Dinner:	
1 serving Coconut-Curried Chicken (recipe in Chapter 13)	
¾ cup brown rice	
1 cup cooked carrots	
1 tsp. margarine spread	
Total dinner calories:	*424*
Snack 1:	
¾ cup plain, nonfat yogurt	
½ cup strawberries	
2 TB. unsalted slivered almonds	
Total snack 1 calories:	*177*
Snack 2:	
1 serving Peach Shortcake (recipe in Chapter 22)	
Total snack 2 calories:	*193*
Total calories for day 8:	**1,525**

Day 9

	Calories
Breakfast:	
1 serving Grilled Bananas and Almond Butter on Cinnamon Toast (recipe in Chapter 5)	
½ cup skim milk	
Total breakfast calories:	*348*
Lunch:	
1 serving Roasted Squash Soup with Sage (recipe in Chapter 9)	
¾ cup seedless grapes	
Total lunch calories:	*338*
Dinner:	
1 serving Braised Chicken with Apples and Sweet Potatoes (recipe in Chapter 18)	
1 cup garden salad (lettuce, tomato, cucumber, etc.)	
2 TB. reduced-fat dressing	
1 cup skim milk	
Total dinner calories:	*395*
Snack 1:	
1 serving Broiled Tomatoes (recipe in Chapter 20)	
Total snack 1 calories:	*208*
Snack 2:	
1 serving Strawberry Carbo-rita Smoothie (recipe in Chapter 8)	
Total snack 2 calories:	*179*
Total calories for day 9:	**1,468**

Day 10

	Calories
Breakfast:	
1 serving Mushroom Frittata (recipe in Chapter 4)	
1 light multigrain English muffin	
1½ TB. peanut butter	
Total breakfast calories:	*415*
Lunch:	
1 Crunchy Tuna Pocket (recipe in Chapter 11)	
½ cup skim milk	
½ medium cucumber	
1 TB. reduced-fat ranch dip/dressing	
1 cup melon cubes	
Total lunch calories:	*351*
Dinner:	
1 serving Crispy Baked Cod (recipe in Chapter 15)	
1 cup steamed broccoli	
1 tsp. margarine spread	
½ cup brown rice	
½ cup skim milk	
Total dinner calories:	*446*
Snack 1:	
1 oz. low-sodium cheddar, sliced	
4 low-sodium wheat crackers	
Total snack 1 calories:	*151*
Snack 2:	
1 serving Mango Power Smoothie (recipe in Chapter 8)	
Total snack 2 calories:	*175*
Total calories for day 10:	**1,538**

Day 11

	Calories
Breakfast:	
1 serving Dreamsicle Smoothie (recipe in Chapter 8)	
1 large hard-boiled egg	
1 tsp. margarine spread	
Total breakfast calories:	*347*
Lunch:	
1 Chopped Egg and Olives Wrap (recipe in Chapter 12)	
½ cup strawberries	
Total lunch calories:	*386*
Dinner:	
1 serving Hearty Sloppy Joes (recipe in Chapter 14)	
½ cup skim milk	
1 cup garden salad (lettuce, tomato, cucumber, etc.)	
2 TB. reduced-fat dressing	
Total dinner calories:	*435*
Snack 1:	
2 (2½-inch) square graham crackers	
¾ cup skim milk	
1 TB. chocolate syrup	
Total snack 1 calories:	*177*
Snack 2:	
1 serving Classic Hummus (recipe in Chapter 19)	
¼ cup baby carrots	
Total snack 2 calories:	*207*
Total calories for day 11:	**1,552**

Day 12

	Calories
Breakfast:	
1½ cups wheat bran flakes cereal with raisins	
¾ cup skim milk	
Total breakfast calories:	*352*
Lunch:	
1 serving Asian-Style Chicken Soup (variation in Chapter 9)	
4 whole-grain crackers	
1 medium apple	
Total lunch calories:	*396*
Dinner:	
1 serving Turkey Cutlets with Apple Compote (recipe in Chapter 13)	
½ cup brown rice	
1 cup steamed green beans	
1 tsp. margarine spread	
½ cup skim milk	
Total dinner calories:	*410*
Snack 1:	
1 Peanut Butter Banana Roll-Up (recipe in Chapter 21)	
Total snack 1 calories:	*192*
Snack 2:	
1 serving Spinach-Stuffed Mushrooms (recipe in Chapter 19)	
Total snack 2 calories:	*175*
Total calories for day 12:	**1,525**

Day 13

	Calories
Breakfast:	
1 serving Breakfast Parfait (recipe in Chapter 6)	
1 cup 100 percent orange juice	
Total breakfast calories:	*314*
Lunch:	
1 serving Cannellini Bean Salad (recipe in Chapter 10)	
1/2 cup skim milk	
Total lunch calories:	*372*
Dinner:	
1 serving Texas Chili (recipe in Chapter 17)	
3 low-sodium saltines	
1 cup garden salad (lettuce, tomato, cucumber, etc.)	
2 TB. reduced-fat dressing	
3/4 cup skim milk	
Total dinner calories:	*433*
Snack 1:	
1 serving Cape Cod Trail Mix (recipe in Chapter 21)	
Total snack 1 calories:	*286*
Snack 2:	
1 serving Pumpkin Custard (recipe in Chapter 22)	
Total snack 2 calories:	*177*
Total calories for day 13:	**1,582**

Day 14

	Calories
Breakfast:	
1 serving Crispy Potato Cups Stuffed with Spinach and Ham (recipe in Chapter 7)	
1 cup skim milk	
Total breakfast calories:	*358*
Lunch:	
2 slices whole-grain bread	
1 TB. peanut butter	
1 tsp. all-fruit spread	
1 cup melon cubes	
$\frac{1}{2}$ cup skim milk	
Total lunch calories:	*367*
Dinner:	
1 serving Beef Stroganoff (recipe in Chapter 14)	
1 cup garden salad (lettuce, tomato, cucumber, etc.)	
2 TB. reduced-fat dressing	
Total dinner calories:	*466*
Snack 1:	
1 serving Roasted Red Pepper Hummus (variation in Chapter 19)	
Total snack 1 calories:	*177*
Snack 2:	
1 small banana dipped into 1 TB. hazelnut chocolate spread	
Total snack 2 calories:	*175*
Total calories for day 14:	**1,543**

1,800-Calorie Meal Plan

Men or taller women or those who are fairly active should try 1,800 calories a day. Your body needs the extra calories for energy, but this amount of calories should still promote weight loss. If you try this and find the pounds not dropping, you can always go down to the 1,500-calorie menu.

Day 1

	Calories
Breakfast:	
1 serving All-in-One Egg Breakfast (recipe in Chapter 4)	
1 cup skim milk	
1 medium apple	
Total breakfast calories:	*380*
Lunch:	
1 serving Mediterranean Tuna Tomato Cups (recipe in Chapter 10)	
¾ cup skim milk	
1 medium orange	
Total lunch calories:	*476*
Dinner:	
1 serving Italian Chicken Stew (recipe in Chapter 18)	
1 cup skim milk	
1 cup garden salad (lettuce, tomato, cucumber, etc.)	
2 TB. reduced-fat dressing	
1 cup melon cubes	
Total dinner calories:	*509*
Snack 1:	
1 serving Loaded Potato (recipe in Chapter 20)	
Total snack 1 calories:	*194*
Snack 2:	
1 serving Angel Food Cake Trifle (recipe in Chapter 22)	
½ cup skim milk	
Total snack 2 calories:	*243*
Total calories for day 1:	**1,802**

Day 2

	Calories
Breakfast:	
1 serving Fill 'Em Up Muffins (variation in Chapter 6)	
$\frac{1}{2}$ cup skim milk	
Total breakfast calories:	*389*
Lunch:	
1 serving Egg Salad Pita Pocket (recipe in Chapter 11)	
$\frac{3}{4}$ cup seedless grapes	
$\frac{1}{2}$ cup skim milk	
Total lunch calories:	*401*
Dinner:	
1 serving Spicy Beef Satay (recipe in Chapter 14)	
1 medium baked potato	
1 TB. light sour cream	
1 cup garden salad (lettuce, tomato, cucumber, etc.)	
2 TB. reduced-fat dressing	
Total dinner calories:	*506*
Snack 1:	
1 serving Sweet Bruschetta (recipe in Chapter 22)	
Total snack 1 calories:	*172*
Snack 2:	
6 low-sodium saltines	
2 TB. peanut butter	
Total snack 2 calories:	*262*
Total calories for day 2:	**1,730**

Day 3

	Calories
Breakfast:	
1 serving New England Breakfast Bowl (recipe in Chapter 6)	
¾ cup 100 percent orange juice	
Total breakfast calories:	*370*
Lunch:	
1 serving Broiled Chicken Kabob Wrap (recipe in Chapter 12)	
1 cup melon cubes	
1 cup skim milk	
Total lunch calories:	*463*
Dinner:	
1 serving Southwestern Broiled Tilapia (recipe in Chapter 15)	
¾ cup brown rice	
1 cup skim milk	
1 cup garden salad (lettuce, tomato, cucumber, etc.)	
2 TB. reduced-fat dressing	
Total dinner calories:	*473*
Snack 1:	
1 Granola Bar (recipe in Chapter 21)	
Total snack 1 calories:	*278*
Snack 2:	
1 serving Mulled Cider (recipe in Chapter 23)	
3 (2½-inch) square graham crackers	
Total snack 2 calories:	*218*
Total calories for day 3:	**1,802**

Day 4

	Calories
Breakfast:	
1½ cups toasted oat cereal	
1 cup skim milk	
1 medium banana	
Total breakfast calories:	*350*
Lunch:	
1 Avocado Sandwich with Lime Vinaigrette (recipe in Chapter 11)	
1 cup skim milk	
½ cup seedless grapes	
Total lunch calories:	*478*
Dinner:	
1 serving Chicken Picatta (recipe in Chapter 13)	
1 cup whole-wheat spaghetti	
1 cup steamed broccoli	
1 tsp. margarine spread	
1 cup skim milk	
Total dinner calories:	*509*
Snack 1:	
1 cup plain, nonfat yogurt	
½ cup blueberries	
2 TB. unsalted slivered almonds	
Total snack 1 calories:	*220*
Snack 2:	
1 Fill 'Em Up Muffin (variation in Chapter 6)	
¾ cup skim milk	
Total snack 2 calories:	*240*
Total calories for day 4:	**1,797**

Day 5

	Calories
Breakfast:	
1 serving Poached Eggs with Avocado and Tomato (recipe in Chapter 4)	
½ cup blueberries	
1 cup skim milk	
Total breakfast calories:	*368*
Lunch:	
1 Spicy Meatball Pocket (recipe in Chapter 11)	
1 medium apple	
½ cup skim milk	
Total lunch calories:	*418*
Dinner:	
1 serving Quinoa-Stuffed Tomatoes (recipe in Chapter 16)	
1 medium slice Italian bread	
1 cup garden salad (lettuce, tomato, cucumber, etc.)	
2 TB. reduced-fat dressing	
1 cup skim milk	
Total dinner calories:	*501*
Snack 1:	
1 serving Rice Pudding (recipe in Chapter 22)	
Total snack 1 calories:	*245*
Snack 2:	
1 serving Baba Ganoush (recipe in Chapter 19)	
Total snack 2 calories:	*207*
Total calories for day 5:	**1,739**

Day 6

	Calories
Breakfast:	
1 serving Tropical Smoothie (recipe in Chapter 8)	
1 slice whole-wheat toast	
1 tsp. margarine spread	
Total breakfast calories:	*406*
Lunch:	
1 serving Pepper-Smothered Beef Wrap (variation in Chapter 11)	
1 cup skim milk	
1 cup strawberries	
Total lunch calories:	*449*
Dinner:	
1 serving Cajun Tilapia (recipe in Chapter 15)	
¾ cup brown rice	
1 cup skim milk	
1 cup steamed green beans	
1 tsp. margarine spread	
Total dinner calories:	*559*
Snack 1:	
1 serving Bruschetta Caprese (recipe in Chapter 19)	
Total snack 1 calories:	*170*
Snack 2:	
1 Apple Cider Muffin (recipe in Chapter 6)	
1 serving Ginger Spritzer (recipe in Chapter 23)	
Total snack 2 calories:	*196*
Total calories for day 6:	**1,780**

Day 7

	Calories
Breakfast:	
1 serving Skillet Breakfast (recipe in Chapter 4)	
1 cup 100 percent orange juice	
1 slice whole-wheat toast	
1 tsp. margarine spread	
Total breakfast calories:	*382*
Lunch:	
1 serving Shrimp Po'Boy (recipe in Chapter 11)	
1 cup skim milk	
1 cup melon cubes	
Total lunch calories:	*458*
Dinner:	
1 serving Mexican Meatloaf (recipe in Chapter 14)	
¾ cup corn	
1 cup garden salad (lettuce, tomato, cucumber, etc.)	
2 TB. reduced-fat dressing	
1 cup skim milk	
Total dinner calories:	*497*
Snack 1:	
6 medium strawberries	
1 fat-free chocolate pudding cup	
Total snack 1 calories:	*153*
Snack 2:	
1 serving S'mores Trail Mix (recipe in Chapter 21)	
Total snack 2 calories:	*292*
Total calories for day 7:	**1,782**

Day 8

	Calories
Breakfast:	
1 serving Hot Millet Porridge with Dried Fruit (recipe in Chapter 6)	
Total breakfast calories:	*352*
Lunch:	
1 serving White Bean, Shrimp, and Bacon Salad (recipe in Chapter 10)	
1 small banana	
1 cup skim milk	
Total lunch calories:	*459*
Dinner:	
1 serving Coconut-Curried Chicken (recipe in Chapter 13)	
¾ cup brown rice	
1 cup cooked carrots	
1 tsp. margarine spread	
¾ cup skim milk	
Total dinner calories:	*492*
Snack 1:	
1 cup plain, nonfat yogurt	
½ cup strawberries	
3 TB. unsalted slivered almonds	
Total snack 1 calories:	*241*
Snack 2:	
1 serving Apple Crisp (recipe in Chapter 22)	
Total snack 2 calories:	*267*
Total calories for day 8:	**1,811**

Day 9

	Calories
Breakfast:	
1 serving Cantaloupe with Cottage Cheese and Wheat Germ (recipe in Chapter 7)	
¾ cup 100 percent orange juice	
Total breakfast calories:	*393*
Lunch:	
1 serving Roasted Squash Soup with Sage (recipe in Chapter 9)	
1 cup seedless grapes	
1 cup skim milk	
Total lunch calories:	*456*
Dinner:	
1 serving Braised Chicken with Apples and Sweet Potatoes (recipe in Chapter 18)	
1 cup garden salad (lettuce, tomato, cucumber, etc.)	
2 TB. reduced-fat dressing	
1 cup skim milk	
1 cup strawberries	
Total dinner calories:	*443*
Snack 1:	
1 serving Nuts and Fruit (recipe in Chapter 21)	
Total snack 1 calories:	*315*
Snack 2:	
1 serving Strawberry Carbo-rita Smoothie (recipe in Chapter 8)	
Total snack 2 calories:	*179*
Total calories for day 9:	**1,786**

Day 10

	Calories
Breakfast:	
1 serving Mushroom Frittata (recipe in Chapter 4)	
1 light multigrain English muffin	
1½ TB. peanut butter	
Total breakfast calories:	*415*
Lunch:	
1 Crunchy Tuna Pocket (recipe in Chapter 11)	
1 cup skim milk	
1 cup carrot sticks	
2 TB. reduced-fat ranch dip/dressing	
1 cup melon cubes	
Total lunch calories:	*466*
Dinner:	
1 serving Crispy Baked Cod (recipe in Chapter 15)	
1 cup steamed broccoli	
1 tsp. margarine spread	
½ cup brown rice	
¾ cup skim milk	
Total dinner calories:	*469*
Snack 1:	
1 oz. low-sodium cheddar, sliced	
6 low-sodium wheat crackers	
Total snack 1 calories:	*170*
Snack 2:	
1 serving Tropical Smoothie (recipe in Chapter 8)	
Total snack 2 calories:	*304*
Total calories for day 10:	**1,824**

Day 11

	Calories

Breakfast:

1 serving Peanut Butter and Banana Smoothie (recipe in Chapter 8)

1 slice whole-wheat toast

2 tsp. all-fruit spread

Total breakfast calories: *416*

Lunch:

1 Chopped Egg and Olives Wrap (recipe in Chapter 12)

1 cup strawberries

¾ cup skim milk

Total lunch calories: *478*

Dinner:

1 serving Hearty Sloppy Joes (recipe in Chapter 14)

1 cup skim milk

1 cup garden salad (lettuce, tomato, cucumber, etc.)

2 TB. reduced-fat dressing

Total dinner calories: *480*

Snack 1:

3 (2½-inch) square graham crackers

1 cup skim milk

1 TB. chocolate syrup

Total snack 1 calories: *229*

Snack 2:

1 serving Classic Hummus (recipe in Chapter 19)

¾ cup baby carrots

Total snack 2 calories: *207*

Total calories for day 11:   **1,810**

Day 12

	Calories

Breakfast:

1½ cups wheat bran flakes cereal with raisins

1 cup skim milk

Total breakfast calories: *374*

Lunch:

1 serving *Ribollita* (Italian Bread Soup; recipe in Chapter 17)

1 medium apple

1 cup carrot sticks

1½ TB. reduced-fat ranch dressing

Total lunch calories: *468*

Dinner:

1 serving Turkey Cutlets with Apple Compote (recipe in Chapter 13)

¾ cup brown rice

1 cup steamed green beans

1 tsp. margarine spread

1 cup skim milk

Total dinner calories: *537*

Snack 1:

1 Granola Bar (recipe in Chapter 21)

Total snack 1 calories: *278*

Snack 2:

1 serving Spinach-Stuffed Mushrooms (recipe in Chapter 19)

Total snack 2 calories: *175*

Total calories for day 12:   **1,832**

Day 13

	Calories
Breakfast:	
1 serving Breakfast Parfait (recipe in Chapter 6)	
½ cup 100 percent orange juice	
1 slice whole-wheat toast	
1 tsp. margarine spread	
Total breakfast calories:	*361*
Lunch:	
1 serving Cannellini Bean Salad (recipe in Chapter 10)	
¾ cup skim milk	
¾ cup seedless grapes	
Total lunch calories:	*473*
Dinner:	
1 serving Texas Chili (recipe in Chapter 17)	
6 low-sodium saltines	
1½ cups garden salad (lettuce, tomato, cucumber, etc.)	
2 TB. reduced-fat dressing	
1 cup skim milk	
Total dinner calories:	*504*
Snack 1:	
1 serving Cape Cod Trail Mix (recipe in Chapter 21)	
Total snack 1 calories:	*286*
Snack 2:	
1 serving Pumpkin Custard (recipe in Chapter 22)	
Total snack 2 calories:	*177*
Total calories for day 13:	**1,801**

Day 14

	Calories
Breakfast:	
1 serving Crispy Potato Cups Stuffed with Spinach and Ham (recipe in Chapter 7)	
½ cup skim milk	
1 small banana	
Total breakfast calories:	*388*
Lunch:	
2 slices whole-grain bread	
2 TB. peanut butter	
2 tsp. all-fruit spread	
1 cup melon cubes	
1 cup skim milk	
Total lunch calories:	*499*
Dinner:	
1 serving Beef Stroganoff (recipe in Chapter 14)	
1 cup garden salad (lettuce, tomato, cucumber, etc.)	
2 TB. reduced-fat dressing	
1 cup skim milk	
Total dinner calories:	*556*
Snack 1:	
1 serving Roasted Red Pepper Hummus (variation in Chapter 19)	
Total snack 1 calories:	*177*
Snack 2:	
1 serving Chocolate-Covered-Strawberry Trifle (variation in Chapter 22)	
Total snack 2 calories:	*183*
Total calories for day 14:	**1,803**

As you can see, keeping your calories in check doesn't mean eating the same bland, boring foods day after day. Whatever your calorie needs are to allow you to lose weight or maintain a healthy weight, you're sure to find yourself satisfied with the menus in this chapter.

Once you're through the 2 weeks, feel free to repeat the menu as is or swap out the recipes for other recipes in this book with the same calorie level. When you're comfortable with that, you can try adding in some of your family favorites once in a while, too.

The Least You Need to Know

- Adapting to a new way of eating, especially if you're lowering your calories, can feel daunting, but the easy-to-follow menu plans in this chapter should help.
- Try the 1,300-calorie meal plan if you're small framed or looking for a weight-loss jump-start.
- Try the 1,550-calorie meal plan if you need a few more energizing calories to power you through your day.
- If you're tall or very active, try the 1,800-calorie meal plan.

Unbeatable Breakfasts

Always start your day with a balanced breakfast. Breakfast is your first opportunity, after the long fast of night, to fuel your body for the day ahead. In addition, due to the nature of typical breakfast foods, it's a great chance for you to get your first daily serving of almost every food group—fruit, dairy, lean protein, whole grain, healthy fats, and maybe even some veggies.

In Part 2, we share recipes for eggs, pancakes, breakfast sandwiches, smoothies, and much more. No matter what your morning holds, you'll find a breakfast in these chapters to fit the bill. If it's a relaxing morning, and you have lots of time, you'll find a variety of breakfasts to enjoy. On the other hand, we also give you plenty of quick-fix and grab-and-go ideas for those mornings when time is a luxury you don't have.

You'll also find breakfasts to fit any palate. Go for the pancakes or waffles if you want to start with something a little sweet. Eggs and bacon offer a protein-packed start to your day. And when you need a cool, refreshing beginning, check out the smoothies.

*Eggs*traordinary Eggs

In This Chapter

- Starting your day with protein
- Very veggie morning meals
- Nutrient-rich breakfasts

Eggs have been given a bad rep in the past. For years, they were public enemy number one in the battle against high cholesterol. Fortunately for egg lovers everywhere, more recent research has taught us that eggs can be included in a healthy diet.

As it turns out, eggs don't contain as much cholesterol as once believed, and they're very low in saturated fat, which is the real bad guy when it comes to heart disease. So a fairly healthy person can include up to an egg a day, while someone with a history of heart disease can enjoy one several times a week.

But after all the years of skipping eggs, why should we start eating them again? For at least a dozen reasons. Eggs are a low-fat source of high-quality protein. They're low in calories and sodium. And eggs are a good source of an assortment of vitamins and minerals, including choline and vitamin A, that play roles in eye health, brain function, healthy pregnancies, and more.

Eggs Florentine

Black pepper and Parmesan cheese give flair to these mild eggs served on a delightfully colorful "nest" of spinach.

Yield:	Prep time:	Cook time:	Serving size:
4 ramekins	5 to 10 minutes	15 to 20 minutes	1 ramekin

Each serving has:			
113 calories	10 g protein	4 g carbohydrates	3 g fiber
	7 g total fat	2 g saturated fat	192 mg sodium

1 (10-oz.) bag or box frozen chopped spinach, thawed and squeezed dry	4 large eggs
	⅛ tsp. black pepper
½ tsp. garlic powder	2 TB. grated Parmesan cheese

1. Preheat the oven to 350°F. Lightly coat 4 (6-ounce) ramekins or custard cups with nonstick cooking spray.

2. In a medium bowl, combine spinach and garlic powder.

3. Fill each ramekin with ¼ cup spinach mixture, making an indentation in spinach to hold egg.

4. One at a time, carefully break 1 egg into a small bowl and then slide into each spinach cup. Top with pinch black pepper and 1½ teaspoons Parmesan cheese.

5. Bake for 15 to 20 minutes or until egg whites are set and Parmesan cheese is golden brown. Serve immediately.

MAKE IT A MEAL

A whole-grain English muffin, bowl of melon cubes, and glass of skim milk help complete this nutrient-packed egg dish.

Scrambled Eggs and Potatoes

The heartwarming aroma of baking potatoes is brightened by the addition of parsley, making these scrambled eggs a delicious way to start the day.

Yield:	Prep time:	Cook time:	Serving size:
4 cups	10 minutes	10 to 15 minutes	1 cup

Each serving has:			
114 calories	8 g protein	10 g carbohydrates	1 g fiber
	5 g total fat	2 g saturated fat	199 mg sodium

1 medium russet potato	¼ tsp. kosher salt
2 TB. skim milk	⅛ tsp. black pepper
4 large eggs, beaten	2 TB. chopped fresh parsley

1. Wash russet potato, and prick with a fork. Place potato in a microwave-safe dish and cook on high for 6 to 8 minutes. Turn potato over halfway through the cook time. When potato is cool enough to handle, chop into 1-inch cubes.

2. In a medium bowl, combine skim milk and eggs.

3. Lightly coat a 12-inch nonstick sauté pan with nonstick cooking spray, and set over medium heat. Add egg mixture and potatoes. Using a heat-resistant rubber spatula, gently fold eggs into soft curds. As egg mixture thickens, begin to fold more quickly. Continue this for about 3 to 5 minutes or until eggs are cooked.

4. Season with kosher salt and black pepper, garnish with parsley, and serve.

Variation: For **Scrambled Eggs and Turkey Bacon,** eliminate the potato and add 4 strips turkey bacon. Heat a 12-inch, nonstick sauté pan lightly coated with nonstick cooking spray over medium heat. Sauté bacon in the pan for 3 or 4 minutes per side or until crisp. Remove bacon from the pan, and keep it warm. Add eggs to the pan, and cook for 3 to 5 minutes. *Each serving has: 109 calories, 9 g protein, 1 g carbohydrates, 0 g fiber, 8 g total fat, 2 g saturated fat, 365 mg sodium.*

MAKE IT A MEAL

A cup of vanilla nonfat yogurt topped with sliced bananas is all you need to round out this meal.

Shirred Eggs

The spark of Parmesan and black pepper radiate throughout the smooth flavor of this aromatic, protein-packed comfort food.

Yield:	Prep time:	Cook time:	Serving size:
4 ramekins	5 to 10 minutes	12 to 15 minutes	1 ramekin

Each serving has:			
161 calories	14 g protein	1 g carbohydrates	0 g fiber
	11 g total fat	4 g saturated fat	315 mg sodium

¼ tsp. kosher salt	2 TB. grated Parmesan cheese
⅛ tsp. black pepper	2 TB. chopped fresh chives
8 large eggs	

1. Preheat the oven to 350°F. Lightly coat 4 (6-ounce) ramekins or custard cups with nonstick cooking spray.

2. Sprinkle pinch kosher salt and pinch black pepper into each ramekin.

3. Carefully crack 2 eggs into each ramekin, and top each with 1½ teaspoons Parmesan cheese and 1½ teaspoons chives.

4. Bake for 20 to 25 minutes or until egg whites are set.

MAKE IT A MEAL

A piece of whole-grain toast and some fresh fruit will turn this yummy egg dish into a delicious way to start the day.

Skillet Breakfast

The aroma of baked potato merges with the tantalizing sizzle of bacon in this delectable one-pan breakfast.

Yield:	Prep time:	Cook time:	Serving size:
4 eggs	10 to 15 minutes	20 to 25 minutes	1 egg

Each serving has:			
169 calories	11 g protein 9 g total fat	10 g carbohydrates 3 g saturated fat	1 g fiber 410 mg sodium

1 medium baking potato	¼ cup shredded reduced-fat cheddar cheese
4 slices turkey bacon, cooked and crumbled	¼ tsp. kosher salt
4 large eggs	⅛ tsp. black pepper

1. Preheat the oven to 350°F. Lightly coat a 12-inch skillet with nonstick cooking spray and place in the preheating oven.

2. Wash potato, and prick with a fork. Place potato in a microwave-safe dish, and cook on high for 6 to 8 minutes. Turn potato over halfway through the cook time. When potato is cool enough to handle, slice into circles.

3. In a medium bowl, combine potato and turkey bacon.

4. Carefully remove the skillet from the oven, and add potato and bacon.

5. One at a time, carefully break eggs into a small bowl and then pour into the skillet. Top with cheddar cheese, kosher salt, and black pepper.

6. Bake for 12 to 15 minutes or until whites are set.

CULINARY KNOW-HOW

Cracking your eggs into a small bowl first makes it easier to remove any shells that may have fallen in. Plus, if you happen to get a bad egg, you haven't ruined your whole dish.

Mushroom Frittata

The tang of spinach and Parmesan cheese give this smooth and creamy oven omelet extra flavor.

Yield:	Prep time:	Cook time:	Serving size:
8 slices	10 minutes	20 to 25 minutes	2 slices

Each serving has:			
172 calories	15 g protein	3 g carbohydrates	1 g fiber
	11 g total fat	4 g saturated fat	212 mg sodium

8 large eggs, beaten

2 cups fresh cooked spinach or ½ cup frozen spinach, thawed, drained, cooked, and chopped

½ cup cooked crimini or button mushrooms, chopped

2 TB. chopped fresh parsley

2 TB. grated Parmesan cheese

¼ tsp. black pepper

1. Preheat the oven to 350°F.

2. Lightly coat a 12-inch, nonstick, oven-safe sauté pan with nonstick cooking spray, and set over medium heat. Allow to heat for about 20 seconds.

3. Meanwhile, in a medium bowl, combine eggs, spinach, crimini mushrooms, parsley, Parmesan cheese, and black pepper. Pour egg mixture into the pan, and place in the oven. Bake for 20 to 25 minutes or until eggs begin to pull away from the side of the pan.

4. Remove the pan from the oven, and loosen frittata from the pan using a heat-resistant rubber spatula. Slide frittata onto a cutting board, cut into 8 slices, and serve.

Variations: For a **Loraine Frittata,** substitute 4 slices turkey bacon, cooked and crumbled, for ½ cup cooked spinach and ½ cup cooked mushrooms. Also swap ¼ cup grated Swiss cheese for 2 tablespoons Parmesan cheese. *Each serving has: 235 calories, 19 g protein, 2 g carbohydrates, 0 g fiber, 16 g total fat, 6 g saturated fat, 343 mg sodium.*

For a **Spinach and Potato Frittata,** substitute 1 medium potato, cooked, for ½ cup cooked mushrooms. *Each serving has: 207 calories, 15 g protein, 11 g carbohydrates, 2 g fiber, 11 g total fat, 4 g saturated fat, 216 mg sodium.*

MAKE IT A MEAL

For a full breakfast, simply add 1 or 2 slices whole-grain toast and a medium orange. Or enjoy for lunch with a simple green salad and whole-grain roll.

All-in-One Egg Breakfast

The delightful textures and scrumptious flavors of bacon, potato, and cheese make this melt-in-your-mouth egg dish a luscious, fragrant way to start your day.

Yield:	Prep time:	Cook time:	Serving size:
4 slices	10 minutes	10 to 15 minutes	1 slice

Each serving has:			
195 calories	13 g protein 11 g total fat	10 g carbohydrates 5 g saturated fat	1 g fiber 460 mg sodium

1 medium russet potato

4 slices turkey bacon, cooked and chopped

¼ cup shredded reduced-fat cheddar cheese

4 large eggs, beaten

2 TB. skim milk

¼ tsp. kosher salt

¼ tsp. black pepper

2 TB. chopped fresh parsley

1. Wash potato and prick with a fork. Place potato in a microwave-safe dish, and cook on high for 6 to 8 minutes. Turn potato over halfway through the cook time. Remove potato from the microwave, and chop into 1-inch pieces.

2. In a large bowl, combine turkey bacon, cheddar cheese, eggs, and skim milk.

3. Lightly coat a 12-inch nonstick sauté pan with nonstick cooking spray, and set over medium heat. Add egg mixture and potatoes. When edges of eggs begin to set, slide a rubber spatula under edges to allow uncooked eggs to flow onto pan surface. Continue this until eggs are cooked.

4. Season with kosher salt and black pepper, garnish with parsley, and serve.

 MAKE IT A MEAL

All you need is a cold glass of 100 percent fruit juice to wash down this hearty breakfast.

Hearty Canadian Breakfast

The mild saltiness of Canadian bacon merges with the smoothness of a lightly boiled egg and crisp, sweet whole wheat in this delightful, fragrant morning meal.

Yield:	Prep time:	Cook time:	Serving size:
8 eggs, 4 strips bacon, 4 English muffins	15 to 20 minutes	5 to 10 minutes	2 eggs, 1 strip bacon, 1 English muffin

Each serving has:			
219 calories	20 g protein 12 g total fat	8 g carbohydrates 4 g saturated fat	1 g fiber 598 mg sodium

2 qt. water

8 large eggs

4 slices Canadian bacon

4 100 percent whole-wheat English muffins, toasted

1. In a large pot over medium heat, bring water to a boil. Add eggs, in shells, and cook for 3 to $3\frac{1}{2}$ minutes.

2. Lightly coat a nonstick sauté pan with nonstick cooking spray, and set over medium heat. Add Canadian bacon and cook for 1 or 2 minutes per side.

3. Remove eggs from water. Break shell on one end of each egg, and scoop out eggs into 4 separate bowls.

4. Serve eggs with Canadian bacon and toasted English muffins.

 TASTY TIDBIT

Canadian bacon is more like ham than bacon, and it's actually pretty low in fat. In Canada, it's known as "back bacon" because it's a cured pork loin, whereas in the United States, bacon is from the belly.

California Scramble

Rich, creamy avocado blends with the sharpness of Monterey Jack cheese and the fresh crispness of sprouts in this exciting scramble.

Yield:	Prep time:	Cook time:	Serving size:
2 eggs	5 minutes	8 minutes	2 eggs

Each serving has:			
220 calories	15 g protein 16 g total fat	4 g carbohydrates 5 g saturated fat	2 g fiber 202 mg sodium

2 large eggs
1 TB. shredded reduced-fat
 Monterey Jack cheese

¼ medium avocado, peeled, pitted, and diced
1 TB. alfalfa sprouts

1. Heat a small, nonstick skillet over medium-low heat.

2. In a small bowl, whisk eggs until well blended. Pour into the skillet and cook, stirring often, for 3 to 5 minutes or until eggs are almost set.

3. Sprinkle Monterey Jack cheese and avocado on top, and stir until well combined and heated through.

4. Top with alfalfa sprouts, and serve.

 TASTY TIDBIT

Avocados are high in fat, but it's a heart-healthy type of fat. So although they're fantastic to include in your diet, keep your portion sizes on the small side.

Poached Eggs with Avocado and Tomato

Rich, tangy, and bright flavors top golden brown pieces of warm toast.

Yield:	Prep time:	Cook time:	Serving size:
4 open-face sandwiches	10 minutes	12 to 15 minutes	1 open-face sandwich

Each serving has:			
236 calories	11 g protein	13 g carbohydrates	8 g fiber
	13 g total fat	3 g saturated fat	350 mg sodium

2 qt. water

1 TB. cider, white wine, or rice vinegar, or lemon juice

4 large eggs

4 slices 100 percent whole-wheat bread, toasted

1 medium avocado, peeled, pitted, and sliced

4 ($\frac{1}{4}$-in.-thick) slices tomato

$\frac{1}{4}$ tsp. kosher salt

$\frac{1}{8}$ tsp. black pepper

1. In a large, shallow pot over medium-high heat, bring water to a boil. (Water should be about 2 inches deep.) Add cider vinegar, and reduce heat to a simmer.

2. One at a time, crack egg into a cup and slowly slide egg into water. Repeat with remaining eggs. Cook for 4 to $4\frac{1}{2}$ minutes. Using a slotted spoon, carefully remove eggs from water.

3. Top each toasted whole-wheat bread slice with avocado and tomato slices, followed by 1 poached egg. Season with kosher salt and black pepper, and serve.

TASTY TIDBIT

Adding vinegar to the water helps set the egg whites quickly around the yolk.

Huevos Rancheros Wraps

Rich and hearty with the kick of tomato salsa, these breakfast wraps will have you ready to roll!

Yield:	Prep time:	Cook time:	Serving size:
4 wraps	5 to 10 minutes	10 minutes	1 wrap

Each serving has:			
271 calories	15 g protein	27 g carbohydrates	5 g fiber
	12 g total fat	5 g saturated fat	696 mg sodium

4 large eggs, beaten	4 (8-in.) whole-wheat tortillas
¼ tsp. black pepper	½ cup mild salsa
¼ cup shredded reduced-fat cheddar cheese	¼ cup canned black beans, drained and rinsed

1. Lightly coat a nonstick sauté pan with nonstick cooking spray, and set over medium heat. Add eggs, and stir with a heat-resistant rubber spatula. Cook for 3 or 4 minutes or until eggs are cooked and set.

2. Season egg mixture with black pepper, turn off heat, top with cheddar cheese, and set aside to melt cheese.

3. Meanwhile, place whole-wheat tortillas between paper towels, and microwave on high for 20 seconds.

4. Divide egg mixture among tortillas, top each with equal amounts salsa and black beans, roll, and serve.

CULINARY KNOW-HOW

To vary the taste of this dish, try it with one of the many different flavor tortillas available. Tomato or spinach tortillas would be great, or try different types of salsa—hot, chipotle, corn, or whatever suits your fancy.

Breakfast Tacos

Bright, spicy, smooth, and creamy are what you'll find in this hearty, Mexican-inspired breakfast.

Yield:	Prep time:	Cook time:	Serving size:
4 tacos	5 minutes	20 minutes	1 taco

Each serving has:			
301 calories	17 g protein	30 g carbohydrates	6 g fiber
	12 g total fat	5 g saturated fat	511 mg sodium

1 cup canned pinto beans, drained and rinsed	½ tsp. kosher salt
1 cup cooked brown rice	¼ tsp. black pepper
½ cup mild salsa	4 100 percent whole-wheat tortillas
½ cup water	¼ cup grated low-fat cheddar cheese
2 tsp. chili powder	4 TB. low-fat sour cream
4 large eggs, beaten	

1. In a medium microwave-safe bowl, combine pinto beans, brown rice, salsa, water, and chili powder. Cover with a plastic lid and microwave on high for 2 to 4 minutes.

2. Lightly coat a nonstick sauté pan with nonstick cooking spray, and set over medium heat. Add eggs, and using a heat-resistant rubber spatula, gently fold eggs into soft curds. As egg mixture thickens, begin to fold more quickly. Continue until eggs are cooked, about 3 to 5 minutes. Season with kosher salt and black pepper.

3. Meanwhile, place whole-wheat tortillas between paper towels, and microwave on high for 20 seconds.

4. Fill tortillas with eggs and bean-and-rice mixture. Top with cheddar cheese and sour cream, and serve.

TASTY TIDBIT

The brown rice and beans bump up the fiber in this Mexican-inspired breakfast.

Denver Omelets

Bursting with flavor, this colorful, rich omelet is enhanced by the tangy addition of citrus and the aromatic, crispy goodness of whole-wheat toast.

Yield:	Prep time:	Cook time:	Serving size:
4 omelets	5 to 10 minutes	10 to 20 minutes	1 omelet

Each serving has:			
313 calories	21 g protein	37 g carbohydrates	9 g fiber
	11 g total fat	4 g saturated fat	624 mg sodium

1 small yellow onion, diced

1 small green bell pepper, diced

½ cup diced low-sodium ham

6 large eggs, beaten

⅛ tsp. kosher salt

⅛ tsp. black pepper

2 TB. shredded reduced-fat cheddar cheese

4 slices 100 percent whole-wheat bread, toasted

4 medium oranges, sliced into wedges

1. Lightly coat a 12-inch nonstick sauté pan with nonstick cooking spray, and set over medium heat. Add yellow onion and green bell pepper, and cook for 5 to 10 minutes.

2. Mix in ham.

3. Stir in eggs using a heat-resistant rubber spatula. When edges of eggs begin to set, slide a rubber spatula under eggs and allow uncooked eggs to flow onto pan surface, and cook for 5 to 10 minutes or until eggs are set.

4. Season with kosher salt and black pepper, remove from heat, and fold in cheddar cheese.

5. Serve omelets with whole-wheat toast and orange slices.

CULINARY KNOW-HOW

If you don't have any leftover ham for this recipe, ask for ¼ pound of low-sodium ham, sliced thick, at your grocer's deli.

Oatmeal Surprise

The salty crunch of bacon and the soft richness of egg blend with the mildness of oatmeal in this savory concoction.

Yield:	Prep time:	Cook time:	Serving size:
4 cups	5 minutes	15 to 20 minutes	1 cup

Each serving has:			
409 calories	21 g protein	53 g carbohydrates	8 g fiber
	14 g total fat	5 g saturated fat	482 mg sodium

8 slices center-cut bacon

2 qt. water

1 TB. cider, white, rice vinegar, or lemon juice

2 cups plain instant oatmeal

4 large eggs

¼ tsp. kosher salt

⅛ tsp. black pepper

1. Lightly coat a nonstick sauté pan with nonstick cooking spray, and set over medium heat. Add center-cut bacon, and sauté for 3 or 4 minutes per side or until crisp. Remove bacon from the pan, and place on paper towels to drain. Break into pieces.

2. In a large shallow pot over medium-high heat, bring water to a boil. (Water should be about 2 inches deep.) Add cider vinegar.

3. Prepare instant oatmeal according to the package directions.

4. Reduce heat under the pot to low. One at a time, crack egg into a cup and then slowly slide egg into water. Repeat with remaining eggs. Cook for 4 to 4½ minutes. Using a slotted spoon, carefully remove eggs from water.

5. Divide oatmeal among bowls, top each with 1 poached egg and 2 slices bacon, season with kosher salt and black pepper, and serve.

 TASTY TIDBIT

The vinegar helps keep the egg white from spreading during cooking.

From the Griddle

In This Chapter

- Tasty breakfast sandwiches
- Starting the day with nutritious whole grains
- Fresh and fruity griddle breakfasts

Pancakes (and waffles) are breakfast's blank canvases. Although they're fairly simple on their own—flour, eggs, and liquid—with a nice, albeit mostly plain flavor, they're ideal for the addition of spices, fruits, sauces, meats, and an assortment of other flavor boosters, both sweet and savory. In addition, the basic recipe is low in fat, calories, and sodium and can be a great source of whole grains. Plus they're incredibly easy to make!

In this chapter, we give you an array of recipes pairing different fruits with pancakes and other griddle breads, some using different grains and others incorporating spreads. Plenty of delicious and nutritious breakfasts await you using these recipes as is, but don't be afraid to get creative. Experiment with different spices, fruits, and grains. With your trusty griddle (or waffle iron), you'll have no shortage of healthy, yummy breakfasts.

Gingered Whole-Wheat Toast with Ham

The sweetness of the ginger preserve complements the rich saltiness of the ham.

Yield:	Prep time:	Cook time:	Serving size:
4 pieces toast	5 minutes	5 minutes	1 piece toast

Each serving has:			
228 calories	17 g protein 6 g total fat	27 g carbohydrates 2 g saturated fat	4 g fiber 684 mg sodium

4 (2-oz.) slices low-sodium ham

4 slices 100 percent whole-wheat
    bread, toasted

4 TB. ginger preserves

1. Lightly coat a 12-inch nonstick sauté pan with nonstick cooking spray, and set over medium heat. Add ham, and cook for 2 minutes per side.

2. Divide whole-wheat toast slices among 4 plates. Top each with 1 tablespoon ginger preserves and 1 slice ham, and serve.

MAKE IT A MEAL

A cup of plain or vanilla nonfat yogurt mixed with ½ cup of your favorite berries goes well alongside this tasty toast.

The Breakfast Club

Juicy tomato, sharp Swiss, and protein-rich eggs are sandwiched in an English muffin with just the right amount of crunch.

Yield:	Prep time:	Cook time:	Serving size:
4 sandwiches	5 to 10 minutes	10 minutes	1 sandwich

Each serving has:			
261 calories	19 g protein 11 g total fat	28 g carbohydrates 5 g saturated fat	9 g fiber 403 mg sodium

4 large eggs, beaten	4 (1-oz.) slices low-fat Swiss cheese
$\frac{1}{8}$ tsp. kosher salt	4 ($\frac{1}{4}$-in.-thick) slices tomato
$\frac{1}{8}$ tsp. black pepper	
4 100 percent whole-wheat English muffins, split in $\frac{1}{2}$ and toasted	

1. Lightly coat a 10-inch, nonstick sauté pan with nonstick cooking spray, and set over medium heat. Stir in eggs, and using a heat-resistant rubber spatula, gently fold eggs into soft curds. As egg mixture thickens, begin to fold more quickly. Continue until eggs are cooked, about 3 to 5 minutes. Season with kosher salt and black pepper.

2. Divide toasted English muffin bottoms among 4 plates. Top each with 1 slice Swiss cheese, $\frac{1}{4}$ of eggs, and 1 slice tomato. Add English muffin tops, and serve.

MAKE IT A MEAL

If you need a little more to go along with this hearty sandwich, try about 1 cup watermelon cubes on the side.

Waffle Ham Sandwiches

Sweet syrup and salty ham pair perfectly between whole-grain waffles.

Yield:	Prep time:	Cook time:	Serving size:
4 sandwiches	5 minutes	5 minutes	1 sandwich

Each serving has:			
281 calories	11 g protein 8 g total fat	41 g carbohydrates 2 g saturated fat	3 g fiber 697 mg sodium

4 (1-oz.) slices low-sodium ham	4 TB. maple syrup
8 whole-grain toaster waffles, toasted	

1. Lightly coat a nonstick sauté pan with nonstick cooking spray, and set over medium heat. Add ham, and cook for 2 minutes per side.

2. Divide 4 toasted waffles among 4 plates. Top each waffle with 1 tablespoon maple syrup and 1 slice ham. Add remaining 4 waffles on top to make 4 sandwiches, and serve.

Variation: For **Waffle Sausage Sandwiches,** replace the ham with 4 links low-fat turkey breakfast sausage, cooked according to package directions and sliced lengthwise. *Each serving has: 299 calories, 9 g protein, 42 g carbohydrates, 3 g fiber, 11 g total fat, 2 g saturated fat, 588 mg sodium.*

CULINARY KNOW-HOW

Try to use real maple syrup in this recipe instead of maple-flavored pancake syrup. It's all-natural and has a much more maple-y flavor.

Strawberry-Stuffed French Toast

Strawberries add a hint of natural sweetness to this creamy filled French toast.

Yield:	Prep time:	Cook time:	Serving size:
8 pieces toast	10 to 15 minutes	10 minutes	2 pieces toast

Each serving has:			
283 calories	17 g protein 8 g total fat	35 g carbohydrates 4 g saturated fat	9 g fiber 583 mg sodium

1 cup egg substitute

½ cup water

½ tsp. vanilla extract

1 cup whipped low-fat cream
cheese

8 slices 100 percent whole-wheat
bread

1 cup sliced fresh strawberries

1. Lightly coat a nonstick sauté pan with nonstick cooking spray, and set over medium heat.

2. In a shallow dish, whisk together egg substitute, water, and vanilla extract. Set aside.

3. Spread cream cheese on 1 side of each of 4 pieces of whole-wheat bread. Top each with ¼ cup sliced strawberries, followed by remaining bread slices to make 4 sandwiches. Gently press down on each sandwich.

4. Place stuffed bread slices into egg mixture, and carefully turn several times until all liquid is absorbed. Add to the sauté pan, cover, and cook for 3 to 5 minutes. Uncover, turn over sandwiches, and cook, uncovered, for 2 to 4 more minutes. Serve immediately.

Variation: For **Blueberry Stuffed French Toast,** replace the strawberries with 1 cup fresh blueberries. *Each serving has: 291 calories, 17 g protein, 38 g carbohydrates, 9 g fiber, 8 g total fat, 4 g saturated fat, 583 mg sodium.*

TASTY TIDBIT

Strawberries are a terrific source of vitamin C, which helps you stay healthy and may help you recover faster when you're sick.

Blueberry Pancakes

Pancakes filled with sweet, fresh blueberries are a great way to start the day.

Yield:	Prep time:	Cook time:	Serving size:
12 pancakes	5 to 10 minutes	4 or 5 minutes per batch	3 pancakes

Each serving has:			
284 calories	9 g protein	46 g carbohydrates	1 g fiber
	8 g total fat	5 g saturated fat	583 mg sodium

1½ cups all-purpose flour	1 cup skim milk
2½ tsp. baking powder	1 large egg, beaten
2 TB. sugar	2 TB. melted butter
¼ tsp. kosher salt	¼ cup fresh blueberries
¼ tsp. ground cinnamon	

1. In a large bowl, sift together all-purpose flour, baking powder, sugar, and kosher salt.

2. In a medium bowl, combine skim milk, egg, and melted butter. Mix skim milk mixture into dry ingredients. Do not overmix; batter should be light and fluffy.

3. Fold in blueberries.

4. Heat a nonstick sauté pan over medium heat, and lightly coat with nonstick cooking spray. Or preheat an electric griddle to 325°F.

5. For each pancake, spoon about ¼ cup batter into the pan. Using the back of a spoon, spread batter to 3 inches in diameter. Cook for 2 or 3 minutes or until top begins to look dry and bubbles have broken. Turn over pancakes and cook for 2 more minutes. Remove to a plate, cover with a towel to keep warm, and repeat with remaining batter.

6. Serve with maple syrup or jam.

Variations: For **Butterscotch-Chip Pancakes,** substitute ¼ cup butterscotch chips for the blueberries and omit ¼ teaspoon ground cinnamon. *Each serving has: 364 calories, 10 g protein, 64 g carbohydrates, 1 g fiber, 12 g total fat, 9 g saturated fat, 595 mg sodium.*

For **Cornmeal Pancakes,** reduce the flour to 1 cup and add $\frac{1}{2}$ cup yellow cornmeal. Omit the blueberries. *Each serving has: 308 calories, 8 g protein, 49 g carbohydrates, 1 g fiber, 8 g total fat, 5 g saturated fat, 585 mg sodium.*

For **Make-Ahead Pancakes,** omit the blueberries. Allow pancakes to cool; wrap in plastic wrap, layering waxed paper between pancakes; and freeze. To reheat, pop into the toaster on medium setting, and toast twice. *Each serving has: 284 calories, 9 g protein, 44 g carbohydrates, 1 g fiber, 8 g total fat, 5 g saturated fat, 585 mg sodium.*

Crepes with Fresh Berries and Crème Fraîche

The *crème fraîche* adds a nice tartness to the sweet berries in these breakfast crepes.

Yield:	Prep time:	Cook time:	Serving size:
4 crepes	35 minutes	10 to 15 minutes	2 crepes

Each serving has:			
287 calories	10 g protein 8 g total fat	44 g carbohydrates 4 g saturated fat	4 g fiber 200 mg sodium

1 large egg

½ cup skim milk

⅛ tsp. kosher salt

½ cup all-purpose flour

2 cups fresh strawberries, blueberries, or raspberries

4 TB. crème fraîche

1. In a medium bowl, beat together egg, skim milk, and kosher salt. Add all-purpose flour, and beat until smooth. Cover and set aside for 30 minutes.

2. Lightly coat a 7-inch nonstick sauté pan with nonstick cooking spray, and set over medium heat. Ladle ¼ batter into the pan, and tilt the pan so batter evenly spreads out over the bottom of the pan. Cook for 2 or 3 minutes or until bottom begins to brown and edges begin to curl. Flip over crepe using a heat-resistant rubber spatula, and cook for 1 more minute.

3. Lay 1 crepe at a time on a plate, top with ¼ of strawberries and 1 tablespoon crème fraîche, roll, and serve.

DEFINITION

Crème fraîche is a thickened, slightly tangy cream. If you can't find it, you can use light sour cream or plain, nonfat yogurt in its place.

Pumpkin-Spiced Pancakes

The heavenly scents of fall will float through your kitchen as you cook these delicious pancakes, and the flavors will tingle your tongue with each bite.

Yield:	Prep time:	Cook time:	Serving size:
12 pancakes	5 to 10 minutes	4 or 5 minutes per batch	3 pancakes

Each serving has:			
294 calories	9 g protein 8 g total fat	47 g carbohydrates 5 g saturated fat	2 g fiber 586 mg sodium

1½ cups all-purpose flour	½ tsp. ground nutmeg
2½ tsp. baking powder	1 cup skim milk
2 TB. sugar	1 large egg, beaten
¼ tsp. kosher salt	2 TB. melted butter
1 tsp. ground cinnamon	½ cup pumpkin purée
½ tsp. ground ginger	

1. In a large bowl, combine all-purpose flour, baking powder, sugar, kosher salt, cinnamon, ginger, and nutmeg.

2. In a medium bowl, combine skim milk, egg, melted butter, and pumpkin purée. Mix skim milk mixture into dry ingredients. Do not overmix. Batter should be light and fluffy.

3. Heat a nonstick sauté pan over medium heat, and lightly coat with nonstick cooking spray. Or preheat an electric griddle to 325°F.

4. For each pancake, spoon about ¼ cup batter into the pan. Using the back of a spoon, spread batter to 3 inches in diameter. Cook for 2 or 3 minutes or until top begins to look dry and bubbles have broken. Turn over pancakes and cook for 2 more minutes. Remove to a plate, cover with a towel to keep warm, and repeat with remaining batter.

TASTY TIDBIT

Canned pumpkin purée is an extremely simple, inexpensive, and delicious way to add more vitamin A into your diet. Try adding it to soups, muffin batters, oatmeal, and more.

Grilled Bananas and Almond Butter on Cinnamon Toast

The nuttiness of the almond butter blends well with the sweet cinnamon raisin bread.

Yield:	Prep time:	Cook time:	Serving size:
4 sandwiches	5 minutes	5 to 10 minutes	1 sandwich

Each serving has:			
303 calories	10 g protein	43 g carbohydrates	5 g fiber
	12 g total fat	1 g saturated fat	245 mg sodium

4 TB. almond butter

8 slices cinnamon raisin bread, toasted

2 small bananas, peeled and sliced

1. Lightly coat a 12-inch nonstick sauté pan with nonstick cooking spray, and set over medium heat.

2. Spread 1 tablespoon almond butter on 1 side of each of 4 slices of cinnamon raisin toast. Top with $\frac{1}{4}$ of sliced banana and 1 more slice toast. Repeat with remaining ingredients.

3. Place sandwich into the pan, gently press down, and cook for 2 or 3 minutes per side.

4. Slice in $\frac{1}{2}$, and serve.

Almond Butter and Apricot Toast

This crisp toast is topped with creamy almond butter, sweet apricots, and just a hint of brown sugar.

Yield:	Prep time:	Cook time:	Serving size:
4 pieces toast	5 to 10 minutes	2 or 3 minutes	1 piece toast

Each serving has:			
310 calories	11 g protein 19 g total fat	27 g carbohydrates 1 g saturated fat	8 g fiber 205 mg sodium

4 slices 100 percent whole-wheat
   bread, toasted

8 TB. almond butter

4 medium apricots, pitted, peeled,
   and sliced

4 tsp. dark brown sugar

1. Preheat the broiler to 400°F. Position the broiler rack 3 inches from the heat source.

2. Spread each slice of whole-wheat toast with 2 tablespoons almond butter. Top with $\frac{1}{4}$ apricot slices and 1 teaspoon dark brown sugar.

3. Place toast on a baking sheet, and place under the broiler for 2 or 3 minutes.

4. Slice in $\frac{1}{2}$, and serve.

Very Berry Wheat-Germ Pancakes

Wheat germ adds a unique texture to these molasses-laced pancakes that are topped deliciously with sweet fruit and tangy crème fraîche.

Yield:	Prep time:	Cook time:	Serving size:
12 pancakes	5 to 10 minutes	4 or 5 minutes per batch	3 pancakes

Each serving has:			
354 calories	11 g protein 12 g total fat	52 g carbohydrates 7 g saturated fat	3 g fiber 593 mg sodium

1¼ cups all-purpose flour
¼ cup wheat germ
2½ tsp. baking powder
1 TB. molasses
2 TB. sugar
¼ tsp. kosher salt
¼ tsp. ground cinnamon

1 cup skim milk
1 large egg, beaten
2 TB. melted butter
1 cup fresh strawberries, blueberries, and/or raspberries
¼ cup crème fraîche

1. In a large bowl, combine all-purpose flour, wheat germ, baking powder, molasses, sugar, and kosher salt.

2. In a medium bowl, combine skim milk, egg, and melted butter. Mix skim milk mixture into dry ingredients. Do not overmix. Batter should be light and fluffy.

3. Heat a nonstick sauté pan over medium heat, and lightly coat with nonstick cooking spray. Or preheat an electric griddle to 325°F.

4. For each pancake, spoon about ¼ cup batter into the pan. Using the back of a spoon, spread batter to 3 inches in diameter. Cook for 2 or 3 minutes or until top begins to look dry and bubbles have broken. Turn over pancakes and cook for 2 more minutes. Remove to a plate, cover with a towel to keep warm, and repeat with remaining batter.

5. Serve with fresh berries and crème fraîche.

Variation: For **Buckwheat Pancakes,** reduce the flour to 1 cup, omit the wheat germ, and add $\frac{1}{2}$ cup buckwheat flour. Add 1 tablespoon molasses, and omit the fresh berries and crème fraîche. *Each serving has: 292 calories, 9 g protein, 45 g carbohydrates, 3 g fiber, 9 g total fat, 5 g saturated fat, 587 mg sodium.*

TASTY TIDBIT

Wheat germ is one of the inner parts of the wheat grain. It's a great source of vitamin E.

The Presley Panini

This healthier version of The King's favorite still has all that peanut butter and banana goodness.

Yield:	Prep time:	Cook time:	Serving size:
4 sandwiches	10 to 15 minutes	10 minutes	1 sandwich

Each serving has:			
373 calories	14 g protein	46 g carbohydrates	11 g fiber
	17 g total fat	3 g saturated fat	402 mg sodium

½ cup peanut butter	2 medium bananas, peeled and sliced
8 slices 100 percent whole-wheat bread	4 tsp. margarine

1. Spread 2 tablespoons peanut butter on 1 side of each of 4 pieces of whole-wheat bread. Top each with ¼ of sliced bananas, and add 1 slice bread on top of each to make 4 sandwiches. Gently press down on each sandwich.

2. Spread margarine evenly on outer sides of each sandwich.

3. Heat a 10-inch nonstick sauté pan over medium heat. Place sandwiches in the pan, and use a smaller pan to press down on sandwiches. Cook for 3 to 5 minutes or until golden brown on the bottom. Remove small pan, turn over sandwiches, and cook for 2 to 4 more minutes or until second side is golden brown.

4. Remove from the pan, slice in ½, and serve.

 TASTY TIDBIT

Bananas are a great source of potassium, which helps regulate blood pressure.

Great Grains

In This Chapter

- Hearty hot grains to warm you from the inside out
- Fiber-rich grain bowls
- Quick-and-easy grab-and-go breakfasts

The grains and seeds called for in this chapter's recipes—oats, quinoa, whole-wheat flour, and other whole-grain ingredients—are incredible sources of fiber as well as an assortment of B vitamins. They provide a mega dose of nutrition to start the day while satisfying your morning hunger and keeping you full for hours. Delaying hunger is a great way to help you say "no, thanks" to too many mid-morning munchies.

Steel-Cut Oatmeal

Slow cooking oats brings out their natural sweetness, which balances perfectly with the sour cherries and warm cinnamon in this hearty oatmeal.

Yield:	Prep time:	Cook time:	Serving size:
4 cups	5 minutes	25 minutes	1 cup

Each serving has:			
203 calories	5 g protein 1 g total fat	43 g carbohydrates 0 g saturated fat	6 g fiber 35 mg sodium

4 cups water	¼ tsp. ground cinnamon
1 cup steel-cut oats	¼ cup maple syrup
½ cup dried sour cherries	1 cup skim milk
¼ tsp. ground nutmeg	

1. In a 2-quart pot over medium-high heat, bring water to a boil. Stir in steel-cut oats, reduce heat to low, and cook for 20 to 25 minutes, stirring occasionally.

2. Stir in sour cherries, nutmeg, cinnamon, and maple syrup.

3. In a glass measuring cup, microwave skim milk on high for 30 seconds.

4. Divide oatmeal among 4 bowls, top with ¼ cup warm skim milk, and serve.

CULINARY KNOW-HOW

Soaking the oats overnight in the refrigerator in half the liquid reduces the cooking time by about half.

Breakfast Parfait

Creamy, crunchy, and with a touch of sweetness—what a better way to start the day!

Yield:	Prep time:	Serving size:
4 parfaits	10 minutes	1 parfait

Each serving has:			
204 calories	17 g protein	33 g carbohydrates	4 g fiber
	1 g total fat	0 g saturated fat	99 mg sodium

1 cup low-fat granola	2 cups fresh blueberries,
3 cups plain fat-free Greek yogurt	strawberries, or raspberries

1. Spoon ¼ cup granola into each of 4 (12-ounce) glasses.

2. Layer in ¾ cup Greek yogurt, followed by ½ cup blueberries, and serve.

TASTY TIDBIT

Parfaits are a great dish to make with your kids. They'll have a great time layering the different ingredients and then eating their colorful (and nutritious!) creation.

Quinoa Porridge

Quinoa's delicate flavor is enhanced with a touch of cinnamon.

Yield:	Prep time:	Cook time:	Serving size:
4 cups	5 minutes	12 to 15 minutes	1 cup

Each serving has:			
243 calories	10 g protein 7 g total fat	36 g carbohydrates 1 g saturated fat	5 g fiber 13 mg sodium

2 cups water	½ cup plain fat-free Greek yogurt
1 cup quinoa	¼ cup chopped toasted walnuts
¼ tsp. ground cinnamon	
1 medium Honeycrisp apple, cored and diced	

1. In a 2-quart pot over medium-high heat, bring water to a boil.

2. Lightly coat a 12-inch nonstick sauté pan with nonstick cooking spray, and set over medium heat. Add quinoa, and cook, stirring, for 1 minute.

3. Add quinoa, cinnamon, and Honeycrisp apple to the boiling water, cover, and reduce heat to low. Simmer for 10 to 12 minutes or until liquid is absorbed.

4. Spoon 1 cup quinoa porridge into each of 4 bowls, top with 2 tablespoons Greek yogurt and 1 tablespoon toasted walnuts, and serve.

TASTY TIDBIT

Quinoa is a seed rich in protein and other nutrients. Plus, it's naturally gluten free, perfect for those with celiac disease.

Cornmeal Porridge with Fruit and Honey

This porridge is bursting with the flavors of cornbread, plus highlights of honey and naturally sweet berries.

Yield:	Prep time:	Cook time:	Serving size:
4 cups	5 minutes	15 to 20 minutes	1 cup

Each serving has:			
261 calories	8 g protein 1 g total fat	56 g carbohydrates 0 g saturated fat	2 g fiber 189 mg sodium

1 cup coarse cornmeal

2 cups water

2 cups skim milk

¼ cup honey

¼ tsp. kosher salt

½ cup fresh strawberries, raspberries, or blueberries

1. In a small bowl, combine cornmeal with 1 cup water. Set aside.

2. In a 2-quart pot over medium-high heat, bring remaining 1 cup water and skim milk to a boil. Stir in cornmeal, reduce heat to low, and cook for 15 minutes.

3. Stir in honey and kosher salt.

4. If cornmeal porridge becomes too thick, add an additional ½ cup water. Stir vigorously after adding water.

5. Divide cornmeal porridge among 4 bowls, top with strawberries, and serve.

TASTY TIDBIT

This is a sweeter version of a popular savory Italian dish called polenta. Like other hot cereals, it's a great vehicle to get much-needed milk and fruit at the start of the day.

New England Breakfast Bowl

Tart cranberries and crunchy walnuts with a touch of cinnamon create a yummy way to warm your belly on a cold morning.

Yield:	Prep time:	Cook time:	Serving size:
1 bowl	1 minute	3 minutes	1 bowl

Each serving has:			
287 calories	14 g protein	46 g carbohydrates	4 g fiber
	7 g total fat	0 g saturated fat	210 mg sodium

1 (.98-oz.) pkg. plain instant
   oatmeal

1 cup skim milk

2 TB. dried cranberries

1 TB. chopped walnuts

$\frac{1}{4}$ tsp. vanilla extract

Dash ground cinnamon

1. In a microwave-safe bowl, combine instant oatmeal, $\frac{2}{3}$ cup skim milk, cranberries, walnuts, vanilla extract, and cinnamon. Cook, uncovered, on high for 1 minute. Stir, and cook for 1 more minute. Stir and continue heating in 30-second increments until desired consistency is reached.

2. Top with remaining $\frac{1}{3}$ cup milk, and serve.

Variations: For a **Banana-Walnut Breakfast Bowl,** replace the cranberries with $\frac{1}{2}$ small banana, peeled and chopped, and add 1 tablespoon maple syrup. Depending on your preference, banana can be added before or after cooking. *Each serving has: 335 calories, 15 g protein, 58 g carbohydrates, 5 g fiber, 7 g total fat, 1 g saturated fat, 213 mg sodium.*

For a **Wild Blueberry Breakfast Bowl,** replace the cranberries, walnuts, and cinnamon with $\frac{1}{4}$ cup frozen wild blueberries. *Each serving has: 208 calories, 13 g protein, 37 g carbohydrates, 5 g fiber, 2 g total fat, 0 g saturated fat, 211 mg sodium.*

TASTY TIDBIT

Flavored instant oatmeal packets contain a good deal of added sugar and, therefore, calories. You're better off doctoring up plain oatmeal yourself for a quick, hearty, and healthy breakfast.

Hot Millet Porridge with Dried Fruit

Sweet fruit and tropical coconut create a wonderful flavor combination with the millet.

Yield:	Prep time:	Cook time:	Serving size:
4 cups	5 minutes	25 to 30 minutes	1 cup

Each serving has:			
352 calories	12 g protein	67 g carbohydrates	7 g fiber
	4 g total fat	2 g saturated fat	103 mg sodium

2½ cups skim milk

1 cup water

1 cup millet

¼ cup dried apricots

¼ cup raisins

¼ cup dried cherries

¼ cup dried shredded coconut

1. In a 2-quart pot over medium-high heat, bring skim milk and water to a boil. Stir in millet, reduce heat to low, partially cover, and cook for 25 to 30 minutes.

2. Meanwhile, in a small bowl, combine apricots, raisins, cherries, and coconut.

3. Spoon 1 cup millet porridge into each of 4 bowls, top with ¼ cup dried fruit mixture, and serve.

TASTY TIDBIT

Millet is a small round grain and a good source of the minerals manganese, phosphorus, and magnesium. You should be able to find it in the cereal aisle of your grocery store.

Comforting Couscous

Here, couscous is enhanced with the rich flavor of molasses, the sweetness of honey, and the crunch of almonds.

Yield:	Prep time:	Cook time:	Serving size:
4 cups	1 minute	10 minutes	1 cup

Each serving has:			
359 calories	10 g protein 4 g total fat	70 g carbohydrates 0 g saturated fat	5 g fiber 47 mg sodium

1 cup almond milk	1½ cups couscous
1 cup water	¼ cup golden raisins
1 TB. honey	¼ cup unsalted toasted slivered
1 TB. molasses	almonds

1. In a 2-quart pot with a tight-fitting lid over medium-high heat, bring almond milk and water to a boil. Stir in honey, molasses, couscous, and golden raisins. Remove from heat, cover, and set aside for 10 minutes. Fluff couscous with a fork.

2. Spoon 1 cup couscous into each of 4 bowls, top with 1 tablespoon slivered almonds, and serve.

TASTY TIDBIT

Almond milk is a lactose-free alternative to cow's milk. It contains no saturated fat or cholesterol.

Apple Cider Muffins

Cinnamon, nutmeg, and apples bring the flavors of a crisp fall day at the apple orchard.

Yield:	Prep time:	Cook time:	Serving size:
12 muffins	15 minutes	18 to 22 minutes	2 muffins

Each serving has:			
364 calories	6 g protein	63 g carbohydrates	2 g fiber
	10 g total fat	1 g saturated fat	373 mg sodium

1 cup all-purpose flour

1 cup whole-wheat pastry flour or whole-wheat flour

$\frac{1}{2}$ tsp. baking soda

$1\frac{1}{2}$ tsp. baking powder

$\frac{1}{4}$ tsp. salt

$1\frac{1}{4}$ tsp. ground cinnamon

$\frac{1}{2}$ tsp. ground nutmeg

$\frac{1}{4}$ cup canola oil

$\frac{1}{2}$ cup brown sugar, firmly packed

1 large egg, beaten

1 tsp. vanilla extract

$\frac{1}{2}$ cup apple cider

$\frac{1}{2}$ cup plain or vanilla fat-free yogurt

$\frac{1}{2}$ cup apple butter

2 TB. sugar

1. Preheat the oven to 400°F. Line a 12-cup muffin pan with paper liners.

2. In a medium bowl, combine all-purpose flour, whole-wheat pastry flour, baking soda, baking powder, salt, 1 teaspoon cinnamon, and nutmeg. Set aside.

3. In a large bowl, combine canola oil, brown sugar, egg, vanilla extract, and apple cider.

4. Add dry ingredients to wet ingredients, alternating with yogurt.

5. Stir in apple butter just until combined, and spoon batter into muffin cups until $\frac{2}{3}$ full.

6. In a small bowl, combine sugar with remaining $\frac{1}{4}$ teaspoon cinnamon. Sprinkle each muffin with $\frac{1}{2}$ teaspoon cinnamon-sugar mixture.

7. Bake for 18 to 22 minutes or until a toothpick or cake tester inserted in center comes out clean.

8. Let muffins cool in the pan for 5 minutes before removing to a wire rack to cool completely.

Variation: For **Fill 'Em Up Muffins,** omit the apple butter and apple cider. Increase the yogurt to ¾ cup, and add 1 medium apple, peeled, cored, and chopped or grated; 1 medium carrot, peeled and shredded; and ¼ cup raisins, soaked in hot water and drained. Omit the sugar and cinnamon topping. *Each serving has: 344 calories, 7 g protein, 58 g carbohydrates, 3 g fiber, 10 g total fat, 1 g saturated fat, 381 mg sodium.*

MAKE IT A MEAL

To make this great breakfast even better, add a cold glass of skim milk.

Breakfast Barley

Tart cranberries and crunchy walnuts are the perfect accompaniment to nutty, chewy barley.

Yield:	Prep time:	Cook time:	Serving size:
5 cups	5 minutes	55 to 60 minutes	1¼ cups

Each serving has:			
400 calories	9 g protein 6 g total fat	83 g carbohydrates 1 g saturated fat	13 g fiber 127 mg sodium

3 cups water

1½ cups pearl barley

¼ tsp. kosher salt

¼ cup honey

¼ cup chopped walnuts, toasted

¼ cup dried cranberries

1. In a 2-quart pot over medium-high heat, bring water to a boil. Stir in pearl barley, kosher salt, and honey. Reduce heat to low, cover, and simmer for 55 to 60 minutes.

2. Spoon barley into each of 4 bowls, top with 1 tablespoon walnuts and 1 tablespoon dried cranberries, and serve.

TASTY TIDBIT

Cranberries contain a type of antioxidant called proanthcyanidins that can help prevent urinary tract infections.

Lazy Weekend Breakfasts

In This Chapter

- Easy and elegant breakfasts
- Simple starts for long and lazy mornings
- Fruity breakfast dishes
- Comforting soufflés and casseroles

It's always nice when you don't have to get up at the crack of dawn or when you have some extra time in the morning when you don't have to rush. Starting those days with the right amount of carbohydrates for energy and protein and healthy fats to help you feel fuller longer is just as crucial as it is on more harried weekday mornings. A morning meal with mouthwatering ingredients like pomegranate, Greek yogurt, melon, and cheeses is not only delicious but is nutritious, too, as you'll see by the recipes in this chapter.

Fresh Melon Salad with Mint, Basil, and Pomegranate Dressing

The mint and basil add an unexpected layer of flavor to this sweet salad.

Yield:	Prep time:	Serving size:
4 cups	5 to 10 minutes	1 cup

Each serving has:			
67 calories	1 g protein	16 g carbohydrates	1 g fiber
	0 g total fat	0 g saturated fat	30 mg sodium

½ medium cantaloupe, peeled, seeded, and diced (about 2 cups)

½ small honeydew melon, peeled, seeded, and diced (about 2 cups)

2 TB. chopped fresh mint

2 TB. chopped fresh basil

¼ cup pomegranate juice

1. In a large bowl, place cantaloupe, honeydew melon, mint, and basil.

2. Pour pomegranate juice over top, toss, and serve.

MAKE IT A MEAL

A couple slices of whole-grain toast and 1 cup of your favorite low-fat yogurt make this a relaxing breakfast.

Easy Soufflé

Light, fluffy eggs topped with a rich, cheesy sauce—delicious.

Yield:	Prep time:	Cook time:	Serving size:
4 cups	15 to 20 minutes	15 to 20 minutes	1 cup

Each serving has:			
173 calories	13 g protein	4 g carbohydrates	0 g fiber
	12 g total fat	5 g saturated fat	313 mg sodium

6 large eggs, separated	¼ cup shredded reduced-fat cheddar cheese
⅛ tsp. cream of tartar	
1 TB. butter	¼ tsp. kosher salt
1 TB. all-purpose flour	⅛ tsp. black pepper
½ cup skim milk	2 TB. chopped fresh chives

1. Preheat the oven to 350°F. Lightly coat a 1-quart oven-safe casserole dish with nonstick cooking spray.

2. In a large metal bowl, place egg whites. Using an electric mixer on low speed, begin whipping egg whites. Add cream of tartar, increase speed to high, and whip for 3 to 5 minutes or until egg whites are thick and glossy-looking (soft peak stage).

3. In a separate large bowl, beat egg yolks by hand for about 30 seconds or until blended. Using a rubber spatula, fold ⅓ of egg whites into egg yolks, and continue folding in until combined.

4. Pour whipped egg mixture into the prepared casserole dish, and bake for 12 to 15 minutes.

5. Meanwhile, in small saucepan over medium heat, melt butter. Whisk in 1 tablespoon flour, and cook for 1 minute.

6. Slowly add skim milk, and whisk until well blended and mixture begins to thicken. Remove from heat and stir in cheddar cheese, kosher salt, and black pepper.

7. Remove eggs from the oven. Spoon onto 4 separate plates, top each with 2 tablespoons cheese sauce, garnish with chives, and serve.

TASTY TIDBIT

Cream of tartar increases the stability and volume of the egg whites. In addition, be sure your bowls and utensils are free of all fat, grease, and oil to maximize volume.

Crispy Potato Cups Stuffed with Spinach and Ham

Nutrient-rich spinach and a salty bite from ham combine in a crispy potato cup.

Yield:	Prep time:	Cook time:	Serving size:
4 potato cups	5 to 10 minutes	30 to 35 minutes	1 potato cup

Each serving has:			
268 calories	16 g protein	40 g carbohydrates	5 g fiber
	5 g total fat	2 g saturated fat	462 mg sodium

4 medium russet potatoes	½ cup baked ham, chopped
Nonstick cooking spray	4 oz. light Boursin cheese
1 cup cooked spinach, chopped and drained	⅛ tsp. black pepper

1. Preheat the oven to 450°F.

2. Cut potatoes in ½ crosswise, and using a melon baller, scoop out the center. Leave the side about ¼ inch thick. (Save scooped-out potato for another use.) Cut a piece off the bottom so potatoes won't roll around.

3. In a large pot over medium-high heat, place potato cups with water to cover. Bring to a boil, and cook for 5 minutes. Remove potatoes from water, and set aside for 5 minutes.

4. Spray potato cups inside and out with nonstick cooking spray. Place potatoes in ramekins or custard cups, scooped side up. Bake for 20 minutes or until golden brown.

5. Meanwhile, in a small bowl, combine spinach, ham, Boursin cheese, and black pepper.

6. When potato cups are golden brown, reduce temperature to 350°F. Spoon ½ cup spinach mixture into each potato cup, and bake for 5 to 8 more minutes. Serve hot.

TASTY TIDBIT

Feel free to use frozen, chopped spinach (thawed and squeezed dry) in this recipe. It's a huge time-saver in the kitchen and still has all the nutrition of fresh.

French Toast Casserole

Protein-packed Greek yogurt provides a mild tang, which is balanced by sweet maple syrup.

Yield:	Prep time:	Cook time:	Serving size:
8 slices	35 to 40 minutes	12 to 15 minutes	2 slices

Each serving has:			
287 calories	23 g protein 2 g total fat	45 g carbohydrates 0 g saturated fat	8 g fiber 533 mg sodium

8 slices 100 percent whole-wheat bread	½ cup plain fat-free Greek yogurt
2 cups egg substitute	¼ tsp. ground cinnamon
½ cup skim milk	½ tsp. vanilla extract
	¼ cup maple syrup

1. Lightly coat a 10×14-inch oven-safe casserole dish with nonstick cooking spray.

2. Arrange whole-wheat bread slices in a single layer in the prepared casserole dish.

3. In a small bowl, combine egg substitute, skim milk, Greek yogurt, cinnamon, and vanilla extract. Pour egg mixture over bread, cover, and refrigerate for 30 minutes.

4. Preheat the oven to 350°F.

5. Remove casserole from the refrigerator, and bake for 12 to 15 minutes.

6. Serve with maple syrup.

 MAKE IT A MEAL

A sprinkle of fresh berries and a cup of warm skim milk with a dash of your favorite flavoring turn this into a meal to savor.

Cantaloupe with Cottage Cheese and Wheat Germ

Crystallized ginger provides an explosion of sweet and heat in each bite of this cantaloupe dish.

Yield:	Prep time:	Serving size:	
4 cantaloupe halves	10 minutes	1 cantaloupe half	
Each serving has:			
310 calories	27 g protein	43 g carbohydrates	5 g fiber
	4 g total fat	1 g saturated fat	72 mg sodium

3 cups low-fat, low-sodium cottage cheese

¼ cup crystallized ginger, chopped

2 medium cantaloupes, cut in ½ and seeds scooped out

½ cup wheat germ

1. In a medium bowl, combine low-fat cottage cheese and crystallized ginger.

2. Fill cantaloupe halves with cottage cheese mixture, top with wheat germ, and serve.

CULINARY KNOW-HOW

Crystallized ginger is pretty sticky stuff. To make chopping easier, spray your knife with nonstick cooking spray first.

Harvest Brie

Mild, creamy Brie is the perfect complement to the crisp sweet/tart fruit.

Yield:	Prep time:	Cook time:	Serving size:
8 ounces Brie, with 2 sliced apples and pears, and French bread	5 minutes	5 to 10 minutes	¼ cheese and fruit and 1 slice bread

Each serving has:			
320 calories	16 g protein 10 g total fat	41 g carbohydrates 5 g saturated fat	5 g fiber 460 mg sodium

8 oz. light Brie	2 medium Barlett pears, cored and sliced
2 medium Golden Delicious apples, cored and sliced	4 (1-in.) slices French bread

1. Preheat the oven to 350°F.

2. Place Brie in an oven-safe dish. If Brie is at room temperature, bake for 5 minutes. If it's chilled, bake for 10 minutes.

3. Evenly divide Brie, ¼ of apple slices, and ¼ of pear slices among 4 plates, and serve with French bread slices.

TASTY TIDBIT

Brie is a bit rich for daily consumption, but for a special occasion, treat yourself with this breakfast.

Grecian Breakfast

Thick, creamy yogurt and sweet, refreshing fruit combine to make a delicious start to the day.

Yield:	Prep time:	Serving size:
2 bagels, 2 cups yogurt, and 2 cups fresh berries	5 minutes	1 bagel, 1 cup yogurt, and 1 cup fresh berries

Each serving has:

380 calories	28 g protein	67 g carbohydrates	6 g fiber
	1 g total fat	0 g saturated fat	494 mg sodium

2 cups plain fat-free Greek yogurt

2 cups fresh blueberries, strawberries, or raspberries

2 (3-in.) whole-wheat bagels, toasted

1. In a medium bowl, combine Greek yogurt and blueberries.

2. Evenly divide yogurt and berries between 2 bowls, and serve each alongside 1 toasted whole-wheat bagel.

CULINARY KNOW-HOW

If you only have those big bakery-style bagels on hand, use only ½ of one to keep the calories in check. You also can use only ½ of the 3-inch bagel to save about 90 calories.

Drink It All In

In This Chapter

- Fruit-packed smoothies
- Quick grab-and-go breakfast drinks
- Sweet and creamy smoothies

When you buy smoothies at your local donut shop or juice joint, you might not know what you're in for. You could be getting the protein-packed, fruit-filled drink you expect. Or you might get something more like a fast-food, super-size milkshake (calorie, fat, and sugar-wise) than a healthy drink.

That's not the case with the easy-to-make smoothies in this chapter. They give you everything you crave in a delicious breakfast smoothie—a variety of fruits and fruit juices, protein, calcium, and more.

Morning Wake-Up Smoothie

This surprising smoothie with a mochalike taste with a hint of coconut will get you up and at 'em!

Yield:	Prep time:	Serving size:
4 cups	5 minutes	1 cup

Each serving has:			
164 calories	5 g protein	29 g carbohydrates	2 g fiber
	5 g total fat	4 g saturated fat	83 mg sodium

2 small bananas, peeled   2 cups chocolate skim milk

2 TB. instant espresso powder   1 cup lite coconut milk

1. In a blender, combine bananas, instant espresso powder, chocolate skim milk, and lite coconut milk.

2. Blend until smooth, and serve.

MAKE IT A MEAL

A simple omelet would accompany this drink perfectly.

Mango Power Smoothie

The tropical flavors of this smoothie are enhanced by the sweetness of strawberries.

Yield:	Prep time:	Serving size:
3 cups	5 minutes	1 cup

Each serving has:			
175 calories	5 g protein	40 g carbohydrates	4 g fiber
	1 g total fat	0 g saturated fat	36 mg sodium

1 small mango, peeled and pitted	¾ cup plain low-fat yogurt
1 cup chopped pineapple	1 TB. honey
1 small banana, peeled	2 TB. wheat germ
¼ cup fresh strawberries	

1. In a blender, combine mango, pineapple, banana, strawberries, yogurt, honey, and wheat germ.

2. Blend until smooth, and serve.

TASTY TIDBIT

Mangoes are tropical fruits native to India, but today they're grown all over the world. They're high in vitamins A and C.

Mango Morning Smoothie

Honey gives just a hint of sweetness to this mango-riffic smoothie.

Yield:	Prep time:	Serving size:	
2 cups	5 minutes	1 cup	
Each serving has:			
177 calories	3 g protein	45 g carbohydrates	3 g fiber
	0 g total fat	0 g saturated fat	18 mg sodium

1 small banana, peeled

1 cup frozen mango chunks

½ cup orange juice

¼ cup plain low-fat yogurt

1 TB. honey

1. In a blender, combine banana, mango, orange juice, yogurt, and honey.

2. Blend until smooth, and serve.

TASTY TIDBIT

Frozen produce, like canned, is often perceived as less healthy than fresh. It's actually just as, if not more, healthy because it's picked and flash frozen or canned immediately, preserving the maximum amount of nutrients, unlike fresh, especially out of season, that may have been chilled and on trucks for a few days before landing in your store. To maximize nutrition, be sure to purchase fruit with no added salt or sugar and without extra sauces or syrups.

Strawberry Carbo-rita Smoothie

This smoothie is loaded with fresh, sweet strawberry flavor plus a touch of extra sweetness from the honey.

Yield:	Prep time:	Serving size:	
3 cups	5 minutes	1 cup	
Each serving has:			
179 calories	3 g protein 0 g total fat	48 g carbohydrates 0 g saturated fat	5 g fiber 23 mg sodium

2 cups frozen strawberries

2 small bananas, peeled

1 medium Gala apple, peeled, cored, and cut into chunks

½ cup skim milk

2 TB. honey

1. In a blender, combine strawberries, bananas, Gala apple, skim milk, and honey.

2. Blend until smooth, and serve.

 MAKE IT A MEAL

This smoothie is perfect alongside a hard-boiled or scrambled egg.

Sunshine Smoothie

This bright smoothie has a thick, rich banana taste and a hint of sweet strawberry.

Yield:	Prep time:	Serving size:	
3 cups	5 minutes	1 cup	

Each serving has:			
199 calories	9 g protein	43 g carbohydrates	4 g fiber
	1 g total fat	0 g saturated fat	70 mg sodium

2 small bananas, peeled

½ cup fresh or frozen strawberries

1½ cups plain low-fat yogurt

2 TB. honey

4 TB. wheat germ

1. In a blender, combine bananas, strawberries, yogurt, honey, and wheat germ.

2. Blend until smooth, and serve.

TASTY TIDBIT

When you blend smoothies with frozen fruit, you get a smoothie with the same thick and creamy consistency as a milkshake—but is so much better for you!

Very Berry Smoothie

The deep color of this smoothie is a clue that it's packed with berry flavor as well as an array of nutrients.

Yield:	Prep time:	Serving size:
2 cups	5 minutes	1 cup

Each serving has:			
205 calories	5 g protein	41 g carbohydrates	4 g fiber
	4 g total fat	2 g saturated fat	36 mg sodium

1 small banana, peeled
¼ cup sliced fresh strawberries
¼ cup fresh raspberries
¼ cup fresh blueberries

¾ cup vanilla low-fat ice cream
1 TB. honey
2 TB. wheat germ

1. In a blender, combine banana, strawberries, raspberries, blueberries, vanilla ice cream, honey, and wheat germ.

2. Blend until smooth, and serve.

CULINARY KNOW-HOW

If you want to make your smoothie thicker, use frozen berries.

Protein Power Smoothie

Chocolate, banana, and strawberry combine in this yummy yet protein-rich smoothie.

Yield:	Prep time:	Serving size:	
4 cups	5 minutes	1⅓ cups	
Each serving has:			
234 calories	12 g protein	43 g carbohydrates	4 g fiber
	3 g total fat	0 g saturated fat	98 mg sodium

2 cups chocolate soy milk	1 cup frozen strawberries
1 cup plain fat-free Greek yogurt	2 TB. honey
1 small banana, peeled	1 TB. wheat germ

1. In a blender, combine chocolate soy milk, Greek yogurt, banana, strawberries, honey, and wheat germ.

2. Blend until smooth, and serve.

 CULINARY KNOW-HOW

To keep it fresh, store your wheat germ in the refrigerator. It will last several months.

Raspberry Cocoa Surprise Smoothie

Deep, rich chocolate and sweet raspberries come together in this cool and creamy drink.

Yield:	Prep time:	Serving size:	
2 cups	5 minutes	1 cup	

Each serving has:			
235 calories	8 g protein	45 g carbohydrates	6 g fiber
	4 g total fat	2 g saturated fat	100 mg sodium

1 small banana, peeled	1 TB. honey
¼ cup frozen raspberries	1 TB. cocoa powder
1 cup chocolate skim milk	2 TB. flaxseed powder
¼ cup plain low-fat yogurt	

1. In a blender, combine banana, raspberries, chocolate skim milk, yogurt, honey, cocoa powder, and flaxseed powder.

2. Blend until smooth, and serve.

TASTY TIDBIT

Flaxseeds are a great source of omega-3 fatty acids, which have been shown to benefit the brain, heart, and more. By using flaxseed powder or ground flaxseeds, your body can absorb and benefit from far more of those beneficial nutrients than if you were to simply use the whole seeds.

Dreamsicle Smoothie

The combination of creamy vanilla and sweet orange are a blast from the past, just like those old-fashioned treats from the ice-cream man.

Yield:	Prep time:	Serving size:
2 cups	5 minutes	1 cup

Each serving has:			
236 calories	6 g protein	47 g carbohydrates	3 g fiber
	4 g total fat	2 g saturated fat	37 mg sodium

1 small banana, peeled

1 cup orange juice

¾ cup vanilla low-fat ice cream

1 TB. honey

2 TB. wheat germ

1. In a blender, combine banana, orange juice, vanilla ice cream, honey, and wheat germ.

2. Blend until smooth, and serve.

TASTY TIDBIT

The germ is the most vitamin- and mineral-rich part of the entire wheat kernel. In addition to adding it to smoothies, you also can sprinkle it on yogurt or cereal; add it to quick breads, muffins, and meatloaves; and more.

Passion Fruit Smoothie

The sweet and exotic flavor of passion fruit is balanced by the tang of yogurt in this delicious drink.

Yield:	Prep time:	Serving size:
1 cup	3 minutes	1 cup

Each serving has:			
263 calories	8 g protein	60 g carbohydrates	3 g fiber
	0 g total fat	0 g saturated fat	98 mg sodium

½ cup vanilla nonfat yogurt

½ cup passion fruit juice

1 small banana, peeled, cut into chunks, and frozen

1. In a blender, combine yogurt, passion fruit juice, and banana.

2. Blend until smooth, and serve.

Variation: For a **Pomegranate Smoothie,** replace the passion fruit juice with ½ cup pomegranate juice. *Each serving has: 210 calories, 7 g protein, 50 g carbohydrates, 3 g fiber, 1 g total fat, 1 g saturated fat, 84 mg sodium.*

CULINARY KNOW-HOW

Juicing a pomegranate can be an interesting experience, so for this recipe, you're better off buying bottled juice.

Peanut Butter Cup Smoothie

The perfect combination of chocolate and peanut butter are the basis of this smoothie with a just hint of banana.

Yield:	Prep time:	Serving size:	
1 cup	3 minutes	1 cup	

Each serving has:			
290 calories	15 g protein	43 g carbohydrates	5 g fiber
	9 g total fat	2 g saturated fat	206 mg sodium

1 small banana, peeled, cut into chunks, and frozen

1 TB. smooth peanut butter

1 cup skim milk

1 TB. unsweetened cocoa powder

1. In a blender, combine banana, peanut butter, skim milk, and cocoa powder.

2. Blend until smooth, and serve.

TASTY TIDBIT

Including a frozen banana in smoothies thickens the drink without the need for ice, which can water it down.

Tropical Smoothie

The aroma and flavors of coconut and pineapple will have you feeling like you're on a tropical island—without the jet lag!

Yield:	Prep time:	Serving size:
1 cup	3 minutes	1 cup

Each serving has:			
304 calories	8 g protein	64 g carbohydrates	1 g fiber
	2 g total fat	1 g saturated fat	115 mg sodium

¾ cup banana reduced-fat yogurt
½ cup frozen pineapple chunks

¼ cup skim milk
¼ to ½ tsp. coconut extract

1. In a blender, combine banana yogurt, pineapple, skim milk, and coconut extract.

2. Blend until smooth, and serve.

Variation: If you don't care for coconut, you can substitute vanilla extract in place of the coconut extract. The nutritional information stays the same.

Peanut Butter and Banana Smoothie

Creamy bananas are blended with a little nuttiness and a touch of honey in this smoothie you'll want seconds of.

Yield:	Prep time:	Serving size:
3 cups	5 minutes	1 cup

Each serving has:			
334 calories	14 g protein	38 g carbohydrates	5 g fiber
	17 g total fat	3 g saturated fat	202 mg sodium

2 small bananas, peeled	2 TB. honey
½ cup creamy peanut butter	4 TB. wheat germ
1½ cups plain low-fat yogurt	

1. In a blender, combine bananas, peanut butter, yogurt, honey, and wheat germ.

2. Blend until smooth, and serve.

CULINARY KNOW-HOW

If you'd like to boost the protein even more, use plain fat-free Greek yogurt in place of regular yogurt.

Luscious Lunches

What's not to like about lunch? It can be a refreshing salad, warming soup, tasty sandwich, or any one of a number of creative and delicious food combinations. A healthy lunch gives you the perfect opportunity to refuel your body just as breakfast wears off.

No need to hit the nearest drive-thru or office vending machine because you can't think of something to eat. And no more skipping lunch in hopes it'll help those pounds melt away—it won't! Whether you find yourself at home or away for the midday meal, we're sure the chapters in Part 3 will provide an assortment of meal ideas to satisfy your needs and tastes. Any of these meals pairs perfectly with some fresh fruit to boost your fiber and vitamin intake and also help keep you feeling fuller longer.

Satisfying Soups

In This Chapter

- Thick and hearty soups that eat like meals
- Fiber-ful bowls that fill you up
- Delicious international flavors you'll love

Soup is the ideal comfort food on blustery winter days or when you're feeling blah. Soup warms you from the inside out and is a fantastic way to get nutrient-packed ingredients into your diet. Fiber-rich beans and brown rice, vegetables loaded with vitamins, and lean sources of protein all fit easily and deliciously into a steaming bowl of soup.

For many, canned soups are the norm. That's fine once in a while, but the canned versions have some downfalls. For one, the flavor profiles tend to be pretty basic. More importantly, canned soups are notoriously high in sodium. It's not uncommon to find a can of soup with half a day's worth of sodium per serving, which is usually half a can. So if you eat a whole can, you've reached your sodium limit for the day.

In this chapter, you'll find sensational soups with an Asian spin, Latin flavor, Italian style, and more. Plus, you won't hit your sodium ceiling with just one bowl!

Vegetable Squash Soup

This hearty vegetable soup gets a twist thanks to curry and yogurt. They go very well with the subtle sweetness of the butternut squash.

Yield:	Prep time:	Cook time:	Serving size:
6 cups	15 to 20 minutes	20 to 25 minutes	1½ cups

Each serving has:			
71 calories	6 g protein 1 g total fat	11 g carbohydrates 1 g saturated fat	3 g fiber 289 mg sodium

1 small yellow onion, diced

1 medium celery stalk, diced

1 small carrot, diced

½ small butternut squash, diced

1 bay leaf

1 TB. curry powder

4 cups canned low-sodium chicken broth

¼ tsp. kosher salt

⅛ tsp. black pepper

4 TB. plain fat-free Greek yogurt

1. In a 2-quart pot over medium-high heat, combine yellow onion, celery, carrot, butternut squash, bay leaf, curry powder, chicken broth, kosher salt, and black pepper. Bring to a boil, reduce heat to low, cover, and cook for 20 minutes or until squash is cooked.

2. Remove bay leaf. Ladle into 4 bowls, top each with 1 tablespoon Greek yogurt, and serve.

MAKE IT A MEAL

This soup makes a perfect starter to a simple meal of grilled fish and a green salad.

Quick Bean Soup

Thyme and bay infuse a wonderful flavor to this simple bean soup.

Yield:	Prep time:	Cook time:	Serving size:
6 cups	15 to 20 minutes	25 to 30 minutes	1½ cups

Each serving has:			
93 calories	8 g protein	14 g carbohydrates	4 g fiber
	1 g total fat	1 g saturated fat	447 mg sodium

1 small yellow onion, diced	1 bay leaf
1 medium celery stalk, diced	1 TB. fresh thyme or 1 tsp. dried
1 small carrot, diced	4 cups canned low-sodium chicken broth
½ cup canned kidney beans, drained and rinsed	¼ tsp. kosher salt
½ cup canned navy beans, drained and rinsed	⅛ tsp. black pepper
	¼ cup chopped fresh parsley

1. In a 2-quart pot over medium-high heat, combine yellow onion, celery, carrot, kidney beans, navy beans, bay leaf, thyme, chicken broth, kosher salt, and black pepper. Bring to a boil, reduce heat to low, cover, and cook for 20 minutes or until vegetables are tender.

2. Remove bay leaf. Ladle into 4 bowls, garnish each with 1½ teaspoons parsley, and serve.

MAKE IT A MEAL

Add a thick slice of 100 percent whole-grain bread, a green salad, and a crisp apple to turn this soup into a filling meal.

Thai Sweet-and-Sour Soup

Don't let the serrano chiles in this soup scare you away. The lemongrass, Kaffir lime leaves, basil, and cilantro tone down the heat.

Yield:	Prep time:	Cook time:	Serving size:
6 cups	15 to 20 minutes	10 to 15 minutes	1½ cups

Each serving has:			
108 calories	13 g protein 1 g total fat	12 g carbohydrates 1 g saturated fat	1 g fiber 466 mg sodium

4 cups canned low-sodium chicken broth

2 (3-in.) stalks lemongrass, white portion pounded

4 Kaffir lime leaves, or zest of 2 limes

4 or 5 small tomatoes, peeled, seeded, and diced

6 small serrano chiles, seeded and chopped fine

½ lb. (31 to 40 count, about 9) shrimp, peeled, deveined, and tails on

Juice of 1 lime

2 TB. light brown sugar

6 TB. chopped fresh cilantro

¼ cup chopped fresh basil

1. In a 2-quart pot over medium-high heat, bring chicken broth to a boil. Add lemongrass and Kaffir lime leaves. Reduce heat to low, and cook for 4 minutes. Strain, and return soup to the pot.

2. Add tomatoes, serrano chiles, and shrimp, and cook for 3 or 4 minutes or until shrimp turn pink. Remove from heat.

3. Mix in lime juice and brown sugar.

4. Ladle into 4 bowls, garnish with 1 tablespoon cilantro and 1½ teaspoons basil, and serve.

Variation: For **Hot-and-Sour Lemongrass Shrimp Soup,** add 1½ cups button mushroom, sliced, to the soup with the tomatoes, and omit the light brown sugar and basil. *Each serving has: 119 calories, 19 g protein, 7 g carbohydrates, 2 g fiber, 2 g total fat, 1 g saturated fat, 684 mg sodium.*

MAKE IT A MEAL

A whole-grain roll and 2 or 3 fresh whole apricots finish off this meal nicely.

Chicken Ginger Soup

With lemongrass, ginger, and cilantro, this is anything but your grandma's chicken soup.

Yield:	Prep time:	Cook time:	Serving size:
6 cups	15 to 20 minutes	20 to 25 minutes	1½ cups

Each serving has:			
114 calories	16 g protein	3 g carbohydrates	0 g fiber
	4 g total fat	1 g saturated fat	702 mg sodium

4 cups canned low-sodium chicken broth

¼ cup peeled and minced fresh ginger

1 (3-in.) stalk lemongrass, white portion pounded, or 2 TB. lemon zest

10 fresh cilantro sprigs

1 (½-lb.) boneless, skinless chicken thigh, cut into ¼- to ½-in. pieces

4 large napa cabbage leaves, sliced thin

1 small red chile, seeded and sliced thin

2 tsp. fish sauce

½ cup chopped fresh cilantro

1 medium scallion, sliced

1. In a 2-quart pot over medium-high heat, bring chicken broth to a boil.

2. Reduce heat to low. Add ginger, lemongrass, and cilantro stems, and simmer for 10 minutes. Remove ginger, lemongrass, and cilantro stems.

3. Add chicken, napa cabbage, and red chile, and cook for 7 to 10 minutes.

4. Add fish sauce, cilantro, and scallion.

5. Ladle into 4 bowls, and serve.

Variation: For **Asian-Style Chicken Soup,** add ginger to the chicken broth, omitting the lemongrass and cilantro. Add 4 ounces Asian rice noodles, cooked according to the package instructions; omit the fish sauce, and add 1 tablespoon hoisin sauce. Finish with ½ cup fresh chopped cilantro and 1 diced scallion, both white and green parts. *Each serving has: 221 calories, 16 g protein, 29 g carbohydrates, 1 g fiber, 4 g total fat, 1 g saturated fat, 534 mg sodium.*

CULINARY KNOW-HOW

When using lemongrass, only use the bottom white portion. Peel the outside layer, smash the remaining portion, and mince.

Vegetable Rice Soup

This comforting vegetable soup gets a nutritional boost from fiber-rich brown rice.

Yield:	Prep time:	Cook time:	Serving size:
6 cups	15 to 20 minutes	10 minutes	1½ cups

Each serving has:			
120 calories	6 g protein 1 g total fat	21 g carbohydrates 1 g saturated fat	2 g fiber 285 mg sodium

1 small yellow onion, diced	4 cups canned low-sodium chicken broth
1 medium celery stalk, diced	¼ tsp. kosher salt
1 small carrot, diced	⅛ tsp. black pepper
1½ cups cooked brown rice	¼ cup chopped fresh parsley
1 bay leaf	
¼ tsp. dried thyme	

1. In a 2-quart pot over medium-high heat, combine yellow onion, celery, carrot, brown rice, bay leaf, thyme, chicken broth, kosher salt, and black pepper. Bring to a boil, reduce heat to low, cover, and cook for 5 minutes.

2. Remove bay leaf. Ladle into 4 bowls, garnish with 1½ teaspoons parsley, and serve.

CULINARY KNOW-HOW

You can make a large batch of brown rice all at once and refrigerate it for up to a week or freeze it for up to 6 months. When ready to use, simply reheat in the microwave or on the stovetop with a little bit of water.

White Bean Soup

Creamy white beans are enhanced with the flavors of bay leaf and thyme in this tasty soup.

Yield:	Prep time:	Cook time:	Serving size:
6 cups	15 to 20 minutes	25 to 30 minutes	1½ cups

Each serving has:			
129 calories	13 g protein 1 g total fat	11 g carbohydrates 1 g saturated fat	6 g fiber 560 mg sodium

1 small yellow onion, diced

1 medium celery stalk, diced

1 small carrot, diced

1 (15-oz.) can cannellini beans, drained and rinsed

1 bay leaf

1 TB. fresh thyme or 1 tsp. dried

4 cups canned low-sodium chicken broth

¼ tsp. kosher salt

⅛ tsp. black pepper

1. In a 2-quart pot over medium-high heat, combine yellow onion, celery, carrot, cannellini beans, bay leaf, thyme, chicken broth, kosher salt, and black pepper. Bring to a boil, reduce heat to low, cover, and cook for 20 minutes or until vegetables are cooked.

2. Remove bay leaf. Ladle into 4 bowls, and serve.

MAKE IT A MEAL

Start the meal with a cup of mixed berries and then dig into a bowl of this hearty soup with a few whole-grain crackers on the side.

Barley Soup

Beef broth provides a deep, rich flavor to this light barley soup.

Yield:	Prep time:	Cook time:	Serving size:
6 cups	10 to 15 minutes	1 hour, 15 minutes	1½ cups

Each serving has:			
137 calories	4 g protein	14 g carbohydrates	3 g fiber
	7 g total fat	1 g saturated fat	583 mg sodium

2 TB. canola oil	¼ cup pearl barley, rinsed
1 small yellow onion, diced	¼ cup chopped fresh parsley
1 medium celery stalk, diced	¼ tsp. kosher salt
1 small carrot, diced	¼ tsp. black pepper
4 cups canned low-sodium beef broth	

1. In a 4-quart pot over medium heat, heat canola oil. Add yellow onion, celery, and carrot, and sauté for 10 to 15 minutes or until tender.

2. Pour in low-sodium beef broth and pearl barley, and simmer for 1 hour.

3. Add parsley, kosher salt, and black pepper, and serve.

MAKE IT A MEAL

A small, vegetable-filled salad topped with lean protein such as a hard-boiled egg and a piece of fresh fruit turns this soup into a delicious lunch or light dinner.

Sicilian Chicken Soup

The flavors of garlic and nutty Romano cheese headline this Italian take on chicken noodle soup.

Yield:	Prep time:	Cook time:	Serving size:
6 cups	15 to 20 minutes	30 to 35 minutes	1½ cups

Each serving has:			
168 calories	20 g protein 4 g total fat	13 g carbohydrates 2 g saturated fat	2 g fiber 496 mg sodium

1 small yellow onion, diced

1 medium celery stalk, diced

1 small carrot, diced

1 clove garlic, sliced

1 (8-oz.) can low-sodium diced tomatoes, with juice

1 bay leaf

1 TB. fresh marjoram or 1 tsp. dried

4 cups canned low-sodium chicken broth

½ lb. boneless, skinless chicken breast, cut into ¼-in. pieces

¼ tsp. kosher salt

⅛ tsp. black pepper

2 TB. uncooked pastina (star-shape) pasta

1 large egg, beaten

4 tsp. grated Romano cheese

1. In a 2-quart pot over medium heat, combine yellow onion, celery, carrot, garlic, tomatoes with juice, bay leaf, marjoram, chicken broth, chicken, kosher salt, and black pepper. Cover, bring to a simmer, and cook for 20 minutes or until chicken is cooked.

2. Add pastina pasta, and simmer for 5 minutes. Remove from heat.

3. While stirring soup, drizzle in egg.

4. Remove bay leaf. Ladle into 4 bowls, top each with 1 teaspoon Romano cheese, and serve.

MAKE IT A MEAL

Be sure you have a soft, thick slice of Italian bread to soak up this soup's juices, and finish the meal off with a cup of grapes.

Pho

Star anise lends a mild licorice-like flavor to this Vietnamese beef soup.

Yield:	Prep time:	Cook time:	Serving size:
6 cups	15 to 20 minutes	20 to 25 minutes	1½ cups

Each serving has:			
190 calories	14 g protein	28 g carbohydrates	1 g fiber
	2 g total fat	1 g saturated fat	560 mg sodium

4 cups canned low-sodium beef broth

2 whole star anise

1 (2-in.) cinnamon stick

1 (3-in.) stalk lemongrass, pounded and chopped

1 TB. peeled and grated fresh ginger

1 TB. hoisin sauce

½ lb. thinly sliced raw beef tenderloin

½ cup mung bean sprouts

8 fresh basil leaves

8 fresh mint leaves

1 medium jalapeño pepper, seeded and chopped

4 oz. Asian rice noodles, soaked in hot water for 2 or 3 minutes

1. In a 2-quart pot over medium-high heat, bring beef broth to a boil.

2. Reduce heat to low, and add star anise, cinnamon stick, lemongrass, and ginger. Cover, and simmer for 20 minutes.

3. Strain broth and return to the pot. Add hoisin sauce.

4. Evenly divide beef tenderloin, mung bean sprouts, basil, mint, and jalapeño among 4 plates. Drain and divide Asian rice noodles among 4 bowls. Ladle 1 cup broth into each bowl, and have diners add their own ingredients from their own plate.

TASTY TIDBIT

This is the Vietnamese version of the French dish called *Pot de Fue*. The hot broth cooks the beef.

Leek and Parsnip Soup

Leeks offer a mild onion flavor to this vegetarian soup, balancing out the bit of a kick from the parsnips.

Yield:	Prep time:	Cook time:	Serving size:
6 cups	10 to 15 minutes	45 to 55 minutes	1½ cups

Each serving has:			
218 calories	4 g protein 6 g total fat	38 g carbohydrates 4 g saturated fat	6 g fiber 464 mg sodium

2 medium parsnips	½ tsp. kosher salt
1 medium russet potato	¼ tsp. black pepper
1 lb. (3 medium) leeks, white part	4 cups canned low-sodium vegetable broth
2 TB. butter	

1. Peel parsnips and russet potato, and cut into ½-inch pieces.

2. Remove dark green parts from leeks. Cut off root end, and cut leeks in ½ lengthwise. Chop across to make half moons. Submerge cut leeks in water, and agitate. Lift leeks out of water, and set in a strainer to drain.

3. In a large pot over medium heat, melt butter. Add parsnips, russet potato, leeks, kosher salt, and black pepper, and sauté for 15 to 20 minutes or until leeks are soft.

4. Pour in low-sodium vegetable broth, cover, and bring to a boil. Reduce heat to low, and simmer for 20 to 25 minutes.

5. Ladle into bowls, and serve.

TASTY TIDBIT

Parsnips look like big white carrots and have a mild, almost sweet flavor.

Delicata Squash Chili Bowl

Chipotle peppers add a spicy kick to this chili with a bonus: you can eat the bowl!

Yield:	Prep time:	Cook time:	Serving size:
4 squash bowls	15 to 20 minutes	25 to 30 minutes	1 bowl

Each serving has:			
229 calories	10 g protein 0 g total fat	49 g carbohydrates 0 g saturated fat	10 g fiber 505 mg sodium

2 large delicata squash, cut in ½ lengthwise and seeded

Nonstick cooking spray

1 small yellow onion, diced

1 medium celery stalk, diced

1 small carrot, diced

1 cup canned pinto beans, drained and rinsed

½ cup cooked rice

½ cup low-sodium diced tomatoes

3 chipotle peppers in adobo, diced

¼ tsp. dried oregano

1 cup canned low-sodium chicken broth

¼ tsp. kosher salt

⅛ tsp. black pepper

¼ cup chopped fresh cilantro

1. Preheat the oven to 350°F. Line a rimmed baking sheet with aluminum foil.

2. Lightly coat delicata squashes' flesh with nonstick cooking spray, place squashes cut side down on the prepared baking sheet, and bake for 20 to 25 minutes.

3. Meanwhile, in a 2-quart pot over medium-high heat, combine yellow onion, celery, carrot, pinto beans, rice, tomatoes, chipotle peppers, oregano, chicken broth, kosher salt, and black pepper. Bring to a boil, reduce heat to low, cover, and cook for 10 minutes or until vegetables are tender.

4. Ladle into 4 squash bowls, garnish each with 1 tablespoon cilantro, and serve.

Variation: For **Easy Vegetable Chili,** eliminate the delicata squash and increase the chicken broth to 4 cups. *Each serving has: 127 calories, 9 g protein, 21 g carbohydrates, 6 g fiber, 0 g total fat, 0 g saturated fat, 538 mg sodium.*

 TASTY TIDBIT

There's no need to peel delicata squash. You can eat the skin and get an extra dose of fiber.

Lemongrass and Coconut Milk Soup with Chicken

This soup just bursts with the flavors of ginger, coconut, cilantro, and a bit of heat from the serranos.

Yield:	Prep time:	Cook time:	Serving size:
6 cups	15 to 20 minutes	20 to 25 minutes	$1\frac{1}{2}$ cups

Each serving has:			
230 calories	26 g protein	5 g carbohydrates	1 g fiber
	11 g total fat	8 g saturated fat	501 mg sodium

2 cups canned low-sodium chicken broth

3 cups lite coconut milk

3 Kaffir lime leaves, or zest of 1 lime

2 (3-in.) stalks lemongrass, pounded and chopped

$\frac{1}{4}$ cup peeled and julienned fresh ginger

1 (1-lb.) boneless, skinless chicken breast, cut into $\frac{1}{4}$- to $\frac{1}{2}$-in. pieces

1 TB. fish sauce

2 cups button mushrooms, chopped

2 small serrano chiles, seeded and chopped

Juice of 1 lime

6 TB. chopped fresh cilantro

1. In a 2-quart pot over medium-high heat, bring chicken broth to a boil.

2. Reduce heat to low, and blend in coconut milk until smooth.

3. Add Kaffir lime leaves, lemongrass, and ginger, and simmer for 5 minutes. Strain, and return broth to the pot.

4. Add chicken, and cook for 10 minutes.

5. Add fish sauce, button mushrooms, and serrano chiles, and cook for 1 minute.

6. Remove from heat, and add lime juice.

7. Ladle into 4 bowls, garnish each with 1 tablespoon cilantro, and serve.

Variation: For **Thai Coconut Soup,** reduce the lite coconut milk to 2 cups. Omit the Kaffir lime leaves, mushrooms, and lime juice, substitute 2 serrano chiles for 1 small red chile, and add scallions with fish sauce. *Each serving has: 221 calories, 25 g protein, 4 g carbohydrates, 0 g fiber, 11 g total fat, 8 g saturated fat, 499 mg sodium.*

TASTY TIDBIT

Coconut milk is a liquid made by puréeing coconut meat and water. The liquid found inside of coconuts is coconut *water.*

Roasted Squash Soup with Sage

Roasting the squash brings a caramelized sweetness to this filling soup.

Yield:	Prep time:	Cook time:	Serving size:
8 cups	20 to 25 minutes	1 hour, 15 minutes	2 cups

Each serving has:			
262 calories	9 g protein 1 g total fat	63 g carbohydrates 1 g saturated fat	19 g fiber 425 mg sodium

1 (3-lb.) butternut squash, cut in $\frac{1}{2}$ and seeded

1 (2-lb.) acorn squash, cut in $\frac{1}{2}$ and seeded

Nonstick cooking spray

$\frac{1}{2}$ tsp. kosher salt

$\frac{1}{4}$ tsp. black pepper

1 small yellow onion, diced

2 medium celery stalks, diced

2 TB. chopped fresh sage

$\frac{1}{4}$ tsp. ground allspice

4 cups canned low-sodium chicken broth

1. Preheat the oven to 350°F. Line a rimmed baking sheet with aluminum foil.

2. Lightly coat butternut squash and acorn squash flesh with nonstick cooking spray, and season with $\frac{1}{4}$ teaspoon kosher salt and $\frac{1}{8}$ teaspoon black pepper. Place squashes cut side down on the prepared baking sheet, and roast for 45 minutes or until fork-tender. Allow to cool, scoop out flesh into a large bowl, and set aside.

3. Meanwhile, lightly coat a 4-quart pot with nonstick cooking spray, and set over medium heat. Add yellow onion, celery, sage, and allspice, and cook for about 10 minutes or until vegetables are tender.

4. Add butternut squash, acorn squash, and chicken broth. Bring to a boil, reduce heat to low, and cook for 20 minutes.

5. Remove from heat. Working in batches, purée soup in a blender and return to the pot. Season with remaining $\frac{1}{4}$ teaspoon kosher salt and remaining $\frac{1}{8}$ teaspoon black pepper.

6. Ladle into 4 bowls, and serve.

TASTY TIDBIT

The two types of squash in this soup are responsible for the big dose of fiber listed. Fiber not only helps keep you feeling fuller longer, but helps keep cholesterol levels in check, too.

Squash Soup with Whipped Goat Cheese

The goat cheese helps bring out and enhance the sweetness of the roasted squash.

Yield:	Prep time:	Cook time:	Serving size:
8 cups	25 to 30 minutes	1 hour, 15 minutes	1½ cups

Each serving has:			
296 calories	11 g protein 4 g total fat	63 g carbohydrates 2 g saturated fat	19 g fiber 486 mg sodium

1 (3-lb.) butternut squash, cut in ½ and seeded

1 (2-lb.) acorn squash, cut in ½ and seeded

Nonstick cooking spray

½ tsp. kosher salt

¼ tsp. black pepper

1 small yellow onion, diced fine

¼ tsp. ground nutmeg

¼ tsp. ground ginger

¼ tsp. ground allspice

4 cups canned low-sodium chicken broth

2 TB. goat cheese

2 TB. low-fat cream cheese

1. Preheat the oven to 350°F. Line a rimmed baking sheet with aluminum foil.

2. Lightly coat butternut squash and acorn squash flesh with nonstick cooking spray, and season with ¼ teaspoon kosher salt and ⅛ teaspoon black pepper. Place squashes cut side down on the prepared baking sheet, and roast for 45 minutes or until fork-tender. Allow to cool, scoop out flesh into a large bowl, and set aside.

3. Meanwhile, lightly coat a 4-quart pot with nonstick cooking spray, and set over medium heat. Add yellow onions, nutmeg, ginger, and allspice, and cook for about 10 minutes or until onions are tender.

4. Add squash and chicken broth, bring to a boil, reduce heat to low, and cook for 20 minutes.

5. Remove from heat. Working in batches, purée soup and return to the pot. Season with remaining ¼ teaspoon kosher salt and ⅛ teaspoon black pepper.

6. In a small bowl, blend together goat cheese and cream cheese.

7. Ladle soup into 4 bowls, top each with 1½ teaspoons cheese mixture, and serve.

TASTY TIDBIT

This soup is loaded with vitamin A, thanks to the two squashes.

De*light*ful Salads

In This Chapter

- Meal-worthy salads
- Incredible ingredient combinations
- Very veggie salads
- Sensational seafood salads

When you think of salads, do you picture boring bowls of leafy greens and the same old raw veggies? If so, prepare to be surprised because the recipes in this chapter will change your image of salads for good!

Several salads start with a canvas of crisp greens. Top that with a wide array of possible toppings, and there's almost no end to the flavor combinations you can create by simply using different raw veggies and delicious dressings. But that's not all. Flavorful ingredients such as briny seafood, sweet roasted vegetables, crunchy nuts, creamy beans, and more take you beyond the basic green salad into a world of tantalizing sides for a simple meal or satisfying entrées for a light lunch or dinner. Sensational salads like these make it easy to get one or more of your daily servings of vegetables.

Green Beans and Fennel Salad

The tang of lemon and Dijon enhance simple green beans and licorice-y fennel in this delightful salad.

Yield:	Prep time:	Cook time:	Serving size:
4 cups	10 to 15 minutes	10 minutes	1 cup

Each serving has:			
110 calories	4 g protein 7 g total fat	8 g carbohydrates 2 g saturated fat	3 g fiber 178 mg sodium

2 qt. water	2 TB. extra-virgin olive oil
1 lb. green beans, stem ends removed	¼ tsp. black pepper
Juice of ½ lemon (about 2 TB.)	½ fennel bulb, sliced thin
½ tsp. Dijon mustard	¼ cup chopped fresh parsley
	¼ cup shaved Pecorino Romano

1. In a large pot over medium-high heat, bring water to a boil. Add green beans, and cook for 4 or 5 minutes or until tender.

2. Remove green beans from the pot, and rinse under cold water to stop the cooking process.

3. In a large bowl, combine lemon juice, Dijon mustard, extra-virgin olive oil, and black pepper. Fold in green beans, fennel, and parsley. Garnish with Pecorino Romano cheese, and serve.

CULINARY KNOW-HOW

Cooling the beans stops the cooking process and quickly sets the chlorophyll (the green pigment in all green vegetables), giving them a beautiful, appetizing color.

Mom's Tuna Salad

Celery and onion add the perfect amount of crunch to this quick and easy tuna salad.

Yield:	Prep time:	Serving size:	
2 cups	10 to 15 minutes	½ cup	
Each serving has:			
139 calories	17 g protein 6 g total fat	3 g carbohydrates 1 g saturated fat	1 g fiber 479 mg sodium

2 (5-oz.) cans tuna packed in water, drained

¼ cup low-fat mayonnaise

1 TB. brown mustard

1 small sweet onion, diced

1 small celery stalk, diced

¼ tsp. black pepper

¼ cup chopped fresh parsley

2 cups chopped romaine lettuce

1. In a medium bowl, combine tuna, low-fat mayonnaise, brown mustard, sweet onion, celery, black pepper, and parsley.

2. Divide romaine lettuce among 4 plates, spoon ½ cup tuna salad on top, and serve.

Variation: For **Tuna in a Tomato,** divide romaine lettuce among 4 plates and drizzle each with 1 tablespoon white wine vinegar. Top each with ½ of 2 large tomatoes, each cut in half with the center spooned out, and fill with ½ cup tuna salad. *Each serving has: 156 calories, 18 g protein, 7 g carbohydrates, 2 g fiber, 6 g total fat, 1 g saturated fat, 724 mg sodium.*

TASTY TIDBIT

Tuna is a great double-duty nutrient powerhouse. It's loaded with protein and also provides heart-healthy fats. And tomatoes are a great source of vitamin C, a powerful antioxidant that helps keep you healthy and may help you recover more quickly when you're sick.

Red Cabbage Slaw

Vitamin-rich red cabbage gives a nice spicy-peppery taste to this slaw that's mellowed by the creamy dressing.

Yield:	Prep time:	Serving size:	
5 cups	15 to 20 minutes	1¼ cups	
Each serving has:			
164 calories	2 g protein 11 g total fat	17 g carbohydrates 2 g saturated fat	4 g fiber 426 mg sodium

2 tsp. celery seed

½ tsp. garlic powder

½ cup low-fat mayonnaise

½ cup chopped fresh parsley

1 tsp. stone-ground mustard

¼ tsp. kosher salt

¼ tsp. black pepper

4 cups red cabbage, grated (about ¾ lb.)

1 medium sweet onion, grated

2 medium carrots, peeled and grated

2 TB. cider vinegar

2 tsp. sugar

1. In a large bowl, combine celery seed, garlic powder, low-fat mayonnaise, parsley, stone-ground mustard, kosher salt, and black pepper.

2. Add red cabbage, sweet onion, carrots, cider vinegar, and sugar. Toss to coat, and serve.

Variation: For **Broccoli Slaw,** omit the mustard, and replace the red cabbage with a 12-ounce bag broccoli coleslaw. *Each serving has: 162 calories, 3 g protein, 16 g carbohydrates, 5 g fiber, 10 g total fat, 2 g saturated fat, 428 mg sodium.*

CULINARY KNOW-HOW

A grated onion infuses a dish with all the flavor and juices of the onion without leaving big chunks of raw onion to bite into.

Old-Fashioned Chicken Salad

In this fresh salad, lean chicken breasts combine with crunchy vegetables in a creamy, smooth dressing.

Yield:	Prep time:	Cook time:	Serving size:
3 cups	15 to 20 minutes	10 minutes	¾ cup

Each serving has:			
169 calories	18 g protein	4 g carbohydrates	1 g fiber
	9 g total fat	2 g saturated fat	454 mg sodium

12 oz. boneless, skinless chicken breasts

1 tsp. kosher salt

¼ tsp. black pepper

⅓ cup low-fat mayonnaise

1 small red onion, diced

1 small celery stalk, diced

1 small carrot, peeled and diced

¼ cup chopped fresh parsley

4 medium Bibb lettuce leaves

1. Heat a 10-inch nonstick sauté pan over medium heat, and lightly coat with nonstick cooking spray.

2. Season chicken breasts with ½ teaspoon kosher salt and ⅛ teaspoon black pepper. Add chicken to the pan, and cook for 5 minutes per side or until an instant-read thermometer inserted into the center reads 165°F.

3. Meanwhile, in a large bowl, combine low-fat mayonnaise, red onion, celery, carrots, parsley, remaining ½ teaspoon kosher salt, and remaining ⅛ teaspoon black pepper.

4. Remove chicken from the pan, and allow to cool for 10 to 15 minutes. Cut into ¼- to ½-inch cubes, and fold chicken into salad.

5. Place 1 Bibb lettuce leaf onto each plate, spoon ¾ cup chicken salad on top, and serve.

Variation: For **Chicken Salad–Stuffed Tomatoes,** reduce the kosher salt to ½ teaspoon and add to the mayo mixture, and replace the Bibb lettuce leaves with 1 cup chopped romaine lettuce. Divide romaine lettuce among 4 plates, and drizzle each with 1 tablespoon white wine vinegar. Top each plate with ½ of 2 large tomatoes, each cut in half with the center spooned out, and fill with ¾ cup chicken salad. *Each serving has: 186 calories, 18 g protein, 7 g carbohydrates, 2 g fiber, 9 g total fat, 2 g saturated fat, 460 mg sodium.*

CULINARY KNOW-HOW

If you don't own an instant-read meat thermometer, you may want to invest in one. They're an important part of your cooking arsenal and are available inexpensively at most food stores.

Crab-Topped Salad

Sweet fresh crabmeat tops this veggie-packed salad, which is enhanced with a slightly sweet balsamic dressing.

Yield:	Prep time:	Serving size:
1 salad	15 minutes	1 salad

Each serving has:			
193 calories	23 g protein	12 g carbohydrates	3 g fiber
	5 g total fat	0 g saturated fat	672 mg sodium

1½ cups chopped romaine lettuce	⅓ cup lump crabmeat
½ medium tomato, chopped	½ tsp. salt-free lemon-pepper seasoning
¼ medium cucumber, sliced	2 TB. reduced-fat balsamic vinaigrette
1 small carrot, peeled and shredded	

1. In a medium bowl, combine romaine lettuce, tomato, cucumber, and carrot.

2. Sprinkle crabmeat with lemon-pepper seasoning. Add crabmeat to salad, drizzle with reduced-fat balsamic vinaigrette, and serve.

TASTY TIDBIT

You can find lump crabmeat refrigerated in plastic tubs at the grocery store, usually near the seafood department.

California Crab Salad

Succulent lump crabmeat stars in this luscious salad, featuring a hint of licorice from the tarragon.

Yield:	Prep time:	Serving size:	
4 cups	15 to 20 minutes	1 cup	

Each serving has:			
194 calories	12 g protein	24 g carbohydrates	5 g fiber
	6 g total fat	2 g saturated fat	453 mg sodium

1 cup lump crabmeat

1 medium avocado, peeled, pitted, and diced

½ cup diced red onion

2 small tomatoes, seeded and diced

1 medium stalk celery, diced

1 TB. fresh parsley or 1 tsp. dried

2 tsp. fresh tarragon or ½ tsp. dried

2 TB. rice vinegar

½ tsp. kosher salt

¼ tsp. black pepper

1½ cups chopped romaine lettuce

1 small Gala apple, cored and sliced

1. In a medium bowl, combine crabmeat, avocados, red onion, tomatoes, celery, parsley, tarragon, rice vinegar, kosher salt, and black pepper.

2. Divide romaine lettuce among 4 plates, and spoon 1 cup crab salad on top.

3. Arrange Gala apple slices on the side, and serve.

TASTY TIDBIT

An avocado does not begin to ripen until after it's picked from the tree. If you keep an avocado in the refrigerator, it will ripen slowly. To speed up the process, put the avocado in a paper bag with an apple. The apple will put off additional ethylene gas and speed up the ripening process.

Carrot, Fennel, and Apple Slaw with Ginger Mayo

The heat of the ginger pairs nicely with the sweetness of the apple and carrot.

Yield:	Prep time:	Serving size:
4 cups	15 to 20 minutes	1 cup

Each serving has:			
208 calories	3 g protein 10 g total fat	28 g carbohydrates 2 g saturated fat	6 g fiber 451 mg sodium

3 or 4 medium carrots, shredded (about 1½ cups)

1 large fennel bulb, cored and sliced thin

2 small Gala apples, cored and sliced thin

Juice of 1 lemon

2 TB. peeled and grated fresh ginger

½ cup low-fat mayonnaise

¼ tsp. kosher salt

¼ tsp. black pepper

1. In a medium bowl, combine carrots, fennel, and Gala apples. Toss with lemon juice.

2. Fold in ginger, low-fat mayonnaise, kosher salt, and black pepper, and serve.

TASTY TIDBIT

The skin of the apple is where a lot of the fiber is found, so leave it on when you can.

Cranberry and Walnut Chicken Salad

The tartness of cranberries and crunchiness of walnuts provide a unique flavor and texture combination in this chicken salad.

Yield:	Prep time:	Cook time:	Serving size:
4 cups	15 to 20 minutes	10 minutes	1 cup

Each serving has:			
238 calories	19 g protein 13 g total fat	10 g carbohydrates 2 g saturated fat	1 g fiber 449 mg sodium

12 oz. boneless, skinless chicken breasts

½ tsp. kosher salt

¼ tsp. black pepper

⅓ cup low-fat mayonnaise

1 small yellow onion, diced

1 small stalk celery, diced

¼ cup chopped fresh parsley

¼ cup dried cranberries

¼ cup chopped walnuts, toasted

4 medium Bibb lettuce leaves

1. Heat a nonstick sauté pan over medium heat, and lightly coat with nonstick cooking spray.

2. Season chicken breasts with ¼ teaspoon kosher salt and ⅛ teaspoon black pepper. Add chicken to the pan, and cook for 5 minutes per side or until an instant-read thermometer inserted into the center reads 165°F.

3. In a large bowl, combine low-fat mayonnaise, yellow onion, celery, parsley, cranberries, walnuts, remaining ¼ teaspoon kosher salt, and remaining ⅛ teaspoon black pepper.

4. Remove chicken from the pan, and allow to cool for 10 to 15 minutes. Cut into ¼- to ½-inch cubes, and fold chicken into salad.

5. Place 1 Bibb lettuce leaf on each plate, spoon 1 cup chicken salad on top, and serve.

TASTY TIDBIT

Walnuts are a great source of omega-3 fatty acids. These good-for-you fats are beneficial in protecting against heart disease.

Roasted Beets, Red Onion, and Blue Cheese Salad

The sweetness of the beets, sharpness of the onion, and creaminess of the blue cheese hit all your taste buds at once.

Yield:	Prep time:	Cook time:	Serving size:
2 cups	10 to 15 minutes	1 hour	½ cup

Each serving has:			
246 calories	8 g protein	18 g carbohydrates	4 g fiber
	15 g total fat	6 g saturated fat	672 mg sodium

2 or 3 medium golden beets	2 TB. walnut oil
2 or 3 medium red beets	¼ tsp. kosher salt
½ cup water	⅛ tsp. black pepper
1 TB. raspberry jam	1 medium red onion, sliced thin
2 TB. sherry or rice wine vinegar	¼ cup blue cheese, crumbled
1 tsp. Dijon mustard	

1. Preheat the oven to 400°F.

2. Wash golden beets and red beets, and cut off all but 1 inch of stems. Place beets in a roasting pan, add water, and cover tightly with aluminum foil. Roast beets for about 1 hour or until beets are pierced easily with a knife. Remove foil, and allow to cool.

3. Peel beets, cutting off stem and root end. Cut each beet into 4 pieces, keeping golden and red beets separate. (Red beets will discolor golden beets.)

4. In a large bowl, combine raspberry jam, sherry, Dijon mustard, walnut oil, kosher salt, and black pepper. Add golden beets, red beets, and red onion, and gently mix.

5. Top with crumbled blue cheese, and serve.

CULINARY KNOW-HOW

Wear latex or plastic gloves when peeling red beets to avoid staining your hands.

Curry Chicken Salad

Protein-rich chicken and crunchy almonds combine with sweet and spice from the raisins and curry in this surprising chicken salad.

Yield:	Prep time:	Cook time:	Serving size:
3 cups	15 to 20 minutes	10 minutes	¾ cup

Each serving has:			
262 calories	20 g protein	16 g carbohydrates	3 g fiber
	14 g total fat	2 g saturated fat	445 mg sodium

12 oz. boneless, skinless chicken
  breasts
½ tsp. kosher salt
¼ tsp. black pepper
⅓ cup low-fat mayonnaise

2 TB. curry powder
⅓ cup slivered almonds, toasted
⅓ cup golden raisins
4 medium Bibb lettuce leaves

1. Heat a nonstick sauté pan over medium heat, and lightly coat with nonstick cooking spray.

2. Season chicken breasts with ¼ teaspoon salt and ⅛ teaspoon pepper. Add chicken to the pan, and cook for 5 minutes per side or until an instant-read thermometer inserted into the center reads 165°F.

3. In a large bowl, combine low-fat mayonnaise, curry powder, remaining ¼ teaspoon kosher salt, and remaining ⅛ teaspoon black pepper.

4. Remove chicken from the pan, and allow to cool for 10 to 15 minutes. Cut into ¼- to ½-inch cubes, and fold chicken into mayonnaise mixture. Add almonds and golden raisins, and fold again.

5. Place 1 Bibb lettuce leaf on each plate, spoon ¾ cup chicken salad on top, and serve.

CULINARY KNOW-HOW

Whenever nuts are called for in a dish, consider toasting them. Toasting imparts the nuts with a richer flavor than they have raw. Preheat the oven to 350°F. Arrange nuts in a single layer on a baking sheet, and toast for 5 minutes, without turning. If you're using nut pieces, reduce the toasting time to 2 or 3 minutes.

Panzanella

This salad features a wealth of textures and flavors—cool, crisp vegetables and soft bread combine with the anise flavor of the fennel.

Yield:	Prep time:	Cook time:	Serving size:
4 salads	15 to 20 minutes	10 minutes	1 salad

Each serving has:			
264 calories	4 g protein	30 g carbohydrates	4 g fiber
	14 g total fat	2 g saturated fat	704 mg sodium

1 (½-lb.) loaf sourdough bread, cut into 1-in. cubes	¼ cup chopped fresh basil
Nonstick cooking spray	¼ cup chopped fresh mint
1 medium red onion, diced	¼ cup chopped fresh parsley
1 medium cucumber, peeled, seeded, and diced	3 TB. extra-virgin olive oil
1 small fennel bulb, sliced	Juice of 1 lemon
	½ tsp. kosher salt
	1 tsp. black pepper

1. Preheat the oven to 350°F.

2. In a large bowl, place sourdough bread. Spray with nonstick cooking spray, stir gently to coat, and arrange in a single layer on a baking sheet. Bake for 10 minutes, and return baked bread to the bowl.

3. Add red onion, cucumber, fennel, basil, mint, and parsley, and toss to combine.

4. In a small bowl, combine extra-virgin olive oil, lemon juice, kosher salt, and black pepper. Pour over salad, toss to coat, and serve.

Variation: For **Fattoush,** substitute 1 (½-pound) pita bread, cut into 1-inch pieces, for the sourdough, spray with nonstick cooking spray, and toast for 5 minutes. Place in a bowl. Add red onion, cucumber, basil, mint, and parsley. Substitute 1 medium tomato, seeded and diced, for the fennel bulb. Toss with extra-virgin olive oil, lemon juice, kosher salt, and black pepper. *Each serving has: 276 calories, 7 g protein, 38 g carbohydrates, 6 g fiber, 12 g total fat, 2 g saturated fat, 788 mg sodium.*

DEFINITION

Panzanella and *fattoush* are both salads made with stale bread. The first is from Florence, and the latter is from the Middle East.

Zippy Egg Salad

Once you taste this creamy egg salad with a burst of fresh dill, you'll want seconds.

Yield:	Prep time:	Cook time:	Serving size:
3 cups	10 to 15 minutes	12 minutes	¾ cup

Each serving has:			
267 calories	13 g protein	6 g carbohydrates	1 g fiber
	21 g total fat	5 g saturated fat	616 mg sodium

2 qt. water	½ tsp. kosher salt
8 large eggs	¼ tsp. black pepper
½ cup low-fat mayonnaise	2 cups chopped romaine lettuce
1 small yellow onion, grated	1 TB. white wine vinegar
1 small stalk celery, grated	
2 TB. chopped fresh dill or 2 tsp. dried	

1. In a large pot over medium-high heat, bring water to a boil. Add eggs, and cook for 12 minutes.

2. Remove eggs from water, and run under cold water to stop the cooking process. Peel and chop eggs.

3. In a large bowl, combine eggs, low-fat mayonnaise, yellow onion, celery, dill, kosher salt, and black pepper.

4. Divide chopped romaine lettuce among 4 plates, drizzle with white wine vinegar, spoon ¾ cup egg salad on top, and serve.

Variation: For **Egg Salad–Stuffed Tomatoes,** use only 1 cup chopped romaine lettuce, and fill 2 large tomatoes, each cut in half with the center spooned out, with the egg salad. *Each serving has: 284 calories, 14 g protein, 9 g carbohydrates, 2 g fiber, 21 g total fat, 5 g saturated fat, 621 mg sodium.*

TASTY TIDBIT

Eggs have been shown *not* to raise blood cholesterol levels as much as once thought. So there's no need to cut this low-fat, protein-packed nutrition nugget from your diet (just remember moderation).

Avocado, Papaya, and Shrimp Salad

Creamy avocado combines with lime juice and sweet papaya in this Caribbean-inspired salad.

Yield:	Prep time:	Serving size:	
4 cups	15 to 20 minutes	1 cup	

Each serving has:			
276 calories	29 g protein 14 g total fat	9 g carbohydrates 2 g saturated fat	3 g fiber 450 mg sodium

Juice of 2 limes

2 TB. extra-virgin olive oil

¼ tsp. kosher salt

¼ tsp. black pepper

1 lb. cooked shrimp (31 to 40 count)

1 medium avocado, peeled, pitted, and diced

1 small papaya, peeled, seeded, and diced

¼ cup chopped fresh cilantro

4 medium Bibb lettuce leaves

1. In a small bowl, combine lime juice, extra-virgin olive oil, kosher salt, and black pepper.

2. In a medium bowl, place shrimp, avocado, papaya, and cilantro. Dress with lime vinaigrette, and gently toss to coat.

3. Place 1 Bibb lettuce leaf on each of 4 plates, spoon 1 cup shrimp salad on top, and serve.

TASTY TIDBIT

Sometimes shrimp are treated in a briny or salty solution that can greatly raise the total sodium content of a meal. To play it safe, look for frozen packaged shrimp and check the nutrition label for the sodium content. Aim for roughly 300 milligrams or less per ¼ pound.

White Bean, Shrimp, and Bacon Salad

Dijon mustard and red wine vinegar create a zesty dressing for this creamy bean salad.

Yield:	Prep time:	Serving size:
3 cups	10 to 15 minutes	¾ cup

Each serving has:			
294 calories	15 g protein	16 g carbohydrates	4 g fiber
	19 g total fat	3 g saturated fat	578 mg sodium

1 TB. Dijon mustard

1 TB. red wine vinegar

¼ cup extra-virgin olive oil

1 TB. fresh tarragon or 1 tsp. dried

¼ tsp. black pepper

1 (15-oz.) can Great Northern or navy beans, drained and rinsed

¼ lb. cooked shrimp (31 to 40 count, about 9)

4 strips cooked bacon, chopped, or ⅓ cup bacon bits

3 medium scallions, thinly sliced

1. In a medium bowl, combine Dijon mustard, red wine vinegar, extra-virgin olive oil, tarragon, and black pepper.

2. Add Great Northern beans, shrimp, bacon, and scallions. Toss to coat, and serve.

TASTY TIDBIT

Rinsing and draining canned beans greatly decreases the sodium content. To cut it even more, look for canned beans labeled "unsalted" or "no salt added."

Cannellini Bean Salad

In this salad, red wine vinegar and red onion work well with the creaminess of the cannellini beans, which provide a hefty dose of fiber.

Yield:	Prep time:	Serving size:	
3 cups	10 minutes	¾ cup	
Each serving has:			
327 calories	10 g protein 16 g total fat	37 g carbohydrates 2 g saturated fat	7 g fiber 486 mg sodium

¼ cup extra-virgin olive oil

2 TB. red wine vinegar

½ small red onion, minced

1½ TB. fresh rosemary or 1¼ tsp. dried

1 medium cucumber, peeled, seeded, and diced

1 (15-oz.) can cannellini beans, drained and rinsed

1 medium red bell pepper, ribs and seeds removed, and diced

½ tsp. kosher salt

¼ tsp. black pepper

4 medium Bibb lettuce leaves

4 small slices French or Italian bread, toasted

1. In a large bowl, whisk together extra-virgin olive oil, red wine vinegar, red onion, and rosemary.

2. Fold in cucumbers, cannellini beans, red bell pepper, kosher salt, and black pepper.

3. Place 1 Bibb lettuce leaf on each plate, and spoon ¾ cup bean salad on top. Serve slices of toasted French bread on the side.

Variation: For **Three Bean Salad,** substitute apple cider vinegar for the red wine vinegar; ¼ cup chopped fresh parsley for the rosemary; 1 medium carrot, peeled and diced, and 1 celery stalk, diced, for the cucumber; and ⅔ cup drained and rinsed kidney beans, ⅔ cup drained and rinsed navy beans, and ⅔ cup drained and rinsed chickpeas for the cannellini beans. Omit the red bell pepper. *Each serving has: 346 calories, 12 g protein, 41 g carbohydrates, 7 g fiber, 16 g total fat, 2 g saturated fat, 802 mg sodium.*

CULINARY KNOW-HOW

It's easy to remove the seeds from a cucumber with a spoon. Simply cut the cuke in half lengthwise and drag the working end of the spoon down the row of seeds to scoop them out.

Mediterranean Tuna Tomato Cups

Olives and artichoke hearts add a delicious layer of flavor to this easy tuna salad.

Yield:	Prep time:	Serving size:	
4 tomato cups	10 to 15 minutes	1 tomato cup	
Each serving has:			
338 calories	35 g protein 19 g total fat	10 g carbohydrates 2 g saturated fat	2 g fiber 636 mg sodium

4 (5-oz.) cans solid white albacore tuna packed in water, drained

½ small red onion, diced

8 kalamata olives, chopped

4 marinated artichoke hearts, chopped

¼ cup chopped fresh parsley

¼ cup chopped fresh basil

2 TB. extra-virgin olive oil

Juice of 1 lemon

¼ tsp. black pepper

1 cup chopped romaine lettuce

2 large tomatoes, cut in half and center spooned out

3 TB. pine nuts, toasted

1. In a large bowl, combine albacore tuna, red onion, kalamata olives, artichokes, parsley, basil, extra-virgin olive oil, lemon juice, and black pepper.

2. Divide romaine lettuce among 4 plates. Top each with a tomato cup, and fill tomatoes with ¾ cup tuna salad.

3. Garnish with pine nuts, and serve.

TASTY TIDBIT

Using tuna packed in water saves a good deal of calories and fat over oil-packed tuna.

Sensational Sandwiches

In This Chapter

- Quick and easy portable meals
- Unique and delicious burgers
- Perfect pockets and po'boys
- Delightful chicken and egg salad sandwiches

There's nothing wrong with a good, old-fashioned PB&J (peanut butter and jelly), but a sandwich can be so much more. It can be more flavorful, filling, and satisfying. It can also be a great way to incorporate a serving of lean protein, veggies, whole grains—or all three!—as you'll see by the recipes in this chapter.

Marinated Portobello Mushroom Burgers

These meaty portobello mushroom burgers are full of zesty garlic, sweet and tangy balsamic, and spicy Dijon mustard.

Yield:	Prep time:	Cook time:	Serving size:
4 burgers	45 to 50 minutes	5 minutes	1 burger

Each serving has:			
159 calories	6 g protein 2 g total fat	30 g carbohydrates 0 g saturated fat	5 g fiber 215 mg sodium

1 tsp. minced garlic	4 100 percent whole-wheat hamburger buns
¼ cup balsamic vinegar	4 thin slices yellow onion
1 tsp. Dijon mustard	4 slices tomato
4 (3-in.) portobello mushroom tops	

1. In a medium bowl, combine garlic, balsamic vinegar, and Dijon mustard. Add portobello tops, and turn to coat. Refrigerate for 30 minutes.

2. Preheat the broiler to 400°F. Position the oven rack 3 inches from the heat source. Line a baking sheet with aluminum foil.

3. Place portobello tops on the prepared baking sheet, with de-stemmed side facing up. Broil for 5 minutes.

4. Divide whole-wheat hamburger buns among 4 plates, and top each with 1 portobello top, 1 slice onion, and 1 slice tomato. Serve.

MAKE IT A MEAL

Pair these burgers with the Green Beans and Fennel Salad (recipe in Chapter 10) for a complete meal.

Open-Faced Italian Sandwiches

This beef sandwich is laced with the sweet pine and citrus of rosemary and marjoram and topped with the deep flavor of roasted red peppers.

Yield:	Prep time:	Cook time:	Serving size:
4 sandwiches	5 to 10 minutes	5 to 10 minutes	1 sandwich

Each serving has:			
177 calories	23 g protein 3 g total fat	17 g carbohydrates 1 g saturated fat	1 g fiber 637 mg sodium

2 cups low-sodium beef stock or broth	8 oz. thin-sliced low-sodium roast beef
1 TB. chopped fresh rosemary or 1 tsp. dried	4 (1-oz.) slices Italian bread
1 TB. fresh marjoram or 1 tsp. dried	½ cup jarred roasted red peppers, packed in water
2 TB. tomato paste	

1. In a large pot over medium-high heat, bring beef stock, rosemary, marjoram, and tomato paste to a boil. Reduce heat to low.

2. Add roast beef, stir, and cook for 2 or 3 minutes.

3. Divide Italian bread slices among 4 plates, top with cooked roast beef, and spoon pan juices over top. Garnish with roasted red peppers, and serve.

Variations: For **Quick Italian Beef Sandwiches,** substitute 4 (2½-inch) rolls for the Italian bread. *Each serving has: 207 calories, 24 g protein, 21 g carbohydrates, 2 g fiber, 4 g total fat, 2 g saturated fat, 632 mg sodium.*

For **Open-Faced Turkey Sandwiches,** substitute chicken stock for the beef stock and ¼ cup parsley for the rosemary and marjoram. Omit the tomato paste, and substitute 8 thick slices low-sodium deli turkey breast for the roast beef and ¼ cup whole canned cranberries for the roasted red peppers. Toast the bread, follow with remaining instructions, and garnish with cranberries. *Each serving has: 280 calories, 30 g protein, 25 g carbohydrates, 2 g fiber, 5 g total fat, 2 g saturated fat, 864 mg sodium.*

Crunchy Tuna Pockets

Tangy, creamy, spicy, and crunchy are the flavors and textures that will fill your mouth with each bite of this tuna pocket.

Yield:	Prep time:	Serving size:
4 pita pockets	15 to 20 minutes	1 pita pocket

Each serving has:			
189 calories	20 g protein	18 g carbohydrates	3 g fiber
	4 g total fat	1 g saturated fat	568 mg sodium

2 (5-oz.) cans tuna, packed in water and drained	⅛ tsp. black pepper
2 TB. low-fat mayonnaise	¼ cup chopped fresh parsley
2 TB. fat-free plain Greek yogurt	4 100 percent whole-wheat pita pockets, cut in ½
1 TB. stone-ground mustard	4 medium romaine lettuce leaves, chopped
1 small yellow onion, diced	4 slices tomato
1 small stalk celery, diced	

1. In a medium bowl, combine tuna, low-fat mayonnaise, Greek yogurt, stone-ground mustard, yellow onion, celery, black pepper, and parsley.

2. Spoon ½ cup salad into each whole-wheat pita pocket, top each with ½ cup chopped romaine and 1 tomato slice, and serve.

Variation: For **Tuna Wraps,** substitute 4 (8-inch) 100 percent whole-wheat tortillas for the pita bread. *Each serving has: 249 calories, 21 g protein, 25 g carbohydrates, 4 g fiber, 7 g total fat, 2 g saturated fat, 742 mg sodium.*

CULINARY KNOW-HOW

Be sure to drain the tuna—even squeeze it a bit—to get out as much water as possible. This prevents the tuna from being watery and runny in your salad.

Veggie Sandwiches with Herb Mayo

Rich herbed mayo, with a hint of licorice, juicy tomatoes, fresh-tasting cucumbers, and sweet carrots combine deliciously in this fiber-rich sandwich.

Yield:	Prep time:	Serving size:
4 sandwiches	15 to 20 minutes	1 sandwich

Each serving has:			
253 calories	11 g protein 7 g total fat	38 g carbohydrates 1 g saturated fat	11 g fiber 566 mg sodium

¼ cup low-fat mayonnaise

¼ cup fat-free plain Greek yogurt

¼ cup mixed fresh herbs (dill, parsley, and rosemary) or 1 TB. dried

2 medium scallions, white and green parts, minced

¼ tsp. kosher salt

⅛ tsp. black pepper

8 slices 100 percent whole-wheat bread, toasted

2 medium carrots, peeled and grated

1 small English cucumber, sliced into 12 (⅛-in.) rounds,

4 slices tomato

1 small fennel bulb, sliced into 12 thin pieces

1. In a large bowl, combine low-fat mayonnaise, Greek yogurt, mixed herbs, scallions, kosher salt, and black pepper.

2. Spread 2 tablespoons mayonnaise mixture on each of 4 whole-wheat toast slices. Top with ¼ cup carrots, 3 English cucumber slices, 1 tomato slice, and 3 fennel slices, and add remaining 4 bread slices. Cut sandwiches in half, and serve.

TASTY TIDBIT

Feel free to experiment with different herbs in this recipe. Use your favorites, or try something new—any way you do it, it'll be delicious!

Pulled Chicken Sandwiches

This pulled chicken sandwich is packed with sweet, smoky, and spicy flavors.

Yield:	Prep time:	Cook time:	Serving size:
6 sandwiches	15 to 20 minutes	10 minutes	1 sandwich

Each serving has:			
267 calories	28 g protein	28 g carbohydrates	4 g fiber
	5 g total fat	1 g saturated fat	361 mg sodium

1 lb. cooked, shredded or diced white meat chicken	1 TB. chili powder
$\frac{1}{2}$ tsp. black pepper	$\frac{1}{2}$ cup low-sodium beef stock or broth
2 TB. dark brown sugar	3 TB. apple cider vinegar
2 TB. stone-ground mustard	1 TB. Worcestershire sauce
1 TB. smoked paprika	6 100 percent whole-wheat hamburger buns
1 TB. tomato paste	

1. In a 2-quart pot over medium-high heat, bring chicken, black pepper, dark brown sugar, stone-ground mustard, smoked paprika, tomato paste, chili powder, and beef stock to a boil. Cover, reduce heat to low, and simmer for 5 minutes.

2. Add apple cider vinegar and Worcestershire sauce, and stir.

3. Divide open whole-wheat hamburger buns among 4 plates, place $\frac{1}{2}$ cup pulled chicken on one side of each bun, add bun tops, and serve.

CULINARY KNOW-HOW

If you have chicken left over from another meal, you can use it for these sandwiches. Otherwise, pick up a rotisserie chicken from the grocery store and use about 1 cup to make this recipe.

Egg Salad Pita Pockets

Sharp onion, sweet crunchy celery, and dill envelop the eggs in these pita pockets, bringing out their creamy and rich flavor.

Yield:	Prep time:	Cook time:	Serving size:
4 pita pockets	15 to 20 minutes	12 minutes	1 pita pocket

Each serving has:			
278 calories	13 g protein 16 g total fat	21 g carbohydrates 4 g saturated fat	3 g fiber 432 mg sodium

2 qt. water	½ tsp. kosher salt
6 large eggs	¼ tsp. black pepper
6 TB. low-fat mayonnaise	4 (4-in.) 100 percent whole-wheat pita pockets, cut in ½
1 small yellow onion, grated	
1 small stalk celery, grated	4 medium romaine lettuce leaves, chopped
2 TB. chopped fresh dill or 2 tsp. dried	4 slices tomato

1. In a large pot over medium-high heat, bring water to a boil. Add eggs, and cook for 12 minutes.

2. Remove eggs from water and run under cold water to stop the cooking process. Peel and chop eggs.

3. In a large bowl, combine eggs, low-fat mayonnaise, yellow onion, celery, dill, kosher salt, and black pepper.

4. Spoon ¾ cup salad into each whole-wheat pita pocket, top with ¼ cup chopped romaine lettuce and 1 tomato slice, and serve.

Variation: For **Egg Salad Sandwiches,** substitute 8 slices of 100 percent whole-wheat bread for the pitas. Reduce the onion and celery to ¼ cup and 2 tablespoons each. Spread egg salad on 4 bread slices, and top with tomatoes, romaine lettuce, and remaining 4 bread slices. *Each serving has: 364 calories, 18 g protein, 33 g carbohydrates, 9 g fiber, 18 g total fat, 4 g saturated fat, 553 mg sodium.*

CULINARY KNOW-HOW

Store your eggs in the body of the refrigerator, not the door. The temperature in the center of your refrigerator is colder and more consistent, which eggs like.

Spicy Meatball Pockets

Sweet bell peppers, rich marinara sauce, and juicy meatballs, all topped with gooey cheese and housed in a whole-wheat pita pocket.

Yield:	Prep time:	Cook time:	Serving size:
4 meatball pockets	5 to 10 minutes	20 minutes	1 meatball pocket

Each serving has:			
278 calories	16 g protein	32 g carbohydrates	6 g fiber
	10 g total fat	3 g saturated fat	612 mg sodium

1 small green bell pepper, ribs and seeds removed, and sliced	½ tsp. crushed red pepper flakes (optional)
1 medium yellow onion, sliced	4 (4-in.) 100 percent whole-wheat pita pockets, cut in ½
¼ tsp. black pepper	¼ cup shredded reduced-fat mozzarella cheese
8 Italian turkey meatballs	1 TB. grated Parmesan cheese
1¼ cups low-sodium spaghetti sauce	
1 TB. chopped fresh rosemary or 1 tsp. dried	

1. Heat a 12-inch nonstick sauté pan over medium heat, and lightly coat with nonstick cooking spray. Add green bell peppers, yellow onions, and black pepper, cover, and cook, stirring occasionally, for 5 to 7 minutes.

2. Add Italian turkey meatballs, spaghetti sauce, rosemary, and crushed red pepper flakes (if using). Cover and simmer for 10 minutes.

3. Place 2 meatballs into each whole-wheat pita pocket. Spoon ⅓ cup sauce over meatballs, top with 3 tablespoons reduced-fat mozzarella cheese and 1 teaspoon Parmesan cheese, and serve.

CULINARY KNOW-HOW

You can purchase turkey meatballs in the freezer section of your grocery store or, if you have time, make a big batch of your own to freeze and have on hand for quick recipes like this.

Shrimp Po'Boys

Sweet, tender shrimp with a hint of spice; a luscious, creamy spicy dressing; and the cooling crunch of lettuce combine to make these po'boys memorable.

Yield:	Prep time:	Cook time:	Serving size:
4 sandwiches	5 to 10 minutes	10 minutes	1 sandwich

Each serving has:			
314 calories	29 g protein 9 g total fat	29 g carbohydrates 2 g saturated fat	4 g fiber 590 mg sodium

2 qt. water

1 lb. raw shrimp (31 to 40 count, about 36), peeled and deveined

1 TB. paprika

1 TB. dried thyme

1 TB. dried oregano

1 TB. celery seed

1 tsp. powdered yellow mustard

1 tsp. ground black pepper

⅛ tsp. cayenne

¼ cup low-fat mayonnaise

¼ cup fat-free plain Greek yogurt

½ tsp. prepared horseradish

1 clove garlic, minced

1 TB. stone-ground mustard

1 TB. dill pickle relish

⅛ tsp. cayenne

⅛ tsp. black pepper

4 100 percent whole-wheat rolls

1½ cups shredded romaine lettuce

2 medium tomatoes, sliced

1. In a large pot over medium-high heat, bring water to a boil. Add paprika, thyme, oregano, celery seed, powdered yellow mustard, black pepper, and cayenne. Boil for 3 minutes.

2. Add shrimp, and cook for 3 or 4 minutes. Remove shrimp from water, and keep warm.

3. In a small bowl, combine low-fat mayonnaise, Greek yogurt, horseradish, garlic, stone-ground mustard, dill pickle relish, cayenne, and black pepper.

4. Divide open whole-wheat rolls among 4 plates, spread 1 tablespoon mayonnaise on one side of each roll, and add romaine lettuce and tomato slices. Top with 9 shrimp and 1 tablespoon mayonnaise, add whole-wheat roll tops, and serve.

MAKE IT A MEAL

Add a serving of Red Cabbage Slaw (recipe in Chapter 10) to have an authentic southern lunch.

Old-Fashioned Chicken Salad Pita Pockets

Sweet onion, celery, and carrot combine with a creamy dressing and perfectly cooked lean chicken breast in these delightful pita pockets.

Yield:	Prep time:	Cook time:	Serving size:
4 pita pockets	15 to 20 minutes	10 minutes	1 pita pocket

Each serving has:			
331 calories	25 g protein	39 g carbohydrates	6 g fiber
	9 g total fat	2 g saturated fat	521 mg sodium

12 oz. boneless, skinless chicken breasts

½ tsp. kosher salt

¼ tsp. black pepper

¼ cup low-fat mayonnaise

¼ cup fat-free plain Greek yogurt

1 small yellow onion, diced

1 small celery stalk, diced

1 small carrot, peeled and diced

¼ cup chopped fresh parsley

4 (6-in.) 100 percent whole-wheat pita breads, cut in ½

4 medium romaine lettuce leaves, chopped

1. Heat a 12-inch nonstick sauté pan over medium heat, and lightly coat with nonstick cooking spray.

2. Season chicken breasts with ¼ teaspoon kosher salt and ⅛ teaspoon black pepper. Add chicken to the pan, and cook for 5 minutes per side or until an instant-read thermometer inserted into the center reads 165°F.

3. In a large bowl, combine low-fat mayonnaise, Greek yogurt, yellow onion, celery, carrots, parsley, remaining ¼ teaspoon kosher salt, and remaining ⅛ teaspoon black pepper.

4. Remove chicken from the pan, and allow to cool for 10 to 15 minutes. Cut into ¼- to ½-inch cubes, and fold chicken into salad.

5. Spoon ¾ cup salad into each whole-wheat pita pocket, top each with ½ cup chopped romaine, and serve.

Variation: For **Old-Fashioned Chicken Salad Sandwiches,** substitute 8 slices 100 percent whole-wheat bread for the pita pockets. Spread ¾ cup chicken salad on each of 4 bread slices, top with romaine lettuce and remaining 4 bread slices, and serve. *Each serving has: 321 calories, 27 g protein, 32 g carbohydrates, 9 g fiber, 9 g total fat, 2 g saturated fat, 450 mg sodium.*

CULINARY KNOW-HOW

Because chicken breasts are so lean, they can dry out easily. Be sure to monitor the internal temperature closely and remove them from heat when they reach 165°F.

Avocado Sandwiches with Lime Vinaigrette

A sweet, crisp lime vinaigrette laced with cilantro, crunchy jicama, and creamy avocado combine in this tasty and filling sandwich.

Yield:	Prep time:	Serving size:
4 sandwiches	10 to 15 minutes	1 sandwich

Each serving has:			
334 calories	11 g protein 17 g total fat	40 g carbohydrates 2 g saturated fat	11 g fiber 392 mg sodium

2 medium ripe avocados, peeled and pitted

8 slices 100 percent whole-wheat bread

1 medium tomato, sliced

1 small jicama, peeled and sliced into 4 ($\frac{1}{4}$-in.) slices

2 medium scallions, white parts only, diced

2 TB. lime juice

1 TB. extra-virgin olive oil

1 tsp. honey

$\frac{1}{4}$ cup chopped fresh cilantro

$\frac{1}{4}$ tsp. kosher salt

$\frac{1}{8}$ tsp. black pepper

1. Slice avocados, and evenly divide slices among 4 whole-wheat bread slices. Top each with 2 tomato slices, 1 jicama slice, and 1 tablespoon scallions.

2. In a small bowl, mix together lime juice, extra-virgin olive oil, honey, cilantro, kosher salt, and black pepper.

3. Spoon 2 teaspoons vinaigrette over each sandwich's vegetables, top with remaining 4 bread slices, carefully cut in half, and serve.

Variation: For **Avocado, Cucumber, and Tomato Sandwiches,** substitute 8 thin slices cucumber for the jicama and 4 thin slices red onion for the scallions. In the vinaigrette, substitute 2 tablespoons lemon juice for the lime juice, omit the honey, and substitute $\frac{1}{4}$ cup parsley for the cilantro. *Each serving has: 329 calories, 11 g protein, 38 g carbohydrates, 11 g fiber, 17 g total fat, 2 g saturated fat, 392 mg sodium.*

TASTY TIDBIT

Jicama is a versatile vegetable that can be eaten raw or cooked. It has very crisp white flesh that's great as a crudité.

Philly Cheese Steak Sandwiches

You don't need to take a trip to Philadelphia to enjoy this cheesy, peppery specialty.

Yield:	Prep time:	Cook time:	Serving size:
4 sandwiches	10 to 15 minutes	15 minutes	1 sandwich

Each serving has:			
344 calories	34 g protein	27 g carbohydrates	2 g fiber
	11 g total fat	5 g saturated fat	669 mg sodium

1 medium yellow onion, sliced

1 medium green bell pepper, ribs and seeds removed, and sliced into strips

1 clove garlic, minced

¼ tsp. kosher salt

⅛ tsp. black pepper

1 lb. sirloin steak, sliced thin

¼ cup low-sodium beef broth

4 (1-oz.) slices low-fat provolone cheese

4 (3-in.) pieces French baguette, sliced open

1. Heat a 12-inch nonstick sauté pan over medium heat, and lightly coat with nonstick cooking spray. Add yellow onion, green bell pepper, garlic, kosher salt, and black pepper, and cook, stirring occasionally, for 10 minutes.

2. Add sirloin steak, and cook for about 5 minutes or until no longer pink.

3. Stir in beef broth, and heat through.

4. Top with provolone cheese slices, and allow to melt.

5. Place open French baguette pieces on plates, and top with ¾ cup meat, vegetables, and cheese. Serve.

Variation: For **Minute Steak and Mushroom Sandwiches,** substitute ½ pound sliced button mushrooms for the green bell peppers and low-fat Swiss cheese for provolone cheese. *Each serving has: 358 calories, 36 g protein, 28 g carbohydrates, 2 g fiber, 11 g total fat, 6 g saturated fat, 506 mg sodium.*

TASTY TIDBIT

We can thank Pat and Harry Olivieri for first putting chopped steak into soft rolls at their hot dog stand in Philly in the 1930s. A few years later, someone added the cheese, and the rest is delicious history.

Open-Face Pepper-Smothered Beef Sandwiches

Sautéed peppers, onions, and fennel marry beef that's enhanced with the robust flavor of rosemary in these open-face sandwiches.

Yield:	Prep time:	Cook time:	Serving size:
4 sandwiches	10 to 15 minutes	15 to 20 minutes	1 sandwich

Each serving has:			
369 calories	32 g protein 6 g total fat	47 g carbohydrates 2 g saturated fat	5 g fiber 634 mg sodium

1 medium yellow onion, sliced	1 small tomato, diced
1 medium red bell pepper, ribs and seeds removed, and sliced	⅛ tsp. kosher salt
	⅛ tsp. black pepper
1 medium fennel blub	4 medium slices French bread, toasted
1 TB. chopped fresh rosemary or 1 tsp. dried	
1 lb. sirloin steak, sliced thin	¼ cup chopped fresh basil

1. Heat a 12-inch nonstick sauté pan over medium heat, and lightly coat with nonstick cooking spray. Add yellow onion, red bell pepper, fennel, and rosemary, cover, and cook, stirring occasionally, for 10 minutes.

2. Add sirloin steak, tomatoes, kosher salt, and black pepper, cover, and simmer for 5 minutes or until liquid is almost evaporated.

3. Evenly divide toasted French bread among 4 plates, and top with ¼ of pepper-smothered beef. Garnish each with 1 tablespoon basil, and serve.

Variation: For **Pepper-Smothered Beef Wraps,** substitute 4 (8-inch) 100 percent whole-wheat tortillas for the toasted French bread. *Each serving has: 311 calories, 28 g protein, 32 g carbohydrates, 6 g fiber, 8 g total fat, 3 g saturated fat, 529 mg sodium.*

CULINARY KNOW-HOW

If the steak is partially frozen, it will be easier to slice.

Curried Chicken Salad Sandwiches

With plenty of tasty chicken, spicy curry, crunchy almonds, and sweet raisins, you get something sweet, savory, spicy, and crunchy in every bite.

Yield:	Prep time:	Cook time:	Serving size:
4 sandwiches	10 to 15 minutes	10 minutes	1 sandwich

Each serving has:			
399 calories	28 g protein 15 g total fat	41 g carbohydrates 2 g saturated fat	11 g fiber 476 mg sodium

12 oz. boneless, skinless chicken breasts

¼ tsp. black pepper

⅓ cup low-fat mayonnaise

2 TB. curry powder

3½ TB. slivered almonds, toasted

¼ cup golden raisins

8 slices 100 percent whole-wheat bread

4 romaine lettuce leaves

4 slices tomato

1. Heat a 12-inch nonstick sauté pan over medium heat, and lightly coat with nonstick cooking spray.

2. Season chicken breasts with ⅛ teaspoon black pepper. Add chicken to the pan, and cook for 5 minutes per side or until an instant-read thermometer inserted into the center reads 165°F.

3. In a large bowl, combine low-fat mayonnaise, curry powder, and remaining ⅛ teaspoon black pepper.

4. Remove chicken from the pan, and allow to cool for 10 to 15 minutes. Cut into ¼- to ½-inch pieces, and fold into salad. Add almonds and golden raisins, and fold again.

5. Spoon ¾ cup salad onto 4 slices whole-wheat bread. Top each with 1 romaine lettuce leaf and 1 tomato slice. Add remaining 4 slices bread, and serve.

Variation: For **Curried Chicken Salad Pockets,** replace the whole-wheat bread with 4 (4-inch) 100 percent whole-wheat pita pockets and the romaine leaves with 1 cup chopped romaine. Cut pita pockets in half, and spoon ¾ cup salad into each pocket.

Top with chopped romaine and tomato, and serve. *Each serving has: 315 calories, 22 g protein, 29 g carbohydrates, 5 g fiber, 13 g total fat, 2 g saturated fat, 355 mg sodium.*

TASTY TIDBIT

For a bit more tang, replace 1 or 2 tablespoons low-fat mayonnaise with 1 or 2 tablespoons plain nonfat or Greek yogurt. You'll save about 40 calories and 5 grams fat per tablespoon.

Wonderful Wraps

In This Chapter

- Meals you can eat with your hands
- Get your veggies
- An easy dose of fiber

Wraps are basically kicked-up versions of sandwiches. Sure, you can fill one with traditional sandwich fixins, but with wraps you can think outside the bread box, too. Load up your wraps with more substantial, hotter, and/or juicier fillings than traditional bread because they'll hold up to the hearty fillings and not get soggy like bread would.

The veggie-filling options in wraps are almost limitless. You could easily whip together a wrap filled with sautéed onions and peppers, carrots, artichoke hearts, or anything else you can think of. Chunky foods like olives, avocados, and tomatillos also are perfect fits.

In addition, the wrap itself is a nutritional goldmine, if you choose tortillas made from 100 percent whole wheat. One such tortilla contains a whopping 3 grams fiber—and that's not counting the fiber-rich fillings you add. But because the tortilla is so thin, it won't leave you feeling uncomfortably stuffed.

Turn the page to find an array of delicious recipes for wraps filled with meat, chicken, seafood, veggies, and so much more.

Lobster and Tomatillo Wraps

In these wraps, tender, succulent lobster mingles with citrusy tomatillos and hot jalapeño, all surrounded by a creamy cilantro dressing.

Yield:	Prep time:	Serving size:	
4 wraps	5 to 10 minutes	1 wrap	

Each serving has:			
149 calories	24 g protein	4 g carbohydrates	1 g fiber
	3 g total fat	1 g saturated fat	519 mg sodium

1 lb. cooked lobster meat

$\frac{1}{2}$ small red onion, diced

2 TB. low-fat mayonnaise

2 TB. plain fat-free Greek yogurt

2 small tomatillos, diced

$\frac{1}{4}$ cup chopped fresh cilantro

1 small jalapeño pepper, seeded and diced

$\frac{1}{8}$ tsp. black pepper

4 (8-in.) 100 percent whole-wheat tortillas

4 medium Bibb lettuce leaves

1. In a large bowl, combine lobster meat, red onion, low-fat mayonnaise, Greek yogurt, tomatillos, cilantro, jalapeño, and black pepper.

2. Place 1 whole-wheat tortilla on each of 4 plates. Spoon $\frac{3}{4}$ cup lobster mixture into center of each tortilla, and spread evenly, leaving a $\frac{1}{2}$-inch border. Top each with 1 Bibb lettuce leaf. Roll, slice, and serve.

 CULINARY KNOW-HOW

Tomatillos are a fruit used in Mexican cooking. To prepare, simply remove the paperlike husk, and rinse the tomatillo to remove the stickiness. You don't have to peel tomatillos, but if you prefer, you can remove the skin with a small paring knife.

California Turkey Wraps

Creamy, rich avocado and sweet and spicy *chutney* combine to lift turkey to new taste heights in these hearty wraps.

Yield:	Prep time:	Serving size:
4 wraps	10 to 15 minutes	1 wrap

Each serving has:			
263 calories	14 g protein	31 g carbohydrates	5 g fiber
	10 g total fat	2 g saturated fat	583 mg sodium

4 (8-in.) 100 percent whole-wheat tortillas	1 medium avocado, peeled, pitted, and diced
4 TB. mango chutney	4 medium Bibb lettuce leaves
6 (1-oz.) slices low-sodium turkey breast	$\frac{1}{8}$ tsp. black pepper

1. Place whole-wheat tortillas on a work surface. Spread 1 tablespoon mango chutney on each, and top with $1\frac{1}{2}$ slices turkey breast.

2. Evenly divide avocado among tortillas, top with 4 Bibb lettuce leaves, and season with pinch black pepper. Roll, slice, and serve.

Variation: For a **Thanksgiving Wrap,** substitute $\frac{1}{4}$ cup canned whole berry cranberries for the chutney and $\frac{1}{4}$ cup reduced-fat cream cheese for the avocado. *Each serving has: 246 calories, 17 g protein, 30 g carbohydrates, 3 g fiber, 6 g total fat, 2 g saturated fat, 735 mg sodium.*

DEFINITION

Chutney is a relish made with fruits, spices, and herbs. You can find peach, mango, cranberry, and many more flavors in either the jams and jelly or international aisles of your local grocer.

Easy Fajitas

In these simple fajitas, onions, peppers, and tasty beef are smothered in a light, flavorfully spiced tomato sauce.

Yield:	Prep time:	Cook time:	Serving size:
4 fajitas	10 to 15 minutes	15 to 20 minutes	1 fajita

Each serving has:			
297 calories	27 g protein	29 g carbohydrates	5 g fiber
	8 g total fat	3 g saturated fat	461 mg sodium

1 medium yellow onion, sliced	1 medium tomato, diced
1 medium red bell pepper, ribs and seeds removed, and sliced	⅛ tsp. kosher salt
2 tsp. chili powder	⅛ tsp. black pepper
1 tsp. ground cumin	4 (8-in.) 100 percent whole-wheat tortillas
1 tsp. ground coriander	¼ cup fresh cilantro
1 lb. sirloin steak, sliced very thin	

1. Heat a 12-inch nonstick sauté pan over medium heat, and lightly coat with nonstick cooking spray. Add yellow onion, red bell pepper, chili powder, cumin, and coriander. Cover and cook, stirring occasionally, for 10 minutes.

2. Add sirloin steak, tomatoes, kosher salt, and black pepper, cover, and simmer for 5 minutes or until liquid is almost evaporated.

3. Place 1 whole-wheat tortilla on each of 4 plates. Spoon ¾ cup fajita filling into center of each tortilla, and spread evenly, leaving a ½-inch border. Top with 1 tablespoon cilantro. Roll, slice, and serve.

CULINARY KNOW-HOW

Cilantro is one of those foods people seem to either love or hate. If you don't like this herb, feel free to substitute curly parsley.

Broiled Chicken Kabob Wraps

In these wraps, garlic, lemon, and cinnamon infuse the chicken that's broiled to a golden brown, trapping those Mediterranean flavors.

Yield:	Prep time:	Cook time:	Serving size:
4 wraps	10 to 15 minutes	6 minutes	1 wrap

Each serving has:			
319 calories	27 g protein	23 g carbohydrates	3 g fiber
	13 g total fat	3 g saturated fat	496 mg sodium

1 lb. boneless, skinless chicken breast, cut into $\frac{1}{2}$-in. cubes

4 small garlic cloves, minced

2 TB. extra-virgin olive oil

$\frac{1}{2}$ tsp. ground allspice

$\frac{1}{2}$ tsp. ground cinnamon

1 TB. fresh lemon juice

$\frac{1}{4}$ tsp. kosher salt

$\frac{1}{8}$ tsp. black pepper

4 (8-in.) 100 percent whole-wheat tortillas

4 medium romaine lettuce leaves, chopped

$\frac{1}{4}$ cup chopped fresh parsley

$\frac{1}{4}$ cup chopped fresh mint

1. In a large bowl, combine chicken breast, garlic, extra-virgin olive oil, allspice, cinnamon, lemon juice, kosher salt, and black pepper.

2. Preheat the broiler to 500°F. Position the oven rack 3 inches from the heat source.

3. Skewer chicken pieces onto 6 (8-inch) bamboo skewers, about $\frac{1}{4}$ inch apart. Leave 1 or 2 inches of the end exposed. Cover the exposed bamboo with aluminum foil.

4. Place skewers on a baking sheet, lightly coat with nonstick cooking spray, and broil for 3 minutes. Turn chicken and broil for 2 or 3 more minutes.

5. Place 1 whole-wheat tortilla on each of 4 plates. Remove chicken from 1 skewer, and place on 1 tortilla. Top each tortilla with $\frac{1}{4}$ cup romaine lettuce, 1 tablespoon parsley, and 1 tablespoon mint. Roll, slice, and serve.

 TASTY TIDBIT

To store fresh herbs, wash them well and let them dry completely. Refrigerate with the stems in a cup of water, and be sure to change the water frequently.

Zesty Chicken Salad Wraps

Chunks of perfectly cooked chicken breast coated with a creamy dressing, paired with fresh vegetables and bright tasting basil, star in these tasty wraps.

Yield:	Prep time:	Cook time:	Serving size:
4 wraps	25 to 30 minutes	10 minutes	1 wrap

Each serving has:			
329 calories	22 g protein	26 g carbohydrates	4 g fiber
	16 g total fat	4 g saturated fat	610 mg sodium

12 oz. boneless, skinless chicken breasts

¼ tsp. black pepper

½ cup low-fat mayonnaise

3 medium scallions, chopped

¼ cup diced celery

1 small tomato, seeded and diced

¼ cup chopped fresh basil

4 (8-in.) 100 percent whole-wheat tortillas

4 medium escarole lettuce leaves, chopped

1. Heat a nonstick sauté pan over medium heat, and lightly coat with nonstick cooking spray.

2. Season chicken breasts with ⅛ teaspoon black pepper. Add chicken to the pan, and cook for 5 minutes per side or until an instant-read thermometer inserted into the center reads 165°F.

3. In a large bowl, combine low-fat mayonnaise, scallions, celery, tomato, basil, and remaining ⅛ teaspoon black pepper.

4. Remove chicken from the pan and allow to cool for 10 to 15 minutes. Cut into ¼- to ½-inch pieces, and fold into mayonnaise mixture.

5. Place 1 whole-wheat tortilla on each of 4 plates, and spoon ¾ cup chicken salad into center. Spread salad evenly over tortilla, leaving a ½-inch boarder. Top with chopped escarole lettuce. Roll, slice, and serve.

MAKE IT A MEAL

A crisp apple or cup of cold grapes provides the ideal side to this creamy filled wrap.

Curried Chicken and Grape Wraps

Plump raisins and crunchy almonds add sweetness to the spicy *curry* mayonnaise, bringing an interesting and delicious texture and flavor to this wrap.

Yield:	Prep time:	Cook time:	Serving size:
4 wraps	15 to 20 minutes	10 minutes	1 wrap

Each serving has:			
345 calories	18 g protein 18 g total fat	30 g carbohydrates 3 g saturated fat	5 g fiber 750 mg sodium

12 oz. boneless, skinless chicken breasts	$\frac{1}{2}$ cup Thompson seedless red grapes, cut in $\frac{1}{2}$
$\frac{1}{4}$ tsp. black pepper	4 (8-in.) 100 percent whole-wheat tortillas
$\frac{1}{3}$ cup low-fat mayonnaise	
2 TB. curry powder	4 medium Bibb lettuce leaves, chopped
$\frac{1}{3}$ cup walnut pieces, toasted	

1. Heat a nonstick sauté pan over medium heat, and lightly coat with nonstick cooking spray.

2. Season chicken breasts with $\frac{1}{8}$ teaspoon black pepper. Add chicken to the pan, and cook for 5 minutes per side or until an instant-read thermometer inserted into the center reads 165°F.

3. In a large bowl, combine low-fat mayonnaise, curry powder, and remaining $\frac{1}{8}$ teaspoon black pepper.

4. Remove chicken from the pan and allow to cool for 10 to 15 minutes. Cut into $\frac{1}{4}$- to $\frac{1}{2}$-inch pieces, and fold chicken into mayonnaise mixture. Add walnuts and red grapes, and fold again.

5. Place 1 whole-wheat tortilla on each of 4 plates. Spoon $\frac{3}{4}$ curried salad into center of each tortilla, and spread evenly, leaving a $\frac{1}{2}$-inch border. Top with Bibb lettuce leaves. Roll, slice, and serve.

DEFINITION

Curry is a traditional Indian way of cooking using spices such as cardamom, cumin, turmeric, and more. These are the same spices found in the seasoning blend curry powder.

Marinated Artichoke Hearts and Broiled Chicken Wraps

Fresh herbs and sharp vinegar fill these wraps with bright, strong, zesty flavors that coat the chicken and artichoke hearts.

Yield:	Prep time:	Cook time:	Serving size:
4 wraps	10 to 15 minutes	6 minutes	1 wrap

Each serving has:			
346 calories	29 g protein	25 g carbohydrates	4 g fiber
	14 g total fat	3 g saturated fat	556 mg sodium

1 lb. boneless, skinless chicken breast, cut into $\frac{1}{4}$- to $\frac{1}{2}$-in. pieces

$\frac{1}{2}$ (6-oz.) jar artichoke hearts packed in water, drained and chopped

2 TB. extra-virgin olive oil

1 TB. chopped fresh oregano or 1 tsp. dried

1 TB. chopped fresh basil or 1 tsp. dried

2 small garlic cloves, minced

1 TB. red wine vinegar

2 TB. grated Parmesan cheese

$\frac{1}{4}$ tsp. kosher salt

$\frac{1}{8}$ tsp. black pepper

4 (8-in.) 100 percent whole-wheat tortillas

1. Preheat the broiler to 500°F. Position the oven rack 3 inches from the heat source. Lightly coat a baking sheet with nonstick cooking spray.

2. Place chicken breast on the prepared baking sheet, and broil for 3 minutes. Turn and broil for 2 or 3 more minutes.

3. In a large bowl, combine artichoke hearts, extra-virgin olive oil, oregano, basil, garlic, red wine vinegar, Parmesan cheese, kosher salt, and black pepper.

4. Remove chicken from the broiler, and fold chicken into the bowl with artichoke hearts.

5. Place 1 whole-wheat tortilla on each of 4 plates. Spoon $\frac{3}{4}$ cup artichokes and chicken mixture into center of each tortilla, and spread evenly. Roll, slice, and serve.

CULINARY KNOW-HOW

For variety, try this sandwich using other flavored tortillas, such as tomato or spinach.

Italian Beef Wraps

Garlic mayonnaise blends with beef and provolone in these wraps for a distinctive savory flavor.

Yield:	Prep time:	Serving size:	
4 wraps	10 to 15 minutes	1 wrap	
Each serving has:			
347 calories	30 g protein 17 g total fat	26 g carbohydrates 7 g saturated fat	4 g fiber 713 mg sodium

¼ cup low-fat mayonnaise

2 garlic cloves, minced

⅛ tsp. black pepper

4 (8-in.) 100 percent whole-wheat tortillas

½ lb. sliced low-sodium deli roast beef

4 (¾-oz.) slices provolone cheese

¼ lb. jarred roasted red peppers, packed in water

8 medium romaine lettuce leaves, chopped

8 fresh basil leaves

1. In a small bowl, combine low-fat mayonnaise, garlic, and black pepper.

2. Place 1 whole-wheat tortilla on each of 4 plates. Spread each with 1 tablespoon mayonnaise mixture. Evenly divide roast beef, provolone cheese, roasted red peppers, romaine lettuce, and basil leaves on top. Roll, slice, and serve.

CULINARY KNOW-HOW

This wrap is also delicious served warm. Heat in the microwave for about 30 seconds or just until the cheese begins to melt.

Egg Salad Wraps

Creamy eggs get a little tang from high-protein, fat-free Greek yogurt in these tasty wraps.

Yield:	Prep time:	Cook time:	Serving size:
4 wraps	15 to 20 minutes	12 minutes	1 wrap

Each serving has:			
349 calories	18 g protein 19 g total fat	26 g carbohydrates 5 g saturated fat	4 g fiber 571 mg sodium

2 qt. water

8 large eggs

¼ cup low-fat mayonnaise

¼ cup plain fat-free Greek yogurt

3 medium scallions, minced

2 TB. capers, rinsed

1 small tomato, diced

2 TB. chopped fresh oregano or 2 tsp. dried

¼ tsp. black pepper

4 (8-in.) 100 percent whole-wheat tortillas

4 medium escarole lettuce leaves, chopped

1. In a large pot over medium heat, bring water to a boil. Add eggs, and cook for 12 minutes.

2. Remove eggs from water and run under cold water to stop the cooking process. Peel and chop eggs.

3. In a large bowl, combine eggs, low-fat mayonnaise, Greek yogurt, scallions, capers, tomato, oregano, and black pepper.

4. Place 1 whole-wheat tortilla on each of 4 plates. Spoon ¾ cup egg salad into center of each tortilla, and spread evenly, leaving a ½-inch border. Top with escarole lettuce leaves. Roll, slice, and serve.

CULINARY KNOW-HOW

You can hard-boil a dozen or more eggs ahead of time to make assembling sandwiches like this quick and easy later. Hard-boiled eggs last in the refrigerator for up to 1 week.

Deli Beef Quesadillas

Crispy tortillas encase warmly seasoned onions, peppers, and beef in these kicky quesadillas.

Yield:	Prep time:	Cook time:	Serving size:
24 wedges	10 to 15 minutes	20 to 25 minutes	6 wedges

Each serving has:			
354 calories	25 g protein 11 g total fat	41 g carbohydrates 4 g saturated fat	7 g fiber 660 mg sodium

1 medium yellow onion, diced

1 medium red bell pepper, ribs and seeds removed, and diced

1 medium tomato, diced

1 tsp. chili powder

½ tsp. ground cumin

½ tsp. ground coriander

½ lb. sliced low-sodium deli roast beef, chopped

¼ cup shredded reduced-fat cheddar cheese

6 (8-in.) 100 percent whole-wheat tortillas

Nonstick cooking spray

¼ cup low-fat sour cream

¼ cup mild salsa

1. Heat a nonstick sauté pan over medium heat, and lightly coat with nonstick cooking spray. Add yellow onion, red bell pepper, tomato, chili powder, cumin, and coriander. Cover and cook, stirring occasionally, for 10 to 15 minutes.

2. Preheat the oven to 350°F. Lightly coat a baking sheet with nonstick cooking spray. (You may need to use 2 baking sheets.)

3. In a large bowl, combine onion mixture, roast beef, and cheddar cheese.

4. Place 3 whole-wheat tortillas on the prepared baking sheet. Spread ¾ cup beef mixture on each tortilla, and cover with remaining 3 tortillas. Lightly spray tops of tortillas with nonstick cooking spray. Bake for 10 minutes.

5. Using a spatula, slide quesadillas onto a cutting board, and cut each into 8 wedges. Place 6 wedges on each of 4 plates. Top each with 1 tablespoon low-fat sour cream and 1 tablespoon mild salsa, and serve.

CULINARY KNOW-HOW

You can use a pizza wheel to cut this quesadilla into the traditional wedges before serving.

Chopped Egg and Olives Wraps

The flavors of onions, celery, and yogurt flood each bite of this flavorful wrap.

Yield:	Prep time:	Cook time:	Serving size:
4 wraps	15 to 20 minutes	12 minutes	1 wrap

Each serving has:			
362 calories	18 g protein	28 g carbohydrates	4 g fiber
	19 g total fat	5 g saturated fat	724 mg sodium

2 qt. water	2 TB. chopped fresh oregano or 2 tsp. dried
6 large eggs	¼ tsp. black pepper
¼ cup low-fat mayonnaise	4 (8-in.) 100 percent whole-wheat tortillas
¼ cup plain fat-free Greek yogurt	
1 small yellow onion, grated	4 medium romaine lettuce leaves, chopped
1 small stalk celery, grated	1 medium tomato, sliced into 4 (¼-in.) slices
8 green olives, pitted	
¼ cup chopped fresh parsley	

1. In a large pot over medium heat, bring water to a boil. Add eggs, and cook for 12 minutes.

2. Remove eggs from water, and run under cold water to stop the cooking process. Peel and chop eggs.

3. In a large bowl, combine eggs, low-fat mayonnaise, Greek yogurt, yellow onion, celery, green olives, parsley, oregano, and black pepper.

4. Place 1 whole-wheat tortilla on each of 4 plates. Spoon 1 cup egg mixture into center of tortilla, and spread evenly, leaving a ½-inch border. Top each with ¼ cup chopped romaine lettuce and 1 slice tomato. Roll, slice, and serve.

TASTY TIDBIT

Greek yogurt is thicker and creamier than regular yogurt. It also contains more protein, which can help keep you feel fuller longer.

Black Bean Hummus and Roasted Red Pepper Wraps

Roasted red peppers add the perfect sweetness to go with garlicky hummus and the flavors of fennel and coriander in these wraps.

Yield:	Prep time:	Serving size:
4 wraps	15 to 20 minutes	1 wrap

Each serving has:			
385 calories	14 g protein	45 g carbohydrates	9 g fiber
	19 g total fat	3 g saturated fat	596 mg sodium

4 small garlic cloves

1 cup canned chickpeas, rinsed and drained

1 cup canned black beans, rinsed and drained

¼ cup jarred roasted red peppers, packed in water

¼ cup tahini

½ tsp. ground cumin

½ tsp. ground coriander seed

¼ tsp. black pepper

2 TB. extra-virgin olive oil

4 (8-in.) 100 percent whole-wheat tortillas

4 medium romaine lettuce leaves, chopped

1. In a food processor fitted with a chopping blade, pulse garlic for 20 seconds or until minced.

2. Add chickpeas, black beans, roasted red peppers, tahini, cumin, coriander seed, and black pepper, and blend for 2 or 3 minutes or until smooth. With the processor running, gradually add extra-virgin olive oil, and blend for 2 minutes or until mixture is smooth.

3. Place 1 whole-wheat tortilla on each of 4 plates. Spoon ⅔ cup black bean hummus into center of each tortilla, and spread evenly, leaving a ½-inch border. Top with ¼ cup chopped romaine lettuce. Roll, slice, and serve.

TASTY TIDBIT

Coriander seeds are from the coriander plant. The leaves of the coriander plant are called cilantro.

Delicious Dinners

The dreaded problem of "What's for dinner?" isn't a problem anymore! Whether you're a meat-and-potatoes gal or guy, a vegetarian, or somewhere in between, Part 4 offers an amazing array of recipes that will fit the bill for your evening meal.

You'll find dinners ideal for a cozy, quiet night alone as well as meals fancy enough for celebrating with family and friends. You'll also find an array of satisfying side dishes for those nights you're just looking for something to pair with a piece of juicy, smoky grilled chicken or light, flaky fish.

And for those of you who like to plan ahead, we've devoted an entire chapter to slow cooker meals so you can have a nutritious and delicious dinner on the table minutes after you walk in the door after a long day of work.

Poultry Perfection

In This Chapter

- Flavorful chicken dishes
- Tempting turkey meals
- When to skin
- White meat versus dark

Chicken and turkey have a mild flavor on their own and make a great base for a wide assortment of tastes—spicy or sweet, Asian, Indian, Italian, Mexican, or whatever type of seasonings and spices you prefer.

Skinless, boneless chicken is almost a mantra in the weight-loss world because the majority of the fat in poultry is in the skin. But should the skin be removed before or after cooking? It's really your preference. Cooking with the skin on and removing it after helps the meat stay a bit juicier, but if you leave the skin on to cook, chances are whatever seasonings and sauces you used are on the skin. When you remove the skin after cooking, you also may remove a lot of the flavor. We recommend taking it off beforehand so you can actually flavor the meat. Use a meat thermometer to ensure you don't overcook the meat.

Of all the chicken parts, the white meat, primarily the breasts, is the lowest in fat. For that reason, they are the go-to chicken piece for healthy eaters and those wanting to lose weight. But that's not to say dark meat should never pass your lips. The dark meat is fattier, has more flavor, and tends to be juicier. So if you're a fan of dark meat, go ahead and enjoy it once in a while.

Jerk Chicken

A mix of sweet and smoky spices blends to create this Caribbean-style chicken dish.

Yield:	Prep time:	Cook time:	Serving size:
4 pieces chicken	1 hour, 15 minutes	15 to 20 minutes	1 piece chicken

Each serving has:			
124 calories	27 g protein	0 g carbohydrates	0 g fiber
	3 g total fat	1 g saturated fat	115 mg sodium

1 small yellow onion, minced

¼ tsp. dried thyme

¼ tsp. ground allspice

⅛ tsp. ground cinnamon

⅛ tsp. ground cumin

⅛ tsp. kosher salt

⅛ tsp. black pepper

⅛ tsp. cayenne

4 (4-oz.) boneless, skinless chicken breasts

Nonstick cooking spray

1. Preheat the oven to 450°F. Line a baking sheet with parchment paper.

2. In a small bowl, combine yellow onion, thyme, allspice, cinnamon, cumin, kosher salt, black pepper, and cayenne.

3. Gently rub spice mixture into chicken breasts, cover with plastic wrap, and refrigerate for 1 hour.

4. Unwrap chicken, place on the prepared baking sheet, and lightly coat tops with nonstick cooking spray. Bake for 15 to 20 minutes or until an instant-read thermometer inserted into the center reads 165°F, and serve.

MAKE IT A MEAL

Turn this flavorful chicken into a delicious meal by pairing it with steamed brown rice and a serving of Red Cabbage Slaw (recipe in Chapter 10).

Chicken Satay with a Zing

Brown sugar brings just the right amount of sweetness to balance the warm ginger and tart lime juice in this chicken dish.

Yield:	Prep time:	Cook time:	Serving size:
12 skewers	4½ hours, plus 4 hours marinate time	6 or 7 minutes	3 skewers

Each serving has:			
149 calories	23 g protein	7 g carbohydrates	0 g fiber
	3 g total fat	1 g saturated fat	55 mg sodium

1 lb. boneless, skinless chicken breast, cut lengthwise into 12 (¼-in.) strips

2 cloves garlic, chopped fine

2 TB. lime juice

1 TB. peeled and grated fresh ginger

2 TB. light brown sugar

1 jalapeño pepper, seeded and diced

1 TB. fresh cilantro, chopped

1. In a 2-quart casserole dish, arrange chicken breast in a single layer.

2. In a medium bowl, combine garlic, lime juice, ginger, light brown sugar, jalapeño, and cilantro. Pour over chicken, cover with plastic wrap, and refrigerate for 4 hours.

3. Preheat the broiler to 500°F. Position the oven rack 3 inches from the heat source. Lightly coat a baking sheet with nonstick cooking spray.

4. Skewer chicken pieces onto 12 (8-inch) bamboo skewers about ¼ inch apart, leaving 1 or 2 inches of bamboo exposed. Cover the exposed bamboo with aluminum foil.

5. Place skewer on a baking sheet, and broil for 4 minutes. Turn chicken, broil for 2 or 3 more minutes, and serve.

MAKE IT A MEAL

A side of steamed brown rice flavored with sautéed onions and a spicy peanut dipping sauce turns this Indonesian-style chicken into a meal. Finish it off with cool pineapple wedges.

Chicken Picatta

Lemon juice, butter, and the saltiness of the capers create a flavorful and elegant sauce for lean chicken breasts.

Yield:	Prep time:	Cook time:	Serving size:
16 pieces chicken	15 minutes	10 minutes	4 pieces chicken

Each serving has:			
169 calories	19 g protein 5 g total fat	11 g carbohydrates 2 g saturated fat	0 g fiber 286 mg sodium

12 oz. boneless, skinless chicken breasts, sliced crosswise into 16 (¼-in.) medallions	1 small shallot, minced
⅛ tsp. kosher salt	2 TB. fresh lemon juice
⅛ tsp. black pepper	½ cup low-sodium chicken broth
¼ cup all-purpose flour	1 TB. unsalted butter
1 clove garlic, minced	2 TB. brined capers, rinsed
	¼ cup chopped fresh parsley

1. Heat a 12-inch nonstick sauté pan over medium heat, and lightly coat with nonstick cooking spray.

2. Season chicken breasts with kosher salt and black pepper, and dust with all-purpose flour. Add to the pan, and cook for 2 or 3 minutes per side or until lightly brown. Remove chicken from the pan.

3. Lightly coat the pan with nonstick cooking spray. Add garlic and shallot, and cook for 1 or 2 minutes.

4. Add reserved chicken, lemon juice, chicken broth, unsalted butter, and capers, and cook for 5 minutes or until an instant-read thermometer inserted into the center reads 165°F. Top with parsley, and serve.

Variation: For **Chicken with Grapes,** substitute 1 cup seedless grapes for the capers and 1 tablespoon fresh or 1 teaspoon dried thyme for the parsley. *Each serving has: 198 calories, 19 g protein, 19 g carbohydrates, 1 g fiber, 5 g total fat, 2 g saturated fat, 129 mg sodium.*

MAKE IT A MEAL

Serve this chicken atop 1 cup cooked thin whole-grain spaghetti with your favorite steamed veggies on the side.

Coconut-Curried Chicken

Coconut milk adds a bit of exotic sweetness to this chicken dish.

Yield:	Prep time:	Cook time:	Serving size:
4 cups	10 to 15 minutes	12 to 15 minutes	1 cup

Each serving has:			
174 calories	25 g protein 5 g total fat	6 g carbohydrates 3 g saturated fat	2 g fiber 231 mg sodium

1 small yellow onion, sliced	½ cup low-sodium chicken broth
1 clove garlic, minced	1 lb. boneless, skinless chicken breasts, cut into ½-in. cubes
2 tsp. peeled and grated fresh ginger	1 cup cooked spinach, chopped
2 TB. curry powder	¼ tsp. kosher salt
½ cup light coconut milk	⅛ tsp. black pepper

1. Heat a 12-inch nonstick sauté pan over medium heat, and lightly coat with nonstick cooking spray. Add yellow onion, and cook for 5 minutes.

2. Stir in garlic, ginger, and curry powder, and cook for 1 minute.

3. Pour in light coconut milk and chicken broth, stir, and bring to a boil. Add chicken, and cook, stirring occasionally, for 5 to 7 minutes.

4. Add cooked spinach, kosher salt, and black pepper, stir, and serve.

MAKE IT A MEAL

Round out this meal with ½ cup couscous, with lemon zest added as it cooks, and roasted asparagus.

Turkey Cutlets with Apple Compote

Fruit blended with sweet spices adds a comforting flavor to turkey cutlets.

Yield:	Prep time:	Cook time:	Serving size:
4 turkey cutlets	5 to 10 minutes	15 to 20 minutes	1 turkey cutlet

Each serving has:			
208 calories	29 g protein 1 g total fat	22 g carbohydrates 0 g saturated fat	2 g fiber 221 mg sodium

4 (4-oz.) turkey cutlets	1 TB. honey
¼ tsp. kosher salt	⅛ tsp. ground nutmeg
⅛ tsp. black pepper	⅛ tsp. ground cloves
¼ cup all-purpose flour	⅛ tsp. ground cinnamon
2 medium Golden Delicious apples, peeled, cored, and diced	

1. Season turkey cutlets with kosher salt and black pepper, and dredge turkey in all-purpose flour.

2. Heat a 12-inch nonstick sauté pan over medium heat, and lightly coat with nonstick cooking spray. Add turkey to the pan, and sauté for 4 minutes per side. Remove turkey from the pan, place on a serving platter, and cover loosely with foil.

3. Lightly spray the pan again with nonstick cooking spray. Add Golden Delicious apples, honey, nutmeg, cloves, and cinnamon to the pan. Sauté, stirring occasionally, for 5 minutes.

4. Return turkey to the pan, and cook for 2 minutes. Serve turkey with ⅓ cup compote on top.

Variation: For **Turkey Cutlets with Cranberry Chutney,** omit the apples, nutmeg, cloves, and cinnamon. After removing turkey from the pan, reapply nonstick cooking spray as in step 3, add 2 tablespoons diced shallots, and cook for 2 minutes. Add ½ cup prepared whole cranberry sauce, 2 tablespoons raisins, pinch cinnamon, pinch clove, pinch ginger, and 2 tablespoons honey to the pan, and sauté, stirring occasionally, for 5 minutes. *Each serving has: 247 calories, 30 g protein, 31 g carbohydrates, 1 g fiber, 1 g total fat, 0 g saturated fat, 226 mg sodium.*

MAKE IT A MEAL

To complete this meal, serve with ½ cup steamed brown rice and 1 cup roasted broccoli.

Buffalo Chicken Tenders

These spicy chicken tenders have a nice crunch, too.

Yield:	Prep time:	Cook time:	Serving size:
about 8 tenders	5 to 10 minutes	15 to 20 minutes	2 tenders

Each serving has:			
243 calories	25 g protein 8 g total fat	16 g carbohydrates 2 g saturated fat	1 g fiber 453 mg sodium

2 TB. hot pepper sauce	⅛ tsp. black pepper
¼ cup low-fat mayonnaise	8 chicken tenders
¼ tsp. garlic powder	1 cup panko breadcrumbs
¼ tsp. onion powder	Nonstick cooking spray
⅛ tsp. kosher salt	

1. Preheat the oven to 400°F. Position the oven rack on the upper level. Line a baking sheet with parchment paper.

2. In a medium bowl, combine hot pepper sauce, low-fat mayonnaise, garlic powder, onion powder, kosher salt, and black pepper. Fold chicken tenders into bowl until evenly coated.

3. Dredge chicken in panko breadcrumbs, gently pressing breadcrumbs into chicken.

4. Arrange breaded chicken on the prepared baking sheet, and lightly coat chicken with nonstick cooking spray. Bake for 15 to 20 minutes or until an instant-read thermometer inserted into the center reads 165°F, and serve.

Variations: For **Cajun Chicken,** substitute 4 (4-ounce) boneless, skinless chicken breasts for the chicken tenders. Omit the hot pepper sauce, and add ½ teaspoon paprika, ½ teaspoon dried basil, and ½ teaspoon dried oregano to the spice mixture. *Each serving has: 243 calories, 25 g protein, 16 g carbohydrates, 1 g fiber, 8 g total fat, 2 g saturated fat, 267 mg sodium.*

For **Crispy Chicken,** eliminate the hot pepper sauce. *Each serving has: 243 calories, 25 g protein, 16 g carbohydrates, 1 g fiber, 8 g total fat, 2 g saturated fat, 267 mg sodium.*

MAKE IT A MEAL

For a hearty lunch or dinner salad, place cut, cooked tenders on a big garden salad and serve with a whole-grain roll on the side.

Chicken Cacciatore

Fennel, tomatoes, onion, rosemary, and thyme help this traditional dish burst with flavor.

Yield:	Prep time:	Cook time:	Serving size:
4 chicken breasts	15 to 20 minutes	25 minutes	1 chicken breast

Each serving has:			
357 calories	47 g protein 5 g total fat	30 g carbohydrates 2 g saturated fat	5 g fiber 632 mg sodium

1 medium sweet onion, diced

1 lb. button mushrooms, caps and stems, chopped

1 small fennel bulb, diced

1 large tomato, diced

1 TB. fresh rosemary or 1 tsp. dried

1 TB. fresh thyme or 1 tsp. dried

¼ cup chopped fresh parsley

1 lb. boneless, skinless chicken breasts, cut into 1-in. cubes

3 cups low-sodium chicken broth

¼ tsp. kosher salt

⅛ tsp. black pepper

4 (1-oz.) slices sourdough bread

1. Heat a 4-quart pot over medium heat, and lightly coat with nonstick cooking spray. Add sweet onion, button mushrooms, and fennel, cover, and cook for 10 minutes or until vegetables are tender.

2. Stir in diced tomatoes, rosemary, thyme, and parsley. Cover and cook for 5 minutes.

3. Add chicken breasts, chicken broth, kosher salt, and black pepper. Cover and simmer for 10 or minutes or until an instant-read thermometer inserted into the center reads 165°F.

4. Place 1 slice sourdough bread on each of 4 plates, spoon 1½ cups Chicken Cacciatore on top, and serve.

MAKE IT A MEAL

All this chicken dish needs is a nice green salad or some green beans to make it a meal.

Chicken Chickpea Ragu

A deep, rich tomato sauce combines with chicken atop a delicious slice of chewy bread.

Yield:	Prep time:	Cook time:	Serving size:
4 open-face sandwiches	15 to 20 minutes	25 minutes	1 open-face sandwich

Each serving has:			
361 calories	35 g protein 5 g total fat	43 g carbohydrates 1 g saturated fat	9 g fiber 634 mg sodium

1 medium sweet onion, diced

1 medium red bell pepper, ribs and seeds removed, and diced

1 small fennel bulb, diced

¼ cup sun-dried tomatoes

2 TB. tomato paste

1 TB. fresh oregano or 1 tsp. dried

1 tsp. ground fennel seed

¼ cup chopped fresh parsley

1 tsp. crushed red pepper flakes

1 lb. boneless, skinless chicken breasts, cut into 1-in. cubes

2 cups low-sodium chicken broth

1 (15-oz.) canned chickpeas, drained and rinsed

¼ tsp. kosher salt

⅛ tsp. black pepper

4 (1-oz.) slices sourdough bread, toasted

1. Heat a 4-quart pot over medium heat, and lightly coat with nonstick cooking spray. Add sweet onion, red bell pepper, fennel, and sun-dried tomatoes. Cover and cook for 10 minutes or until vegetables are tender.

2. Stir in tomato paste, oregano, fennel seed, and parsley, and cook, stirring so tomato paste does not burn, for 5 minutes.

3. Add crushed red pepper flakes, chicken breasts, chicken broth, chickpeas, kosher salt, and black pepper, and simmer for 10 minutes or until an instant-read thermometer inserted into center of chicken thighs reads 165°F.

4. Place 1 slice sourdough bread on each of 4 plates, spoon 1½ cups chicken ragu on top, and serve.

CULINARY KNOW-HOW

Sautéing the tomato paste with the vegetables causes the sugars in the paste to caramelize, imparting a rich depth of flavor to this dish.

Smoky Chicken Enchiladas

The combination of cumin, coriander, and slight dash of cinnamon bring an authentic Mexican flavor to these enchiladas.

Yield:	Prep time:	Cook time:	Serving size:
8 enchiladas	15 to 20 minutes	30 to 35 minutes	2 enchiladas

Each serving has:			
383 calories	27 g protein	37 g carbohydrates	6 g fiber
	15 g total fat	5 g saturated fat	717 mg sodium

1 medium yellow onion, diced	$\frac{1}{8}$ tsp. ground cinnamon
1 small green bell pepper, ribs and seeds removed, and diced	1 TB. all-purpose flour
1 lb. ground chicken	$\frac{1}{2}$ cup low-sodium chicken broth
1 TB. chili powder	8 (6-in.) corn tortillas
$\frac{1}{2}$ tsp. ground cumin	1 cup mild salsa
$\frac{1}{2}$ tsp. ground coriander	$\frac{1}{2}$ cup shredded low-fat cheddar cheese

1. Heat a 12-inch, nonstick sauté pan over medium heat, and lightly coat with nonstick cooking spray. Add yellow onion and green bell pepper, and sauté for 10 minutes or until tender.

2. Add chicken, and cook, stirring to break up clumps, for about 10 minutes or until no longer pink.

3. Stir in chili powder, cumin, coriander, cinnamon, and all-purpose flour, and cook for 1 or 2 minutes.

4. Add chicken broth, and stir until thickened. Remove the pan from heat, and allow chicken to cool.

5. Preheat the oven to 350°F.

6. Loosely stack corn tortillas on a plate, cover with a damp paper towel, and microwave on high for 30 seconds. Place warmed tortillas on a work surface, add 2 or 3 tablespoons filling in center, and roll.

7. Line filled tortillas, seam side down, in a 9×13-inch baking dish. Pour mild salsa over the top, and cover with cheddar cheese. Bake for 10 to 15 minutes or until cheese is bubbling, and serve.

CULINARY KNOW-HOW

If you have leftover cooked chicken, you can shred it and use it in place of the ground chicken.

Chicken, Mushroom, and Brie Quesadillas

Creamy Brie, sweet onion, and earthy mushrooms create a complex combination of texture and flavor these chicken *quesadillas*.

Yield:	Prep time:	Cook time:	Serving size:
4 quesadillas	10 to 15 minutes	20 minutes	1 quesadilla

Each serving has:			
395 calories	25 g protein 12 g total fat	52 g carbohydrates 4 g saturated fat	8 g fiber 744 mg sodium

8 oz. boneless, skinless chicken breasts, sliced crosswise into $\frac{1}{4}$-in. medallions	6 oz. crimini mushrooms, washed and sliced
$\frac{1}{8}$ tsp. black pepper	3 TB. Brie cheese
1 medium sweet onion, diced	8 (8-in.) 100 percent whole-wheat tortillas
6 oz. shiitake mushrooms, washed, stems removed, and sliced	Nonstick cooking spray

1. Season chicken breasts with black pepper.

2. Heat a 12-inch nonstick sauté pan over medium heat, and lightly coat with nonstick cooking spray. Add chicken, sweet onion, shiitake mushrooms, and crimini mushrooms. Cover and cook, stirring occasionally, for 10 minutes.

3. Stir in Brie cheese.

4. Preheat the oven to 350°F. Lightly coat a baking sheet with nonstick cooking spray. (You may need to use 2 baking sheets.)

5. Place 4 whole-wheat tortillas on the prepared baking sheet. Spread 1 cup chicken and mushroom mixture on top of each tortilla, and cover with remaining 4 tortillas. Lightly spray tops of quesadillas with nonstick cooking spray, and bake for 10 minutes.

6. Using a spatula, slide cooked quesadillas onto 4 separate plates, and serve.

Variation: For **Chicken and Black Bean Quesadillas,** replace the mushrooms with ½ cup black beans, drained and rinsed, and replace the Brie with ½ cup reduced-fat shredded Colby-Jack cheese. *Each serving has: 389 calories, 24 g protein, 51 g carbohydrates, 8 g fiber, 11 g total fat, 4 g saturated fat, 848 mg sodium.*

DEFINITION

A **quesadilla** is basically the Mexican version of a grilled cheese sandwich—cheese melted between 2 tortillas. You can add whatever extras you like.

Succulent Beef Dishes

In This Chapter

- Hearty red meat dishes
- Protein- and iron-packed beef
- Sampling flavors from Mexico, Asia, India, and more

Many people think red meat is a no-go when trying to eat healthy or lose weight, but fortunately for meat-lovers, that's not necessarily the case.

Red meat is one of the best sources of iron, and it also contains a great deal of hunger-satisfying protein. As long as you choose lean cuts of beef and trim off extra fat, there's no reason you can't include hearty beef meals in a healthy diet.

Broiled Steak and Mushrooms

Sweet onions, sharp garlic, and mushrooms meld to create an incredibly rich and flavorful topping for juicy steak.

Yield:	Prep time:	Cook time:	Serving size:
4 (3-ounce) steaks	5 to 10 minutes	16 to 24 minutes	1 (3-ounce) steak

Each serving has:			
172 calories	26 g protein	7 g carbohydrates	2 g fiber
	5 g total fat	2 g saturated fat	173 mg sodium

½ lb. button mushrooms, sliced	1 lb. sirloin steak, 1-in. thick, trimmed and cut into 4 pieces
½ lb. shiitake mushrooms, de-stemmed and sliced	¼ tsp. kosher salt
1 medium sweet onion, sliced	¼ tsp. black pepper
1 clove garlic, sliced	

1. Heat a 12-inch nonstick sauté pan over medium heat, and lightly coat with nonstick cooking spray. Add button mushrooms, shiitake mushrooms, sweet onion, and garlic, and sauté for 10 minutes.

2. Preheat the broiler to 400°F. Position the oven rack 3 inches from the heat source.

3. Place sirloin steak on a broiler rack, and season both sides with kosher salt and black pepper. Broil for 3½ minutes per side for rare, 5 minutes per side for medium, and 7 minutes per side for well done.

4. Place 1 piece broiled sirloin steak on each of 4 separate plates, top with ¼ cup mushrooms, and serve.

MAKE IT A MEAL

Add a baked or mashed potato and a big scoop of steamed veggies, and you've got a meal that'll stick to your ribs.

Smoky Stuffed Peppers

Smoked paprika infuses this dish with a delicious smoked pepper flavor.

Yield:	Prep time:	Cook time:	Serving size:
4 peppers	15 to 20 minutes	25 to 30 minutes	1 pepper

Each serving has:			
186 calories	15 g protein 6 g total fat	18 g carbohydrates 3 g saturated fat	3 g fiber 243 mg sodium

2 medium red bell peppers, cut in $\frac{1}{2}$ and ribs and stems removed	$\frac{1}{4}$ tsp. smoked paprika
Nonstick cooking spray	$\frac{1}{4}$ tsp. ground cumin
$\frac{1}{2}$ lb. lean ground beef	$\frac{1}{4}$ tsp. ground coriander
1 cup cooked brown rice	2 TB. tomato paste
3 scallions, white and green parts, diced	$\frac{1}{4}$ tsp. kosher salt
1 clove garlic, sliced	$\frac{1}{8}$ tsp. black pepper
	$\frac{1}{4}$ cup grated Asiago cheese

1. Preheat the oven to 350°F.

2. Place red bell pepper halves on a baking sheet, and lightly coat with nonstick cooking spray. Bake for 15 to 20 minutes, until the sides of the pepper are soft. Remove and keep warm.

3. Meanwhile, heat a 12-inch nonstick sauté pan over medium heat, and lightly coat with nonstick cooking spray. Add lean ground beef, brown rice, scallions, garlic, smoked paprika, cumin, coriander, tomato paste, kosher salt, and black pepper, and sauté, stirring to break up clumps, for 10 minutes or until meat is no longer pink.

4. Stuff red bell pepper halves with 1 cup beef, top with 1 tablespoon Asiago cheese, and return to the oven for 10 minutes.

5. Place 1 stuffed pepper on each of 4 plates, and serve.

CULINARY KNOW-HOW

Asiago is a hard, slightly sharp cheese. If you can't find it, you can use Parmesan or Romano in its place.

Mexican Meatloaf

This moist meatloaf has a real south-of-the-border kick.

Yield:	Prep time:	Cook time:	Serving size:
1 (8×4×2½-inch) meatloaf	10 minutes	1 hour	⅕ of meatloaf

Each serving has:			
210 calories	24 g protein	12 g carbohydrates	3 g fiber
	7 g total fat	3 g saturated fat	463 mg sodium

1 lb. lean ground beef

¾ cup old-fashioned or quick-cooking oats

1 tsp. ground cumin

1 tsp. onion powder

1 large egg, beaten

1 cup mild, medium, or hot salsa

¼ cup shredded reduced-fat Colby-Jack cheese

1. Preheat the oven to 350°F.

2. In a medium bowl, combine lean ground beef, old-fashioned oats, cumin, onion powder, egg, ½ cup salsa, and Colby-Jack cheese.

3. Place mixture in a (8×4×2½-inch) loaf pan, and smooth top. Bake, brushing with remaining ½ cup salsa every 15 minutes, for 1 hour or until done, and serve.

CULINARY KNOW-HOW

Make this as spicy or as mild as you like by choosing different temperatures of salsa.

Spicy Beef Satays

Brown sugar gives a rich caramelized flavor to these satays, and ginger provides a slight heat.

Yield:	Prep time:	Cook time:	Serving size:
12 skewers	35 to 40 minutes, plus 4 hours marinate time	7 minutes	4 skewers

Each serving has:			
218 calories	30 g protein 6 g total fat	10 g carbohydrates 2 g saturated fat	0 g fiber 223 mg sodium

1 lb. sirloin steak, cut lengthwise into 12 (¼-in.) strips	2 TB. light brown sugar
2 cloves garlic, chopped fine	1 medium jalapeño, seeded and diced
2 TB. fresh lime juice	1 TB. chopped fresh cilantro
1 TB. peeled and grated fresh ginger	¼ tsp. kosher salt

1. In a 2-quart casserole dish, arrange sirloin steak in a single layer.

2. In a medium bowl, combine garlic, lime juice, ginger, light brown sugar, jalapeño, cilantro, and kosher salt. Pour over sirloin steak, cover with plastic wrap, and refrigerate for 4 hours.

3. Preheat the broiler to 500°F. Position the oven rack 3 inches from the heat source.

4. Remove sirloin steak from marinade, and discard marinade. Skewer sirloin steak pieces onto 12 (8-inch) bamboo skewers, leaving 1 or 2 inches bamboo exposed. Cover the exposed bamboo with aluminum foil.

5. Place skewers on a baking sheet, and broil for 3 minutes. Turn skewers, and broil for 2 or 3 more minutes.

6. Place 4 skewers on each of 3 separate plates, and serve.

CULINARY KNOW-HOW

Freezing the sirloin steak makes it easier to thinly slice it. Take the beef out of the freezer, and put it in the refrigerator for 3 hours. When it's partially thawed, it's easy to slice thin.

Korean Wraps

This lean beef is infused with Asian flavors and hot rice wrapped in cool and crunchy romaine.

Yield:	Prep time:	Cook time:	Serving size:
4 wraps	15 to 20 minutes, plus 1 or 2 hours chill time	20 minutes	1 wrap

Each serving has:			
280 calories	25 g protein 6 g total fat	30 g carbohydrates 2 g saturated fat	1 g fiber 90 mg sodium

1 lb. sirloin steak, sliced ¼-in. thick	1 tsp. toasted sesame seed oil
1 clove garlic, minced	1 tsp. lite soy sauce
1 medium scallion, white and green parts, diced	⅛ tsp. black pepper
1 tsp. peeled and grated fresh ginger	1 cup short-grain rice
4 TB. rice vinegar	2 cups water
	4 large romaine lettuce leaves

1. In a medium bowl, combine sirloin steak, garlic, scallion, ginger, 2 tablespoons rice vinegar, toasted sesame seed oil, lite soy sauce, and black pepper. Cover with plastic wrap, and refrigerate for 1 or 2 hours.

2. In a 2-quart pot with a tight-fitting lid over medium-high heat, combine short-grain rice and water. Cover, and bring to a boil. Reduce heat to low, and cook for 12 minutes. Do not uncover. Remove from heat, and allow to rest for 5 minutes.

3. Add remaining 2 tablespoons rice vinegar, and fluff with a fork. Re-cover to keep warm.

4. Preheat the broiler to 400°F. Position the oven rack 3 inches from the heat source.

5. Place sirloin steak on a broiler rack, and broil for 3 minutes per side.

6. Place 1 romaine leaf on each of 4 separate plates, and top with ¼ cup rice and several slices of steak. Roll romaine lettuce leaf into a wrap, and serve.

 TASTY TIDBIT

Barbecuing beef is big in Korea, so for a more authentic taste, put the beef on the grill.

Hearty Sloppy Joes

Here, veggies are cooked to bring out their sweetness and combined with smoky seasonings to create a mouthwatering, nutrient-packed meal.

Yield:	Prep time:	Cook time:	Serving size:
4 sloppy joes	15 to 20 minutes	25 minutes	1 sloppy joe

Each serving has:			
283 calories	22 g protein 6 g total fat	36 g carbohydrates 2 g saturated fat	5 g fiber 491 mg sodium

1 medium red bell pepper, ribs and seeds removed, and diced

1 medium sweet onion, diced

1 clove garlic, sliced

¾ lb. lean ground beef

½ cup cooked brown rice

¼ tsp. smoked paprika

¼ cup ketchup

¼ cup water

2 TB. Worcestershire sauce

2 tsp. ground caraway seeds

⅛ tsp. black pepper

4 100 percent whole-wheat hamburger buns

1. Heat a 12-inch nonstick sauté pan over medium heat, and lightly coat with nonstick cooking spray. Add red bell pepper, sweet onion, and garlic, and sauté for 10 minutes.

2. Stir in lean ground beef and brown rice, and cook, stirring to break up clumps, for 10 minutes or until meat is no longer pink.

3. Add smoked paprika, ketchup, water, Worcestershire sauce, ground caraway seeds, and black pepper. Simmer for 5 minutes.

4. Place an open whole-wheat hamburger bun on each of 4 plates, fill with ¾ cup sloppy joe mixture, and serve.

TASTY TIDBIT

Caraway seeds are used to flavor many different dishes, from sauerkraut to havarti cheese to liquors like akvavit.

Mediterranean Burgers

Flavor-rich herbs and slightly crunchy pine nuts make for a juicy burger that explodes with taste.

Yield:	Prep time:	Cook time:	Serving size:
4 burgers	15 to 20 minutes	10 minutes	1 burger

Each serving has:			
305 calories	26 g protein 12 g total fat	23 g carbohydrates 3 g saturated fat	4 g fiber 375 mg sodium

1 lb. lean ground beef

2 TB. sun-dried tomatoes, chopped fine

2 TB. chopped fine fresh marjoram or 2 tsp. dried

2 TB. chopped fine fresh basil or 2 tsp. dried

1 TB. chopped fine toasted pine nuts

1 TB. extra-virgin olive oil

¼ tsp. kosher salt

⅛ tsp. black pepper

4 100 percent whole-wheat hamburger buns

1. In a medium bowl, combine lean ground beef, sun-dried tomatoes, marjoram, basil, toasted pine nuts, extra-virgin olive oil, kosher salt, and black pepper.

2. Divide lean ground beef into 4 equal pieces, and flatten into 2-inch patties.

3. Heat a 12-inch nonstick sauté pan over medium heat, and lightly coat with nonstick cooking spray. Add patties, and sauté for 4 minutes per side or until an instant-read thermometer inserted into the center reads 155°F.

4. Place open whole-wheat hamburger buns on each of 4 plates, top with 1 burger, and serve.

CULINARY KNOW-HOW

To change the flavor of these burgers, mix in ¼ cup of your favorite pasta sauce or salsa, and cook as directed.

Thai Beef Curry

Mint, basil, and coconut milk help cool down this spicy Thai dish.

Yield:	Prep time:	Cook time:	Serving size:
4 cups	10 to 15 minutes	55 minutes	1 cup

Each serving has:			
337 calories	21 g protein	38 g carbohydrates	3 g fiber
	11 g total fat	7 g saturated fat	71 mg sodium

1 cup long-grain brown rice, rinsed 3 times

2¼ cups water

1½ cups lite coconut milk

1 TB. red curry paste

¾ lb. sirloin steak, cut into ½-in. cubes

½ cup fresh mint leaves

½ cup fresh basil leaves

1. In a 2-quart pot with a tight-fitting lid over medium-high heat, combine long-grain brown rice and water. Cover, and bring to a boil. Reduce heat to low, and cook for 45 minutes. Do not uncover. Remove from heat, and allow to rest for 5 minutes. Fluff with a fork.

2. In a 2-quart pot over medium-high heat, bring lite coconut milk to a simmer. Add red curry paste, and stir to blend. Add sirloin steak, and simmer for 30 minutes.

3. Stir in mint and basil, and cook for 30 seconds or until herbs begin to wilt.

4. Place ½ cup rice on each of 4 plates, top with ¾ cup beef curry, and serve.

CULINARY KNOW-HOW

If you're in a rush, you can use long-grain white rice in place of brown. Follow the same directions as with brown rice, except use 1½ cups water and cook for approximately 12 minutes.

Beef Stroganoff

Dijon mustard gives this rich, creamy beef dish its zing.

Yield:	Prep time:	Cook time:	Serving size:
4 cups	5 to 10 minutes	20 minutes	1 cup

Each serving has:			
359 calories	32 g protein 8 g total fat	39 g carbohydrates 3 g saturated fat	2 g fiber 359 mg sodium

1 cup low-sodium beef broth	¼ cup reduced-fat sour cream
2 TB. all-purpose flour	2 tsp. Dijon mustard
1 lb. sirloin steak, cut into ¼-in. strips	¼ tsp. kosher salt
	⅛ tsp. black pepper
1 medium yellow onion, sliced	2 qt. water
½ lb. button mushrooms	6 oz. dried egg noodles

1. In a 2-cup container with a tight-fitting lid, combine beef broth and all-purpose flour. Cover, and shake vigorously.

2. In a 2-quart pot over medium heat, add beef broth–flour mixture. Add sirloin steak, yellow onion, button mushrooms, sour cream, Dijon mustard, kosher salt, and black pepper, and simmer for 15 to 20 minutes.

3. Meanwhile, in a large pot over medium-high heat, bring water to a boil. Add egg noodles, and cook according to the package instructions.

4. Divide egg noodles among 4 plates, top each with 1 cup beef stroganoff, and serve.

CULINARY KNOW-HOW

Mixing cold liquid with corn starch or flour is called a slurry. It's a simple way to help thicken any sauce you're cooking without getting lumps.

Beef Enchiladas

A hint of cinnamon gives these enchiladas an authentic Mexican taste.

Yield:	Prep time:	Cook time:	Serving size:
6 enchiladas	15 to 20 minutes	30 to 35 minutes	1½ enchiladas

Each serving has:			
373 calories	32 g protein	32 g carbohydrates	5 g fiber
	13 g total fat	6 g saturated fat	841 mg sodium

1 medium yellow onion, diced	1 small jalapeño, seeded and diced
1 small green bell pepper, ribs and seeds removed, and diced	2 tsp. all-purpose flour
1 lb. lean ground beef	½ cup water
1 TB. chili powder	6 (6-in.) flour tortillas
½ tsp. ground cumin	¾ cup mild salsa
½ tsp. ground coriander	½ cup shredded reduced-fat cheddar cheese
⅛ tsp. ground cinnamon	¼ cup sliced black olives

1. Preheat the oven to 350°F.

2. Heat a 12-inch nonstick sauté pan over medium heat, and lightly coat with nonstick cooking spray. Add yellow onion and green bell pepper, and sauté for 10 minutes.

3. Add lean ground beef, and cook, stirring to break up clumps, for about 10 minutes or until no longer pink.

4. Stir in chili powder, cumin, coriander, cinnamon, jalapeño, and all-purpose flour, and cook for 1 or 2 minutes.

5. Add water, and stir until thickened. Remove from heat and allow to cool.

6. Place flour tortillas on a work surface, and put ¼ cup filling in center of each. Roll, and place enchiladas seam side down in a 9×13-inch baking dish.

7. Pour mild salsa over top, cover with cheddar cheese, and dot with black olives. Bake for 10 to 15 minutes or until cheese is bubbling, and serve.

TASTY TIDBIT

This is a great dish to freeze and pull out one day when things are busy. Stop before the baking step, wrap the dish, and freeze. Remove from the freezer, cover with aluminum foil, and bake at 350°F for 40 to 45 minutes.

Old-Fashioned Meatloaf

Fiber-rich brown rice help make this meatloaf moist as well as healthy.

Yield:	Prep time:	Cook time:	Serving size:
1 (3×6×1-inch) meatloaf and 4 potatoes	5 to 10 minutes	35 minutes	¼ meatloaf and 1 potato

Each serving has:			
388 calories	25 g protein	57 g carbohydrates	4 g fiber
	7 g total fat	3 g saturated fat	584 mg sodium

1 medium yellow onion, diced	¼ tsp. kosher salt
1 small carrot, peeled and diced	⅛ tsp. black pepper
1 medium celery stalk, diced	¼ cup chopped fresh parsley
1 clove garlic, minced	1 TB. dried oregano
¾ lb. lean ground beef	1 TB. dried basil
¼ cup plain breadcrumbs	2 qt. water
2 large eggs, beaten	4 medium red potatoes, scrubbed
½ cup barbecue sauce	

1. Preheat the oven to 350°F. Line a baking sheet with aluminum foil.

2. Heat a 12-inch nonstick sauté pan over medium heat, and lightly coat with nonstick cooking spray. Add yellow onion, carrot, celery, and garlic, and sauté for 10 minutes. Remove from heat, and allow to cool.

3. In a large bowl, combine cooled onion mixture, lean ground beef, breadcrumbs, eggs, barbecue sauce, kosher salt, black pepper, parsley, oregano, and basil until well blended.

4. Form into a 3×6×1-inch loaf, and place on the prepared baking sheet. Bake for 30 to 35 minutes or until an instant-read thermometer inserted into the center reads 165°F.

5. Meanwhile, in a large pot over high heat, bring water and red potatoes to a boil. Reduce heat to low, and cook for about 15 to 20 minutes or until potatoes are easily pierced with a fork.

6. Place 1 slice meatloaf on each of 4 plates, add 1 potato, and serve.

TASTY TIDBIT

To save time, you can cook a big batch of brown rice on an evening or weekend and refrigerate it for up to a week or freeze it for a couple months. Take it out when you need it for a recipe like this or to serve as a quick side dish and just reheat.

Beef and Broccoli Stir-Fry

Vitamin-rich broccoli and lean beef combine in a sweet and salty Asian-inspired sauce with a bit of heat from the ginger.

Yield:	Prep time:	Cook time:	Serving size:
4 cups	10 to 15 minutes	20 minutes	1 cup

Each serving has:			
398 calories	29 g protein	54 g carbohydrates	2 g fiber
	5 g total fat	2 g saturated fat	427 mg sodium

1 cup long-grain rice, rinsed 3 times

1½ cups water

1 lb. sirloin steak, cut into thin strips

1 medium yellow onion, sliced

2 cloves garlic, minced

1 cup low-sodium beef broth

1 TB. cornstarch

2 TB. lite soy sauce

3 TB. sake, dry sherry, or dry vermouth

1 TB. honey

2 medium scallions, white and green parts, diced

1 tsp. peeled and grated fresh ginger

¼ tsp. ground white pepper

2 cups broccoli florets

1. In a 2-quart pot with a tight-fitting lid over medium-high heat, combine long-grain rice and water. Cover, and bring to a boil. Reduce heat to low, and cook for 12 minutes. Do not uncover. Remove from heat, and allow to rest for 5 minutes. Fluff with a fork.

2. Heat a 12-inch nonstick sauté pan over medium heat, and lightly coat with nonstick cooking spray. Add sirloin steak, yellow onion, and garlic, and sauté for 5 minutes.

3. In a 1½-cup container with a tight-fitting lid, combine beef broth, cornstarch, lite soy sauce, sake, honey, scallions, ginger, and white pepper. Cover, and shake vigorously.

4. Add broccoli and beef stock mixture to the pan, and simmer, stirring, for about 3 minutes or until sauce thickens.

5. Place ½ cup rice on each of 4 plates, top with 1 cup beef and broccoli, and serve.

Variation: For **Sweet and Spicy Beef,** replace the onion, garlic, sake, honey, and ginger with 2 tablespoons light brown sugar. Use 2 teaspoons ground white pepper, and chop the scallions instead of dicing. First sauté the sirloin, and add the beef broth and cornstarch mixture, light brown sugar, and ground white pepper. Simmer for 3 minutes or until sauce thickens. Serve with rice. *Each serving has: 376 calories, 29 g protein, 52 g carbohydrates, 2 g fiber, 5 g total fat, 2 g saturated fat, 425 mg sodium.*

CULINARY KNOW-HOW

To boost the fiber in this recipe, use brown rice in place of white. Up the water to 2¼ cups, and cook rice for 45 minutes.

Beef and Caramelized Onion Quesadillas

Gooey cheese, sweet onions, and juicy beef create a delicious filling in these quesadillas.

Yield:	Prep time:	Cook time:	Serving size:
24 wedges	10 to 15 minutes	30 to 35 minutes	6 wedges

Each serving has:			
398 calories	32 g protein	40 g carbohydrates	6 g fiber
	13 g total fat	5 g saturated fat	740 mg sodium

1 large sweet onion, sliced

1 clove garlic, minced

1 lb. sirloin steak, sliced thin

$\frac{1}{8}$ tsp. black pepper

2 tsp. chili powder

8 (8-in.) 100 percent whole-wheat tortillas

$\frac{1}{4}$ cup reduced-fat shredded cheddar cheese

Nonstick cooking spray

1 chipotle pepper in adobo sauce, diced

$\frac{1}{4}$ cup reduced-fat sour cream

$\frac{1}{4}$ cup mild salsa

1. Preheat the oven to 350°F. Line a baking sheet with parchment paper. (You may need to use 2 baking sheets.)

2. Heat a 4-quart pot over medium heat, and lightly coat with nonstick cooking spray. Add sweet onion and garlic, cover, and cook, stirring occasionally, for 10 to 15 minutes.

3. Add sirloin steak, and season with black pepper and chili powder. Cover and cook for 5 to 10 minutes or until no longer pink.

4. Place 4 whole-wheat tortillas on the prepared baking sheet. Spread $\frac{3}{4}$ cup onion and beef mixture on each tortilla, top with 1 tablespoon cheddar cheese, and cover with remaining 4 tortillas. Lightly spray tops of quesadillas with nonstick cooking spray, and bake for 10 minutes.

5. Using a spatula, slide quesadillas onto a large cutting board. Cut each quesadilla into 4 wedges, and place 4 wedges on each of 4 plates.

6. In a small bowl, combine chipotle pepper and sour cream. Place 1 tablespoon chipotle sour cream and 1 tablespoon mild salsa on each plate, and serve.

Under-the-Sea Suppers

In This Chapter

- Great grilled and broiled fish dishes
- Super smoked seafood
- Shellfish of all kinds
- Mild tilapia, meaty salmon, and everything in between

Seafood seems to often come under attack. Between cholesterol content, fishing practices, and other red flags, it might seem to some that we shouldn't be eating it. That couldn't be further from the truth.

Seafood is an extremely healthy protein source. Most is virtually fat free, and even the fattier fish, like salmon, is loaded with healthy fats that are beneficial in reducing your risk of heart disease. If you have environmental concerns, look for wild-caught versus farm-raised fish. Try to eat seafood at least twice a week to reap the tremendous benefits.

Southwestern Broiled Tilapia

Naturally low in fat, tilapia is kicked up a notch by the smoky chipotle chiles.

Yield:	Prep time:	Cook time:	Serving size:
4 pieces tilapia	5 to 10 minutes	5 to 7 minutes	1 piece tilapia

Each serving has:			
114 calories	23 g protein 2 g total fat	1 g carbohydrates 1 g saturated fat	0 g fiber 143 mg sodium

1 chipotle pepper in adobo sauce, diced	1 lb. tilapia, cut into 4 (4-oz.) pieces
Juice of 1 lime	Nonstick cooking spray
⅛ tsp. kosher salt	¼ cup chopped fresh cilantro

1. Preheat the broiler to 400°F. Position the oven rack 3 inches from the heat source.

2. In a small bowl, combine chipotle pepper, lime juice, and kosher salt. Spread mixture evenly over tilapia.

3. Place tilapia on a baking sheet, and lightly spray with nonstick cooking spray. Broil for 5 to 7 minutes.

4. Place 1 piece tilapia on each of 4 plates, garnish with fresh cilantro, and serve.

MAKE IT A MEAL

To round out this seafood meal, serve with steamed rice mixed with cilantro and sautéed diced peppers and onions, and add a simple garden salad.

Jerk Shrimp

Flavorful island spices enhance these succulent shrimp.

Yield:	Prep time:	Cook time:	Serving size:
about 27 shrimp	5 to 10 minutes plus 30 minutes for marinating	10 to 12 minutes	6 or 7 shrimp

Each serving has:			
154 calories	17 g protein	10 g carbohydrates	0 g fiber
	8 g total fat	1 g saturated fat	186 mg sodium

2 TB. minced yellow onion	⅛ tsp. kosher salt
¼ tsp. dried thyme	Pinch cayenne
¼ tsp. ground allspice	2 TB. canola oil
⅛ tsp. black pepper	¾ lb. raw shrimp (31 to 40 count, about 27), peeled and deveined
⅛ tsp. ground cinnamon	
⅛ tsp. ground cumin	

1. Preheat the oven to 350°F. Line a baking sheet with parchment paper.

2. In a medium bowl, combine yellow onion, thyme, allspice, black pepper, cinnamon, cumin, kosher salt, cayenne, and canola oil. Gently rub spice mixture onto shrimp, and let marinate for 30 minutes.

3. Place shrimp on the prepared baking sheet, and bake for 10 to 12 minutes.

4. Place 6 or 7 shrimp on each of 4 plates, and serve.

MAKE IT A MEAL

This shrimp goes perfectly over a bed of ½ cup steamed brown rice and 1 cup of your favorite veggies.

Sautéed Scallops and Snap Peas

Here, the subtle sweet flavor of scallops and snap peas are enhanced with a rich taste of butter.

Yield:	Prep time:	Cook time:	Serving size:
12 to 16 scallops	15 to 20 minutes	15 minutes	3 or 4 scallops

Each serving has:			
161 calories	17 g protein 3 g total fat	17 g carbohydrates 2 g saturated fat	3 g fiber 591 mg sodium

2 qt. water	⅛ tsp. black pepper
1 lb. snap peas, string removed	1 TB. unsalted butter
12 to 16 fresh sea scallops (1 lb.)	¾ cup low-sodium chicken broth
¼ tsp. kosher salt	

1. In a 2-quart pot over medium-high heat, bring water to a boil. Add snap peas, cover, and cook for 3 minutes. Remove snap peas from water, cover, and keep warm.

2. Heat a 12-inch nonstick sauté pan over medium-high heat, and lightly coat with nonstick cooking spray.

3. Season scallops with kosher salt and black pepper, add to the pan, and cook for 5 minutes. Reduce heat to medium.

4. Add unsalted butter and reserved snap peas. Turn over scallops, add chicken broth, and cook for 4 or 5 more minutes.

5. Place 3 or 4 scallops and ½ cup snap peas on each of 4 plates, and serve.

Variations: For **Sautéed Scallops with Mushrooms,** substitute 2 cups sliced crimini, shiitake tops, and/or button mushrooms for the snap peas. Heat a 12-inch nonstick sauté pan over medium heat and lightly coat with nonstick cooking spray. Add mushrooms, and cook, stirring occasionally, for 4 or 5 minutes. Add scallops, and cook for 5 minutes. Add unsalted butter, substitute low-sodium beef broth for the chicken broth, turn scallops, and cook for 3 or 4 minutes. *Each serving has: 111 calories, 15 g protein, 5 g carbohydrates, 0 g fiber, 4 g total fat, 2 g saturated fat, 593 mg sodium.*

For **Sautéed Scallops and Summer Squash,** substitute 1 small zucchini and 1 medium yellow squash, both sliced into ¼-inch rings, for the snap peas. Heat a 12-inch nonstick sauté pan over medium heat, and lightly coat with nonstick cooking spray. Add zucchini and yellow squash, and cook for 5 minutes. Add scallops, and cook for 5 minutes. Add unsalted butter and chicken broth, turn over scallops, and cook for 3 or 4 more minutes. *Each serving has: 112 calories, 14 g protein, 5 g carbohydrates, 1 g fiber, 4 g total fat, 2 g saturated fat, 593 mg sodium.*

MAKE IT A MEAL

A simple baked potato with a little dollop of reduced-fat sour cream and sprinkle of chives is all this dish needs to make a terrific meal.

Fettuccini with Tuna and Tomatoes

Fresh tender pasta is infused with the robust flavors of garlic and marjoram and combined with fresh tomatoes and protein-packed tuna.

Yield:	Prep time:	Cook time:	Serving size:
4 cups	5 to 10 minutes	15 minutes	1 cup

Each serving has:			
181 calories	20 g protein 1 g total fat	21 g carbohydrates 0 g saturated fat	2 g fiber 463 mg sodium

2 cloves garlic, chopped	¾ cup low-sodium vegetable broth
4 medium plum tomatoes, diced	2 qt. water
2 (5-oz.) cans tuna, packed in water, drained	8 oz. dried fettuccini pasta
1 TB. fresh marjoram or 1 tsp. dried	¼ tsp. kosher salt
	⅛ tsp. black pepper

1. Heat a 12-inch nonstick sauté pan over medium heat, and lightly coat with nonstick cooking spray. Add garlic, plum tomatoes, tuna, and marjoram, and sauté for 5 minutes.

2. Add vegetable broth.

3. In a large pot over medium-high heat, bring water to a boil. Stir in fettuccini pasta, and cook for 8 to 10 minutes. Drain pasta.

4. Fold pasta into tuna mixture, and season with kosher salt and black pepper.

5. Spoon 1 cup pasta and sauce on each of 4 plates, and serve.

MAKE IT A MEAL

A cup of steamed broccoli would look and taste wonderful alongside this pasta dish. Add a garden salad, and you've got yourself a meal.

Mediterranean Swordfish

You'll love this swordfish smothered with sweet marjoram, basil, and garlic.

Yield:	Prep time:	Cook time:	Serving size:
4 pieces swordfish	35 to 40 minutes	6 to 8 minutes	1 piece swordfish

Each serving has:			
208 calories	20 g protein 14 g total fat	1 g carbohydrates 3 g saturated fat	0 g fiber 141 mg sodium

2 cloves garlic, minced

2 TB. extra-virgin olive oil

1 TB. fresh marjoram or 1 tsp. dried

1 TB. chopped fresh basil or 1 tsp. dried

1 lb. fresh swordfish, cut into 4 (4-oz.) pieces

⅛ tsp. kosher salt

⅛ tsp. black pepper

Nonstick cooking spray

1. In a small bowl, combine garlic, extra-virgin olive oil, marjoram, and basil.

2. In a shallow dish, place swordfish pieces. Spread extra-virgin olive oil mixture over top, cover with plastic wrap, and refrigerate for 30 minutes.

3. Preheat the broiler to 400°F. Position the oven rack 3 inches from the heat source. Line a baking sheet with aluminum foil.

4. Place swordfish on the prepared baking sheet, and season with kosher salt and black pepper. Lightly spray with nonstick cooking spray.

5. Broil for 3 or 4 minutes. Turn over swordfish, and broil for 2 or 3 more minutes.

6. Place 1 piece of swordfish on each of 4 plates, and serve.

CULINARY KNOW-HOW

Fish is an extremely healthy part of any diet, but due to a high mercury content, avoid swordfish—as well as shark, king mackerel, and tilefish—if you're pregnant or nursing.

Crispy Baked Cod

Delicious, flaky cod is enveloped by crispy herbed breadcrumbs and fragrant lemon zest.

Yield:	Prep time:	Cook time:	Serving size:
4 pieces cod	5 minutes	12 to 15 minutes	1 piece cod

Each serving has:			
216 calories	20 g protein	15 g carbohydrates	1 g fiber
	8 g total fat	1 g saturated fat	213 mg sodium

1 cup panko breadcrumbs

2 TB. extra-virgin olive oil

Zest of 1 lemon

¼ cup finely chopped fresh parsley

¼ tsp. kosher salt

⅛ tsp. black pepper

1 lb. cod loin, cut into 4 pieces

1. Preheat the oven to 400°F. Position the oven rack on the upper level. Line a baking sheet with parchment paper.

2. In a small bowl, combine panko breadcrumbs, extra-virgin olive oil, lemon zest, parsley, kosher salt, and black pepper.

3. Place cod pieces on the prepared baking sheet, and top with breadcrumb mixture. Bake for 12 to 15 minutes or until golden brown and cod flakes easily.

4. Place 1 piece of cod on each of 4 plates, and serve.

CULINARY KNOW-HOW

Cooking fish correctly requires paying close attention because it is easy to overcook. The internal temperature should be 145°F.

Herbed Steamed Mussels

Succulent mussels swim in rich coconut broth with a hint of ginger and the sweet flavors of basil and mint.

Yield:	Prep time:	Cook time:	Serving size:
40 to 50 mussels with noodles	15 to 20 minutes	15 minutes	10 to 12 mussels with noodles

Each serving has:			
217 calories	12 g protein	31 g carbohydrates	1 g fiber
	3 g total fat	1 g saturated fat	344 mg sodium

2 qt. water

4 oz. rice noodles

2 cloves garlic, minced

1 TB. peeled and grated fresh ginger

40 to 50 mussels, cleaned and debearded

¼ cup white wine

¼ cup lite coconut milk

1 small tomato, chopped

Juice of 1 lime

¼ cup chopped fresh cilantro

¼ cup chopped fresh mint

¼ cup chopped fresh basil

1 tsp. crushed red pepper flakes

¼ tsp. kosher salt

2 scallions, white and green parts, sliced

1. In a 2-quart pot over medium-high heat, bring water to a boil. Add rice noodles, and cook according to package instructions.

2. Meanwhile, heat a large pot with a lid over medium heat, and lightly coat with nonstick cooking spray. Add garlic and ginger, and cook for 30 seconds.

3. Add mussels, remove the pot from heat, and pour in white wine. Cover and cook for about 3 to 5 minutes.

4. Stir in lite coconut milk, tomatoes, lime juice, cilantro, mint, basil, crushed red pepper flakes, and kosher salt. Cover and cook for 10 more minutes. Discard any unopened mussels.

5. Place ½ cup rice noodles on each of 4 plates. Top with 10 to 12 mussels, ¼ cup sauce, and 1 tablespoon scallions, and serve.

CULINARY KNOW-HOW

Mussels anchor themselves in the wild with a hairlike substance that's sometimes still with the mussel after it's been harvested. If your mussels have a beard, simply pull it off and discard before cooking.

Cajun Tilapia

An intensely seasoned crisp crust coats these tender tilapia steaks.

Yield:	Prep time:	Cook time:	Serving size:
4 pieces tilapia	15 to 20 minutes	10 to 15 minutes	1 piece tilapia

Each serving has:			
230 calories	25 g protein 7 g total fat	16 g carbohydrates 2 g saturated fat	1 g fiber 271 mg sodium

¼ cup low-fat mayonnaise	⅛ tsp. kosher salt
¼ tsp. garlic powder	⅛ tsp. black pepper
¼ tsp. onion powder	1 lb. tilapia, cut into 4 even pieces
½ tsp. paprika	1 cup panko breadcrumbs
½ tsp. dried basil	Nonstick cooking spray
½ tsp. dried oregano	

1. Preheat the oven to 400°F. Position the oven rack on the upper level. Line a baking sheet with parchment paper.

2. In a small bowl, combine low-fat mayonnaise, garlic powder, onion powder, paprika, basil, oregano, kosher salt, and black pepper.

3. Spread mayonnaise mixture evenly over tilapia pieces. Dredge fish in panko breadcrumbs, gently pressing crumbs into fish. Place tilapia on the prepared baking sheet, and lightly spray with nonstick cooking spray.

4. Bake for 10 to 15 minutes or until breadcrumbs begin to brown and an instant-read thermometer inserted into the center reads 145°F.

5. Place 1 piece of tilapia on each of 4 plates, and serve.

Variation: For **Crispy Tilapia,** eliminate the paprika, basil, and oregano. *Each serving has: 230 calories, 25 g protein, 16 g carbohydrates, 1 g fiber, 7 g total fat, 2 g saturated fat, 271 mg sodium.*

CULINARY KNOW-HOW

Using mayonnaise helps the panko breadcrumbs stick to the fish and helps baste the fish as it cooks, keeping it moist.

Low Country Shrimp Boil

Tender, spicy shrimp combine with creamy potatoes and garlicky kielbasa.

Yield:	Prep time:	Cook time:	Serving size:
about 36 shrimp	5 to 10 minutes	20 to 25 minutes	about 9 shrimp

Each serving has:			
239 calories	29 g protein 4 g total fat	22 g carbohydrates 1 g saturated fat	2 g fiber 411 mg sodium

3 qt. water

1 TB. paprika

1 TB. dried thyme

1 TB. dried oregano

1 TB. celery seed

1 tsp. powdered yellow mustard

1 tsp. black pepper

⅛ tsp. cayenne

30 new red potatoes, scrubbed

¼ lb. low-fat smoked kielbasa sausage, cut into 1-in. rings

4 medium ears corn, cut in ½

1 lb. raw shrimp (31 to 40 count, about 36), peeled and deveined

1. In a large pot over medium-high heat, combine water, paprika, thyme, oregano, celery seed, powdered yellow mustard, black pepper, and cayenne, and simmer for 5 minutes.

2. Add new red potatoes, cover, and bring to a boil. Reduce heat to low, and cook for 5 minutes.

3. Add kielbasa sausage and corn ears, and cook for 10 minutes.

4. Add shrimp, and cook for 3 or 4 minutes. Drain.

5. Place equal amounts of new red potatoes, kielbasa sausage, corn, and shrimp on each of 4 plates, and serve.

TASTY TIDBIT

This one-pot meal is native to the Carolinas. If you look at other regions, you'll see that all areas have similar meals: New England lobster bowls, Door County Wisconsin whitefish bowl, and crayfish in Louisiana.

Scallop Ceviche

Tender scallops rest in a delicious citrus dressing with creamy avocado.

Yield:	Prep time:	Serving size:
12 to 16 scallops	10 to 15 minutes, plus 8 hours chill time	3 or 4 scallops

Each serving has:			
245 calories	16 g protein 13 g total fat	18 g carbohydrates 2 g saturated fat	2 g fiber 574 mg sodium

12 to 16 fresh sea scallops (1 lb.), sliced crosswise into ¼-in. slices

Zest of 1 medium lime

Juice of 4 medium limes

Zest of 1 medium orange

Juice of 2 medium oranges

2 TB. rice vinegar

2 scallions, white and green parts, diced

1 medium avocado, peeled, pitted, and diced

8 cherry tomatoes, quartered

½ cup sliced fennel

2 TB. extra-virgin olive oil

¼ cup chopped fresh cilantro

¼ tsp. kosher salt

⅛ tsp. black pepper

4 medium Bibb lettuce leaves

1. In a medium glass bowl, combine sea scallops, lime zest, lime juice, orange zest, orange juice, rice vinegar, scallions, avocado, cherry tomatoes, fennel, extra-virgin olive oil, cilantro, kosher salt, and black pepper. Scallops should be submerged in marinade. Cover tightly with plastic wrap, and refrigerate for 8 hours.

2. Place 1 Bibb lettuce leaf on each of 4 plates, spoon 1½ cups scallop *ceviche* on top, and serve.

DEFINITION

Ceviche is a method of preparing seafood in which an acid, such as lemon or lime juice, is used to "cook" the fish. Because no heat is used, be sure to use only the freshest seafood to reduce the risk of food-borne illness.

Pineapple Ginger Salmon

Omega-3–rich salmon is given a tropical spin with crushed pineapple, a hint of ginger, and spicy mustard.

Yield:	Prep time:	Cook time:	Serving size:
4 pieces salmon	5 to 10 minutes	20 minutes	1 piece salmon

Each serving has:			
264 calories	25 g protein	11 g carbohydrates	1 g fiber
	13 g total fat	3 g saturated fat	170 mg sodium

1 lb. salmon fillet, skinned and cut into 4 pieces

1 (15-oz.) can crushed pineapple, drained

1½ TB. fresh lime juice

1 TB. Dijon mustard

1½ tsp. peeled and grated fresh ginger

1 clove garlic, minced

½ tsp. low-sodium soy sauce

¼ tsp. black pepper

1. Preheat the oven to 375°F. Lightly coat a 9×13-inch baking dish with nonstick cooking spray.

2. Place salmon in the prepared baking dish.

3. In a small bowl, combine crushed pineapple, lime juice, Dijon mustard, ginger, garlic, low-sodium soy sauce, and black pepper. Spoon pineapple mixture on top of salmon. Bake for 20 minutes.

4. Place 1 piece of salmon on each of 4 plates, and serve.

 TASTY TIDBIT

Because of its robust flavor, salmon is a fish that lends itself to marinades and toppings.

Cedar Planked Salmon

The rich salmon is infused with a delicate smoky flavor thanks to cedar planks.

Yield:	Prep time:	Cook time:	Serving size:
4 pieces salmon	2 to 4 hours	15 to 20 minutes	1 piece salmon

Each serving has:			
286 calories	25 g protein 20 g total fat	0 g carbohydrates 4 g saturated fat	0 g fiber 298 mg sodium

1 lb. salmon fillet, skinned and cut
  into 4 pieces

½ tsp. kosher salt

¼ tsp. black pepper

2 TB. extra-virgin olive oil

1. Soak a cedar or alder wood plank in water for 2 to 4 hours.

2. Preheat the grill. Clean and oil rack, and position 4 inches from heat. The coals are the right temperature if you can hold your hand above the rack for a count of 3.

3. Place salmon on the wood plank, and season with kosher salt, black pepper, and extra-virgin olive oil. Put planked salmon on the grill, cover, and cook for 15 to 20 minutes or until juices on top of fillet are white. A 1-inch-thick fillet takes 20 minutes.

4. Place 1 piece of salmon on each of 4 plates, and serve.

Variation: For **Oven-Planked Salmon,** preheat the oven to 350°F. Season salmon with kosher salt, black pepper, and extra-virgin olive oil. Place fillets on the plank, and bake for 12 to 15 minutes, depending on thickness of fillets. *Each serving has: 286 calories, 25 g protein, 0 g carbohydrates, 0 g fiber, 20 g total fat, 4 g saturated fat, 298 mg sodium.*

TASTY TIDBIT

Cedar and alder wood planks are available in the seafood section of most grocery stores. These 6×12-inch planks can be reused. Just scrape off any charred areas of wood and scrub the food side of the plank under hot water. Do not use detergent because that would remove the oils from the wood.

Salmon with Broccoli Rabe

The juices from the cooked salmon baste the broccoli rabe, imparting a rich soy flavor with a touch of toasted sesame.

Yield:	Prep time:	Cook time:	Serving size:
4 pieces salmon	5 to 10 minutes	25 minutes	1 piece salmon

Each serving has:			
300 calories	28 g protein 14 g total fat	15 g carbohydrates 3 g saturated fat	3 g fiber 391 mg sodium

2 TB. low-sodium soy sauce	2 qt. water
1 TB. honey	6 cups chopped broccoli rabe
$\frac{1}{2}$ tsp. minced garlic	$\frac{1}{2}$ tsp. toasted sesame seed oil
$\frac{1}{2}$ tsp. peeled and minced fresh ginger	$\frac{1}{8}$ tsp. crushed red pepper flakes
1 lb. salmon fillet, skinned and cut into 4 pieces	

1. Preheat the oven to 350°F. Line a baking sheet with parchment paper.

2. In a small bowl, combine low-sodium soy sauce, honey, garlic, and ginger.

3. Place salmon on the prepared baking sheet, and brush with soy sauce mixture. Bake for 20 minutes.

4. Meanwhile, in a large pot over medium-high heat, bring water to a boil. Add broccoli rabe, and cook for 5 minutes. Remove from water.

5. In a large bowl, toss together broccoli rabe, toasted sesame seed oil, and crushed red pepper flakes.

6. Place $1\frac{1}{2}$ cups broccoli rabe on each of 4 plates, top with 1 piece of salmon, and serve.

TASTY TIDBIT

If broccoli rabe is too strong-tasting for your liking, you can substitute broccoli florets instead. One pound is about 6 cups.

Coconut Curried Shrimp

Jasmine rice is smothered by tender, curry and garlic–flavored shrimp.

Yield:	Prep time:	Cook time:	Serving size:
about 27 shrimp	15 to 20 minutes	30 to 35 minutes	6 or 7 shrimp

Each serving has:			
301 calories	21 g protein	43 g carbohydrates	3 g fiber
	4 g total fat	2 g saturated fat	263 mg sodium

1 cup long-grain jasmine rice, rinsed 3 times	1 small jalapeño pepper, seeded and diced
1½ cups water	2 TB. curry powder
1 medium yellow onion, sliced	½ cup lite coconut milk
1 clove garlic, minced	¾ lb. raw shrimp (31 to 40 count, about 27), peeled and deveined
2 tsp. peeled and grated fresh ginger	¼ cup low-sodium chicken broth
1 small red bell pepper, ribs and seeds removed, and diced	¼ tsp. kosher salt
	⅛ tsp. black pepper

1. In a 1-quart pot with a tight-fitting lid over medium-high heat, combine long-grain jasmine rice and water. Cover, and bring to a boil. Reduce heat to low, and cook for 12 minutes. Do not uncover. Remove from heat, and allow to rest for 5 minutes. Fluff with a fork.

2. Heat a 12-inch nonstick sauté pan over medium heat, and lightly coat with nonstick cooking spray. Add yellow onion, and cook for 3 minutes.

3. Stir in garlic, ginger, red bell pepper, jalapeño, and curry powder, and cook for 3 minutes.

4. Stir in lite coconut milk. Bring to a boil, and reduce heat to low.

5. Add shrimp, and cook for 2 minutes.

6. Pour in chicken broth, and season with kosher salt and black pepper.

7. Place ½ cup cooked jasmine rice on each of 4 plates, top with 6 or 7 shrimp, and serve.

TASTY TIDBIT

Jasmine rice is from Thailand and is a less-expensive alternative to basmati rice from India.

Grilled Haddock with Lemon-Infused Couscous

A light, lemony spice flavor is just enough for mild, flaky haddock.

Yield:	Prep time:	Cook time:	Serving size:
4 (3-ounce) pieces haddock	5 minutes	10 minutes	1 (3-ounce) piece haddock

Each serving has:			
320 calories	24 g protein	34 g carbohydrates	2 g fiber
	9 g total fat	1 g saturated fat	279 mg sodium

1 cup low-sodium chicken broth

1 TB. fresh lemon juice

1 cup couscous

1 tsp. salted butter

Zest of 1 lemon

1 lb. haddock fillet, cut into 4 pieces

2 TB. canola oil

2 or 3 tsp. salt-free lemon-pepper seasoning

1. In a small saucepan over medium-high heat, bring chicken broth and lemon juice to a boil. Stir in couscous, butter, and lemon zest. Cover, remove from heat, and let stand for 5 minutes or until liquid is absorbed.

2. Meanwhile, heat a grill pan or a grill over medium heat.

3. Brush haddock with canola oil, and sprinkle with lemon-pepper seasoning. Grill for 4 or 5 minutes per side or until fish flakes easily with fork.

4. Place 1 piece fish and ¼ of couscous on each of 4 plates, and serve.

CULINARY KNOW-HOW

This is a great base recipe you can use to experiment with seasonings. Try Italian, Cajun, or Greek seasonings, for example. The possibilities are endless.

Mustard Salmon Cakes with Field Greens

Inside these crispy salmon cakes is a garden of fresh herbs with a hint of mustard.

Yield:	Prep time:	Cook time:	Serving size:
4 salmon cakes	10 to 15 minutes	10 minutes	1 salmon cake

Each serving has:			
325 calories	28 g protein 20 g total fat	5 g carbohydrates 5 g saturated fat	1 g fiber 523 mg sodium

1 lb. salmon fillet, skinned and cut into 1-in. cubes

¼ cup low-fat mayonnaise

2 TB. Dijon mustard

½ tsp. powdered yellow mustard

2 large eggs, beaten

2 TB. chopped fresh chives

2 TB. chopped fresh parsley

2 TB. fresh lemon juice

¼ tsp. kosher salt

⅛ tsp. black pepper

Pinch cayenne

1½ cups panko breadcrumbs

2 cups mesclun

4 tsp. apple cider vinegar

1. In a food processor fitted with a chopping blade, pulse salmon 3 times for 3 seconds each time.

2. In a medium bowl, combine salmon, low-fat mayonnaise, Dijon mustard, powdered yellow mustard, eggs, chives, parsley, lemon juice, kosher salt, black pepper, and cayenne. Form mixture into 4 cakes.

3. In a shallow dish, place panko breadcrumbs. Press salmon cakes into breadcrumbs to coat.

4. Heat a 12-inch nonstick sauté pan over medium heat, and lightly coat with nonstick cooking spray. Add salmon cakes, and sauté for 4 minutes per side or until an instant-read thermometer inserted into the center reads 165°F.

5. Place ½ cup field greens on each of 4 plates, spoon 1 teaspoon apple cider vinegar on top of mesclun, top with 1 salmon cake, and serve.

Variation: For **Salmon Cakes with Watercress,** reduce salmon to ¾ pound. Eliminate the Dijon mustard, powdered yellow mustard, chives, parsley, and lemon juice. Substitute 1 tablespoon maple syrup, zest of 1 medium orange, 2 teaspoons prepared horseradish, and pinch cayenne. Substitute watercress for the mesclun and rice vinegar for the apple cider vinegar. *Each serving has: 414 calories, 26 g protein, 36 g carbohydrates, 1 g fiber, 17 g total fat, 4 g saturated fat, 406 mg sodium.*

CULINARY KNOW-HOW

For safety, anytime eggs are used in a dish, be sure to cook them to an internal temperature of 165°F.

Curried Mussels with Basmati Rice

Two curries season fragrant basmati rice that's topped with plump mussels.

Yield:	Prep time:	Cook time:	Serving size:
40 to 50 mussels with rice	5 to 10 minutes	35 to 40 minutes	10 to 12 mussels with rice

Each serving has:			
338 calories	17 g protein 10 g total fat	47 g carbohydrates 7 g saturated fat	4 g fiber 680 mg sodium

1 cup long-grain basmati rice, rinsed 3 times

1½ cups water

1 medium yellow onion, sliced

1 clove garlic, diced

2 tsp. curry powder

½ tsp. red curry powder

1 (14-oz.) can lite coconut milk

½ cup low-sodium chicken broth

½ lb. green beans, stemmed and cut on a diagonal ½ in. long

40 to 50 mussels, cleaned and debearded

1. In a 1-quart pot with a tight-fitting lid over medium-high heat, combine long-grain basmati rice and water. Cover, and bring to a boil. Reduce heat to low, and cook for 12 minutes. Do not uncover. Remove from heat, and allow to rest for 5 minutes. Fluff with a fork.

2. Heat a large pot with a tight-fitting lid over medium heat, and lightly coat with nonstick cooking spray. Add yellow onion, cover, and cook for 5 minutes.

3. Add garlic, curry powder, and red curry powder. Cover and cook for 5 minutes.

4. Add lite coconut milk and chicken broth, bring to a boil, and reduce heat to low.

5. Add green beans, cover, and cook for 5 minutes.

6. Add mussels, cover, and simmer for 10 minutes or until mussels have opened. Discard any unopened mussels.

7. Place ½ cup rice on each of 4 plates. Spoon 10 to 12 mussels, ¼ of vegetables, and sauce on top, and serve.

TASTY TIDBIT

The long-grain basmati rice is rinsed three times to remove any starch that's accumulated on the surface of the grains. This extra starch, if left on, could cause the rice to be sticky and not fluffy.

Teriyaki Salmon with Spinach and Soba

Hearty buckwheat noodles are an authentic taste with the sweet and salty teriyaki salmon.

Yield:	Prep time:	Cook time:	Serving size:
4 pieces salmon	10 to 15 minutes	15 to 20 minutes	1 piece salmon

Each serving has:			
366 calories	29 g protein 14 g total fat	28 g carbohydrates 3 g saturated fat	2 g fiber 331 mg sodium

2 qt. water

2 TB. lite soy sauce

3 TB. sake, dry sherry, or dry vermouth

1 TB. honey

1 clove garlic, minced

1 medium scallion, white and green parts, minced

1 tsp. peeled and grated fresh ginger

1 lb. salmon fillet, skinned and cut into 4 pieces

4 oz. *soba noodles*

3 cups raw spinach

¼ tsp. black pepper

⅛ tsp. onion powder

⅛ tsp. garlic powder

1. In a 2-quart pot fitted with a steamer basket over medium-high heat, bring 1 quart water to a simmer.

2. In a small bowl, combine lite soy sauce, sake, honey, garlic, scallion, and ginger. Spread sauce over salmon pieces, cover, and refrigerate while water comes to a simmer.

3. Place salmon on a piece of aluminum foil, and place foil in the steaming basket. Cover and cook for 8 to 10 minutes. Keep warm.

4. In a 2-quart pot over medium-high heat, bring remaining 1 quart water to a boil. Add soba noodles, and cook for 6 to 8 minutes. Strain and cover to keep warm.

5. In a large bowl, toss spinach with black pepper, onion powder, and garlic powder. Place on another piece of aluminum foil.

6. In the pot with the steaming basket, cook spinach for 2 or 3 minutes.

7. Place ¼ cup spinach, ¼ cup soba noodles, and 1 piece salmon on each of 4 plates, and serve.

Variation: For **Teriyaki Shrimp with Spinach and Soba Noodles,** substitute 1 pound raw shrimp, peeled and deveined (31 to 40 count, about 36), for the salmon. *Each serving has: 264 calories, 28 g protein, 29 g carbohydrates, 2 g fiber, 3 g total fat, 0 g saturated fat, 441 mg sodium.*

DEFINITION

Soba noodles are a thin Japanese noodle made with buckwheat and wheat flour. They can be served in both cold and hot dishes.

Vegetarian Delights

In This Chapter

- Versatile vegetarian entrées
- Meatless main dishes
- Veggie- and bean-based meals

Prepare yourself for an assortment of nutrition-packed and fiber-filled vegetables and whole grains. In the recipes that follow, peppers, tomatoes, eggplant, squash, quinoa, and much more combine to create delicious and nutritious dishes.

Even if you're a meat-and-potatoes kind of person, don't skip this chapter. If you do, you'll miss out on an array of tempting side dishes as well as meatless meals so hearty and filling, you won't even miss the meat.

Grilled Summer Vegetables

Hot, smoky, slightly charred vegetables explode with herb flavor in this delicious vegetable entrée.

Yield:	Prep time:	Cook time:	Serving size:
4 cups	15 to 20 minutes	10 minutes	1 cup

Each serving has:			
107 calories	2 g protein	10 g carbohydrates	2 g fiber
	7 g total fat	1 g saturated fat	245 mg sodium

1 qt. water	Nonstick olive oil cooking spray
4 small shallots, peeled	$\frac{1}{2}$ tsp. kosher salt
2 small red bell peppers	$\frac{1}{4}$ tsp. black pepper
1 small zucchini, cut lengthwise into $\frac{1}{4}$-in.-thick slices	2 TB. chopped fresh basil
	2 TB. chopped fresh parsley
1 small yellow squash, cut lengthwise into $\frac{1}{4}$-in.-thick slices	2 TB. chopped fresh mint
	2 TB. extra-virgin olive oil
4 small plum tomatoes	

1. Preheat the grill. When coals are red hot, clean and oil the grill rack and position it 4 inches from heat. The coals are the right temperature if you can hold your hand above the rack for a count of 3.

2. In a 2-quart pot over medium-high heat, bring water to a boil. Reduce heat to low, add shallots, and simmer for 4 or 5 minutes.

3. Cut red bell peppers through the stem. Remove stem, ribs, and seeds, and cut peppers into 1-inch strips. Place in a large bowl, and add zucchini, yellow squash, shallots, and plum tomatoes. Coat with nonstick olive oil cooking spray, add kosher salt and black pepper, and toss.

4. Place vegetables on the grill. Grill zucchini, yellow squash, and red bell peppers for 3 minutes per side. Grill shallots and tomatoes for about 4 minutes or until they begin to blister.

5. In a small bowl, combine basil, parsley, mint, and extra-virgin olive oil.

6. Return grilled vegetables to the bowl, toss with herb mixture, and serve.

Variations: For **Vegetable Calzones,** follow the grilling instructions. Then preheat the oven to 350°F, and line a baking sheet with parchment paper or aluminum foil. Divide 1 ball uncooked pizza dough into 4 equal pieces, and roll out into discs. Place dough on the prepared baking sheet. Place ½ cup grilled vegetables in center of discs, and evenly divide ½ cup shredded reduced-fat mozzarella cheese and ½ cup low-sodium marinara sauce or pizza sauce among calzones. Fold over dough, crimp edges, cut 2 vent holes in each, and spray with nonstick cooking spray. Bake for 20 minutes. *Each serving has: 394 calories, 14 g protein, 60 g carbohydrates, 3 g fiber, 14 g total fat, 2 g saturated fat, 748 mg sodium.*

For **Grilled Vegetable Pizza,** follow the grilling instructions. Preheat the oven to 350°F, and line a baking sheet with parchment paper or aluminum foil. Place 2 prepared (8-inch) 100 percent whole-wheat pizza crusts on the prepared baking sheet. Evenly divide ½ cup low-sodium marinara sauce or pizza sauce and ½ cup shredded reduced-fat mozzarella cheese between crusts. Spread 2 cups grilled vegetables on crusts, and bake for 20 minutes. *Each serving has: 332 calories, 14 g protein, 46 g carbohydrates, 8 g fiber, 12 g total fat, 3 g saturated fat, 710 mg sodium.*

TASTY TIDBIT

The red bell peppers and tomatoes combine to create a meal that's loaded with vitamin A and with almost an entire day's worth of vitamin C.

Vegetarian Spring Rolls

Sweet carrots, spicy ginger, peppery radish, and the cooling sensation of cilantro are all rolled up in delicate rice wraps.

Yield:	Prep time:	Serving size:
20 spring rolls	5 to 10 minutes	5 spring rolls

Each serving has:			
168 calories	5 g protein	35 g carbohydrates	3 g fiber
	1 g total fat	0 g saturated fat	397 mg sodium

2 TB. rice vinegar	3 napa cabbage leaves, cut into strips
2 TB. *mirin*	½ cup bean sprouts
¼ tsp. kosher salt	1 qt. hot water
1 TB. peeled and grated fresh ginger	20 spring roll wrappers
2 medium carrots, peeled and cut into matchsticks	15 fresh basil leaves
	15 fresh mint leaves
1 small *daikon radish,* peeled and grated	15 fresh cilantro sprigs

1. In a medium bowl, combine rice vinegar, mirin, kosher salt, and ginger. Add carrots, daikon radish, cabbage, and bean sprouts, and toss.

2. In a large bowl, pour hot water. Add spring roll wrappers, 1 at a time, to water and allow to soften for 20 seconds.

3. Arrange softened wrappers on a work surface. In center of each, place 2 tablespoons vegetable mixture, 1 basil leaf, 1 mint leaf, and 1 cilantro sprig. Fold wrapper end closest to you over vegetables, fold sides to the center, and continue to roll into a cylinder. Repeat with remaining wrappers, and serve.

DEFINITION

Mirin is a sweet rice wine used in Japanese cooking. It's available in most grocery stores and Asian markets. The **daikon radish** is also an Asian import. It's much larger and slightly milder than the smaller radish.

Caponata

This hearty and deeply flavored vegetable dish has the finishing tastes of fresh herbs and the pop of a briny caper and can be served warm or at room temperature.

Yield:	Prep time:	Cook time:	Serving size:
4 cups	10 to 15 minutes	50 minutes	1 cup

Each serving has:			
170 calories	6 g protein	27 g carbohydrates	12 g fiber
	7 g total fat	1 g saturated fat	199 mg sodium

2 medium eggplants	1 medium tomato, chopped
1 medium red bell pepper	$\frac{1}{4}$ tsp. black pepper
1 medium yellow bell pepper	1 TB. red wine vinegar
Nonstick cooking spray	2 TB. capers, rinsed
2 cloves garlic, chopped	$\frac{1}{4}$ cup toasted pine nuts
1 medium yellow onion, chopped	$\frac{1}{4}$ cup chopped fresh basil
1 medium fennel bulb, chopped	$\frac{1}{4}$ cup chopped fresh mint

1. Preheat the oven to 350°F.

2. Place eggplants, red bell pepper, and yellow bell pepper on a baking sheet. Spray veggies with nonstick cooking spray, and pierce eggplant several times with a fork. Roast peppers for 20 minutes or until skin blisters and eggplant for 30 minutes or until it collapses.

3. Meanwhile, heat a nonstick sauté pan over medium heat, and lightly coat with nonstick cooking spray. Add garlic, yellow onion, and fennel, and sauté for 10 minutes.

4. Remove bell peppers and eggplants from the oven, and allow to cool for 10 minutes. Peel eggplants, cut in half, and remove all seeds. Chop eggplants, place in a colander, and allow to drain for 10 minutes. Remove stems, ribs, and seeds from bell peppers, peel, and set aside.

5. Add eggplants, bell peppers, tomato, and black pepper to the pan, and cook for 10 minutes.

6. Stir in red wine vinegar, capers, and pine nuts. Allow to cool to room temperature. Right before serving, stir in basil and mint.

MAKE IT A MEAL

Caponata is extremely versatile. It can be a delicious starter served with crusty Italian bread or whole-grain crackers, or for a meal, toss it with some cooked pasta.

Spaghetti Squash Marinara

The tender, almost pastalike spaghetti squash noodles are lifted with a zesty marinara and nutty-flavored Asiago cheese.

Yield:	Prep time:	Cook time:	Serving size:
4 squash bowls	5 minutes	40 minutes	1 squash bowl

Each serving has:			
172 calories	5 g protein	33 g carbohydrates	7 g fiber
	4 g total fat	2 g saturated fat	309 mg sodium

2 small (2-lb.) spaghetti squash, cut in ½ lengthwise and seeded

Nonstick olive oil cooking spray

1 medium red bell pepper, ribs and seeds removed, and sliced

1 medium yellow onion, sliced

¼ tsp. kosher salt

⅛ tsp. black pepper

1 cup low-sodium marinara or spaghetti sauce

¼ cup grated Asiago cheese

1. Preheat the oven to 350°F. Line a baking sheet with aluminum foil.

2. Place cut spaghetti squash halves cut side up on the prepared baking sheet, and spray cut sides with nonstick olive oil cooking spray. Bake for 30 minutes or until squash is easily pierced with a fork.

3. Heat a 12-inch nonstick sauté pan over medium-low heat, and lightly coat with nonstick cooking spray. Add red bell pepper, yellow onion, kosher salt, and black pepper. Cover, and cook, stirring occasionally, for 10 to 15 minutes.

4. Add marinara sauce, stir, and simmer for 5 minutes.

5. Place 1 squash into each of 4 bowls. Using a fork, shred squash into noodles. Pour ⅓ cup sauce into center of each squash bowl, top with 1 tablespoon Asiago cheese, and serve.

MAKE IT A MEAL

A slice of crusty Italian bread and a garden salad make this a meal.

Wild Mushroom Patties

Hearty and robust mushroom flavors mingle with a hint of lemon zest in these tasty patties.

Yield:	Prep time:	Cook time:	Serving size:
4 patties	5 to 10 minutes	20 minutes	1 patty

Each serving has:			
190 calories	10 g protein 3 g total fat	31 g carbohydrates 1 g saturated fat	3 g fiber 234 mg sodium

1 cup button mushrooms, diced	2 TB. fat-free plain Greek yogurt
2 medium portobello mushrooms, chopped	¼ cup chopped fresh parsley
2 shallots, diced (about 2 TB.)	⅛ tsp. kosher salt
1 TB. lemon zest	⅛ tsp. black pepper
1 cup fresh breadcrumbs	½ cup panko breadcrumbs
1 large egg, beaten	4 large romaine lettuce leaves, *chiffonade*

1. In a food processor fitted with a chopping blade, pulse button mushrooms until they resemble coarse breadcrumbs.

2. Heat a 12-inch nonstick sauté pan over medium heat, and lightly coat with nonstick cooking spray. Add button mushrooms, portobello mushrooms, and shallots, and sauté for 10 minutes. Remove from heat, and allow to cool.

3. In a large bowl, combine lemon zest, breadcrumbs, egg, Greek yogurt, parsley, kosher salt, and black pepper until well blended. Form into 8 patties, and coat patties with panko breadcrumbs.

4. Heat the 12-inch nonstick sauté pan over medium heat, and lightly coat again with nonstick cooking spray. Add patties, and sauté for 3 or 4 minutes per side.

5. Place 1 cup chiffonade romaine lettuce leaves on each of 4 plates, top each with 1 mushroom patty, and serve.

DEFINITION

In French, **chiffonade** means "made of rags." In cooking, it means to thinly slice vegetables into strips to be cooked or used as a garnish.

Vietnamese Fried Rice

Fragrant jasmine rice and garden-fresh vegetables are gently combined with eggs and the flavors of fresh herbs, with a touch of *palm sugar*.

Yield:	Prep time:	Cook time:	Serving size:
4 cups	5 to 10 minutes	10 minutes	1 cup

Each serving has:			
228 calories	7 g protein 7 g total fat	34 g carbohydrates 1 g saturated fat	2 g fiber 164 mg sodium

1 TB. canola oil

3 cloves garlic, chopped fine

1 medium yellow onion, sliced thin

2 medium scallions, white and green parts, sliced

2 large eggs, beaten

2 cups cooked jasmine or other long-grain rice

1 medium tomato, seeded and chopped

1 medium yellow bell pepper, ribs and seeds removed, and sliced

1 tsp. palm sugar or light brown sugar

¼ tsp. kosher salt

¼ tsp. ground white pepper

½ cup chopped fresh cilantro

¼ cup chopped fresh basil

1. In a wok or heavy skillet over high heat, heat canola oil. Add garlic, and stir-fry for 30 seconds or until garlic begins to change color.

2. Add yellow onion and scallions, and stir-fry for 3 minutes.

3. Stir in eggs and jasmine rice. Flatten rice into wok and up the sides. Turn it over, and press again.

4. Add tomato, yellow bell pepper, palm sugar, kosher salt, and white pepper, and stir-fry for 3 more minutes.

5. Add cilantro and basil, and toss. Remove from heat, and serve.

DEFINITION

Palm sugar is made from the sap of date palm or coconut palm. It's made similar to maple sugar in that the sap is collected and boiled down to make the sugar.

Quinoa-Stuffed Tomatoes

The super-grain *quinoa*, nutty in flavor and rich in protein, is right at home with Italian hard cheeses and the combination of sun-dried and fresh tomatoes.

Yield:	Prep time:	Cook time:	Serving size:
4 tomato cups	10 to 15 minutes	30 minutes	1 tomato cup

Each serving has:			
250 calories	12 g protein	39 g carbohydrates	6 g fiber
	5 g total fat	2 g saturated fat	390 mg sodium

1 cup quinoa	2 TB. grated Pecorino Romano cheese
1 medium yellow onion, diced	2 TB. grated Parmesan cheese
2 cloves garlic, minced	⅛ tsp. kosher salt
3 TB. chopped sun-dried tomatoes	⅛ tsp. black pepper
1 cup water	2 large tomatoes, cut in ½ and center spooned out
1 cup low-sodium vegetable broth	
1 TB. chopped fresh basil or 1 tsp. dried	

1. In a 12-inch nonstick sauté pan over medium heat, add quinoa and stir for 1 minute. Remove quinoa and set aside.

2. Lightly coat the pan with nonstick cooking spray. Add yellow onion, garlic, and sun-dried tomatoes, and sauté for 10 minutes.

3. Preheat the oven to 350°F.

4. In a 2-quart pot over medium-high heat, bring water and vegetable stock to a boil. Add toasted quinoa and cooked onion mixture, and cook for 10 to 12 minutes or until liquid is absorbed. Remove from heat.

5. Stir in basil, Pecorino Romano cheese, Parmesan cheese, kosher salt, and black pepper.

6. Spoon 1 cup quinoa into each tomato cup, place tomatoes on a baking sheet, and bake for 10 minutes.

7. Place 1 tomato cup on each of 4 plates, and serve.

DEFINITION

Quinoa is a super seed that's a source of complete protein. It's been cultivated for thousands of years—originally in the Andean region of South America.

Oven-Baked Tomato Risotto

This creamy and cheesy risotto has the full flavor of rich risotto—with no stirring.

Yield:	Prep time:	Cook time:	Serving size:
4 cups	5 to 10 minutes	30 minutes	⅔ cup

Each serving has:			
252 calories	7 g protein 10 g total fat	30 g carbohydrates 5 g saturated fat	2 g fiber 374 mg sodium

1 TB. extra-virgin olive oil	1 (14-oz.) can diced tomatoes, with juice
½ medium white onion, finely chopped	1 cup water
1 cup *arborio rice*	2 TB. butter
1 clove garlic, grated	½ cup grated Parmesan cheese
⅓ cup white wine	
2 cups low-sodium vegetable stock or broth	

1. Preheat the oven to 450°F.

2. In a large oven-safe pot over medium-high heat, heat extra-virgin olive oil. Add white onion, and sauté for about 5 minutes or until soft and beginning to turn light brown.

3. Add arborio rice and garlic, and cook, stirring constantly, for 1 more minute.

4. Add white wine, and cook for about 1 minute or until wine has evaporated.

5. Add vegetable stock, tomatoes, and water. Cover, and bring to a boil. Transfer pot to the oven, and bake for about 15 minutes or until rice is tender.

6. Quickly stir in butter and Parmesan cheese until creamy, about 1 or 2 minutes, and serve.

DEFINITION

Arborio rice is a short-grain rice that contains more starch than other types of rice. The starch is what enables it to create such a creamy dish like risotto.

Couscous with Apricots and Goat Cheese

Sweet apricots, creamy goat cheese, and lots of fragrant mint burst from this tasty couscous.

Yield:	Prep time:	Cook time:	Serving size:
3 cups	5 to 10 minutes	10 to 15 minutes	¾ cup

Each serving has:			
260 calories	9 g protein	43 g carbohydrates	4 g fiber
	6 g total fat	2 g saturated fat	135 mg sodium

2 medium shallots, peeled and diced

1 cup low-sodium vegetable broth

1 cup couscous

¼ cup chopped dried apricot

¼ cup crumbled goat cheese

¼ cup chopped fresh mint

¼ cup chopped fresh parsley

¼ tsp. ground allspice

⅛ tsp. kosher salt

⅛ tsp. black pepper

¼ cup toasted slivered almonds

1. Heat a 2-quart pot over medium heat, and lightly spray with nonstick cooking spray. Add shallots, cover, and cook, stirring occasionally, for 5 minutes.

2. Add vegetable broth, and bring to a boil. Stir in couscous, cover, remove from heat, and let rest for 5 minutes.

3. Using a fork, fold in dried apricot, goat cheese, mint, parsley, allspice, kosher salt, and black pepper.

4. Spoon ¾ cup couscous on each of 4 plates, top with 1 tablespoon slivered almonds each, and serve.

CULINARY KNOW-HOW

When fluffing couscous or cooked rice, use a fork. It'll prevent you from smashing the couscous.

Smashed Baked Potatoes
with Feta and Olives

Tender, fluffy potatoes are highlighted with Mediterranean flavors, thanks to feta cheese and kalamata olives.

Yield:	Prep time:	Cook time:	Serving size:
4 cups	5 minutes	6 to 8 minutes	1 cup

Each serving has:			
278 calories	9 g protein 10 g total fat	39 g carbohydrates 5 g saturated fat	4 g fiber 578 mg sodium

4 medium russet potatoes	16 kalamata olives, pitted and chopped
½ cup crumbled feta cheese	¼ tsp. black pepper

1. Wash russet potatoes, and prick with a fork. Place potatoes on a microwave-safe dish, and cook on high for 6 to 8 minutes, turning potatoes over halfway through the cook time. Potatoes should be easily pierced with a fork.

2. In a large bowl, place potatoes, and mash with a potato masher or fork.

3. Fold in feta cheese, kalamata olives, and black pepper, and serve.

Variation: For **Smashed Baked Potatoes with Asiago and Sun-Dried Tomatoes,** substitute ½ cup Asiago cheese for the feta and 16 chopped sun-dried tomatoes for the kalamata olives. *Each serving has: 237 calories, 8 g protein, 42 g carbohydrates, 5 g fiber, 5 g total fat, 3 g saturated fat, 322 mg sodium.*

CULINARY KNOW-HOW

Turning a potato halfway through ensures the potato is cooked and soft throughout. The part of the potato touching the plate tends to be tough.

Spicy Pasta Primavera

Tender, fresh pasta tossed with fresh veggies get an extra kick from crushed red pepper flakes.

Yield:	Prep time:	Cook time:	Serving size:
4 cups pasta	5 to 10 minutes	20 minutes	1 cup pasta

Each serving has:			
287 calories	15 g protein 4 g total fat	47 g carbohydrates 2 g saturated fat	5 g fiber 453 mg sodium

1 small yellow onion, diced

1 small carrot, peeled and diced

1 small yellow squash, sliced into ¼-in. rounds

1 cup broccoli florets

¾ cup low-sodium vegetable stock

2 qt. water

8 oz. dried fettuccine pasta

½ cup fat-free plain Greek yogurt

2 TB. grated Parmesan cheese

½ tsp. crushed red pepper flakes

¼ tsp. kosher salt

⅛ tsp. black pepper

4 chopped fresh basil leaves

1. Heat a 12-inch nonstick sauté pan over medium heat, and lightly coat with nonstick cooking spray. Add yellow onion, carrot, and yellow squash, and sauté for 5 minutes.

2. Add broccoli florets, and sauté for 5 minutes.

3. Stir in vegetable broth.

4. In a large pot over medium-high heat, bring water to a boil. Add fettuccine pasta, and cook for 8 to 10 minutes or until tender. Drain.

5. To the skillet, add fettuccine, Greek yogurt, Parmesan cheese, crushed red pepper flakes, kosher salt, black pepper, and basil.

6. Spoon 1 cup pasta with sauce on each of 4 plates, and serve.

TASTY TIDBIT

In Italian, *primavera* means "in the style of springtime." When it comes to food, it means "served with a mixture of fresh vegetables."

Black Bean and Corn Cakes

A crispy cornmeal crust encases the spicy taste and rich textures of these cakes featuring sweet corn and cooling cilantro mayonnaise.

Yield:	Prep time:	Cook time:	Serving size:
4 cakes	10 to 15 minutes	20 minutes	1 cake

Each serving has:			
309 calories	10 g protein	54 g carbohydrates	8 g fiber
	7 g total fat	2 g saturated fat	481 mg sodium

1 medium yellow onion, diced	⅛ tsp. black pepper
1 clove garlic, minced	½ cup cornmeal
1 (15-oz.) can black beans, drained and rinsed	½ cup fresh or frozen corn
1½ cups cooked brown rice	1 small jalapeño pepper, seeded and diced
1 large egg, beaten	2 TB. chopped fresh cilantro
1 TB. chili powder	¼ cup low-fat mayonnaise
¼ tsp. kosher salt	

1. Heat a 12-inch nonstick sauté pan over medium heat, and lightly coat with nonstick cooking spray. Add yellow onion and garlic, and cook, stirring occasionally, for 10 minutes.

2. In a food processor fitted with a chopping blade, process cooked onions and garlic, 1 cup black beans, brown rice, egg, chili powder, kosher salt, and black pepper for about 1 minute or until well mixed.

3. Place cornmeal in a shallow dish.

4. Transfer mixture from the processor to a large bowl, and add remaining black beans, corn, jalapeño pepper, and cornmeal.

5. Heat the sauté pan over medium heat, and lightly coat again with nonstick cooking spray. Spoon black bean cake mixture into pan in ½ cup portions, smooth out, and cook for 5 minutes per side.

6. In a small bowl, combine cilantro and low-fat mayonnaise, and serve alongside black bean cakes.

TASTY TIDBIT

Cilantro has a cooling effect when you eat it with something spicy-hot, as with the jalapeño in this recipe.

Vegetable Paella

A rainbow of vegetables, enhanced by earthy saffron, fill this fiber-rich dish.

Yield:	Prep time:	Cook time:	Serving size:
8 cups	15 to 20 minutes	60 minutes	1½ cups

Each serving has:			
371 calories	9 g protein 3 g total fat	83 g carbohydrates 1 g saturated fat	10 g fiber 638 mg sodium

1 large yellow onion, diced	1 medium tomato, seeded and diced
2 cloves garlic, minced	1 (15-oz.) can artichoke hearts canned in water, drained and halved
1 small zucchini, diced	
1 small yellow squash, diced	Pinch saffron
1 medium red bell pepper, ribs and seeds removed, and diced	2 bay leaves
1 medium yellow bell pepper, ribs and seeds removed, and diced	2 cups short-grain brown rice
4 cups low-sodium vegetable broth	¼ tsp. black pepper

1. Heat a 3-quart saucepan over medium heat, and lightly coat with nonstick cooking spray. Add yellow onion, garlic, zucchini, yellow squash, red bell pepper, and yellow bell pepper, and sauté for 10 minutes.

2. In a 2-quart pot with a tight-fitting lid over medium-high heat, bring vegetable broth to a boil.

3. Add tomato, artichoke hearts, saffron, bay leaves, heated vegetable stock, short-grain rice, and black pepper to the 3-quart pot. Bring to a boil, reduce heat to low, and simmer for 50 minutes or until all liquid is absorbed and rice is tender. Remove bay leaves.

4. Spoon 1½ cups paella on each of 6 plates, and serve.

TASTY TIDBIT

Saffron comes from the golden-red stigmas of a small purple crocus. Each flower contains 3 stigmas, and it takes more than 10,000 to make 1 ounce. The stigmas are carefully picked by hand, making saffron the most expensive spice on Earth.

Italian-Style Mac and Cheese

Gooey mozzarella and woodsy basil turn traditional macaroni and cheese into a bowlful of Italy.

Yield:	Prep time:	Cook time:	Serving size:
8 cups	20 minutes	40 minutes	1 cup

Each serving has:			
381 calories	18 g protein	48 g carbohydrates	4 g fiber
	15 g total fat	4 g saturated fat	238 mg sodium

1 lb. whole-wheat elbow macaroni	¼ lb. shredded fontina cheese
¼ cup canola oil	1 tsp. garlic powder
4 TB. all-purpose flour	1 tsp. dried basil
1 cup skim milk	¼ tsp. hot sauce (optional)
¼ lb. shredded reduced-fat mozzarella cheese	2 TB. grated Parmesan cheese
	¼ cup panko breadcrumbs

1. Preheat the oven to 350°F.

2. Cook whole-wheat elbow macaroni according to the package directions.

3. Meanwhile, in a medium saucepan over medium heat, heat canola oil. Add all-purpose flour, and whisk for about 1 minute. Whisk in skim milk, and simmer for 5 minutes or until thickened.

4. Add mozzarella cheese, fontina cheese, garlic powder, basil, and hot sauce (if using), and whisk until smooth. Add to cooked macaroni, stir to combine, and pour into a 3-quart casserole dish.

5. In a small bowl, combine Parmesan cheese and panko breadcrumbs, and sprinkle over top of mac and cheese. Cover, and bake for 15 minutes. Uncover, and bake for 15 more minutes. Spoon onto plates, and serve.

TASTY TIDBIT

After you've given this recipe a try, get creative and try different types of cheeses or a variety of bite-size steamed veggies.

Warming Soups, Stews, and Chilies

In This Chapter

- Classic comfort food in a bowl
- Chicken, beef, and seafood soups
- Hearty veggie chili and soups
- Fiber-rich bean bowls

What's better than sitting down to a warm bowl of chili or stew on a cold afternoon, or a soothing, steaming bowl of soup when you're under the weather? Even if you're feeling fine and the sun is shining, you'll find yourself looking for reasons to cook these pots full of flavor.

Three-Squash Stew

This hearty and slightly sweet squash-based stew is accented by fresh thyme.

Yield:	Prep time:	Cook time:	Serving size:
10 cups	15 to 20 minutes	45 to 50 minutes	2 cups

Each serving has:			
59 calories	1 g protein 0 g total fat	14 g carbohydrates 0 g saturated fat	4 g fiber 380 mg sodium

1 small butternut squash, diced	1 medium celery stalk, diced
1 small sugar pumpkin, diced	1 clove garlic, minced
1 small buttercup squash, diced	6 cups low-sodium vegetable broth
Nonstick cooking spray	1 TB. fresh thyme or 1 tsp. dried
1 medium yellow onion, diced	½ tsp. kosher salt
1 small carrot, peeled and diced	¼ tsp. black pepper

1. Preheat the oven to 350°F.

2. Arrange butternut squash, sugar pumpkin, and buttercup squash in a single layer on a baking sheet. Spray with nonstick cooking spray, and bake for 15 minutes.

3. Heat a large pot over medium heat, and lightly coat with nonstick cooking spray. Add yellow onion, carrot, celery, and garlic. Cover, and cook for 10 minutes.

4. Add baked squashes, baked pumpkin, low-sodium vegetable broth, thyme, kosher salt, and black pepper. Cover, and simmer, stirring occasionally, for 20 minutes.

5. Spoon 2 cups stew into each of 5 bowls, and serve.

TASTY TIDBIT

Broth-based, veggie-filled soups make a great starter to any meal. They help fill you up so you eat less of the higher-calorie foods.

Hearty Mushroom Soup

Lemon undertones balance the rich earthiness of the mushrooms in this warming soup.

Yield:	Prep time:	Cook time:	Serving size:
10 cups	5 to 20 minutes	1 hour, 10 minutes	2 cups

Each serving has:			
127 calories	11 g protein 3 g total fat	14 g carbohydrates 2 g saturated fat	2 g fiber 569 mg sodium

1 medium yellow onion, diced

1 small carrot, peeled and diced

1 medium celery stalk, diced

1 clove garlic, minced

1 lb. button mushrooms, sliced

1 cup shiitake mushrooms, stems discarded, and sliced

2 medium tomatoes, diced

8 cups low-sodium chicken broth

1 TB. finely chopped fresh rosemary

¼ cup chopped fresh parsley

2 (½×1½-in.) strips lemon peel

½ tsp. kosher salt

¼ tsp. black pepper

½ cup sour cream

1. Heat a large, heavy pot over medium heat, and lightly coat with nonstick cooking spray. Add yellow onion, carrot, celery, garlic, button mushrooms, and shiitake mushrooms, and cook for 10 minutes.

2. Add diced tomatoes, low-sodium chicken broth, rosemary, parsley, lemon peel, kosher salt, and black pepper. Cover, and simmer for 1 hour.

3. Remove from heat, and stir in sour cream.

4. Spoon 2 cups soup into each of 5 bowls, and serve.

Variation: For **Robust Barley Soup,** add 1 leek, white part only, sliced thin, and washed thoroughly, and sauté with the other vegetables. Substitute 2 bay leaves and 1 tablespoon fresh thyme or 1 teaspoon dried for the rosemary and low-sodium beef broth for low-sodium chicken broth. Add ½ cup pearl barley, and omit the sour cream. Simmer for 40 minutes, remove bay leaves, and serve. *Each serving has: 178 calories, 12 g protein, 30 g carbohydrates, 6 g fiber, 2 g total fat, 1 g saturated fat, 558 mg sodium.*

CULINARY KNOW-HOW

When using citrus peel, only use the part with color. The white pith underneath is bitter, so it's best to avoid that.

Boston Baked Bean Bowl

Here, a dark, rich molasses flavor is highlighted with a nutty, slightly anise taste from the caraway and smoke from the bacon.

Yield:	Prep time:	Cook time:	Serving size:
8 cups	15 to 20 minutes, plus overnight soak time	5 hours	½ cup

Each serving has:			
151 calories	7 g protein	30 g carbohydrates	7 g fiber
	1 g total fat	0 g saturated fat	361 mg sodium

1 lb. dried navy beans	¼ cup molasses
4 strips center-cut bacon, chopped	¼ cup maple syrup
1 large yellow onion, diced	2 TB. Dijon mustard
1 medium celery stalk, diced	1 TB. caraway seeds
3 cups low-sodium chicken broth	½ tsp. kosher salt
1 cup ketchup	¼ tsp. black pepper

1. Soak navy beans in 6 cups water overnight in the refrigerator. Drain.

2. Preheat the oven to 325°F.

3. Heat a large, heavy pot over medium heat, and lightly coat with nonstick cooking spray. Add center-cut bacon, yellow onion, and celery. Cover, and cook for 20 minutes.

4. Add navy beans, low-sodium chicken broth, ketchup, molasses, maple syrup, Dijon mustard, caraway seeds, kosher salt, and black pepper, and bring to a boil.

5. Transfer beans to a large casserole dish, cover, and bake for 4 to 4½ hours. Uncover for the last 15 minutes to achieve a beautiful rich brown color.

6. Spoon ½ cup baked beans into each of 8 bowls, and serve. Refrigerate the remaining 8 ½-cup servings for up to 3 days.

CULINARY KNOW-HOW

When putting a dish like this in the oven, first bring the liquid to a boil on top of stove to save on total cooking time.

Roasted Tomato Soup

Roasted tomatoes lend a layer of deep, rich flavor to this soup.

Yield:	Prep time:	Cook time:	Serving size:
6 cups	5 to 10 minutes	45 minutes	1½ cups

Each serving has:			
162 calories	7 g protein 1 g total fat	26 g carbohydrates 1 g saturated fat	9 g fiber 783 mg sodium

2 (28-oz.) cans whole peeled plum tomatoes, seeded and diced, juice strained and reserved

Nonstick cooking spray

1 medium yellow onion, diced

1 small fennel bulb, diced

2 cloves garlic, chopped

2 cups low-sodium vegetable broth

⅛ tsp. black pepper

¼ cup chopped fresh basil or 2 TB. dried

1 TB. fresh marjoram or 1 tsp. dried

2 TB. grated Parmesan cheese

¼ cup fat-free plain Greek yogurt

1. Preheat the oven to 450°F. Line a baking sheet with aluminum foil.

2. Place plum tomatoes on the prepared baking sheet, and lightly coat with nonstick cooking spray. Bake for 15 to 20 minutes or until tomatoes begin to brown.

3. Heat a large pot over medium heat, and lightly coat with nonstick cooking spray. Add yellow onion, fennel, and garlic. Cover, and cook, stirring occasionally, for 10 minutes.

4. Add roasted tomatoes, reserved juice, low-sodium vegetable broth, and black pepper. Cover, and simmer for 20 minutes.

5. In a small bowl, combine basil, marjoram, Parmesan cheese, and Greek yogurt.

6. Remove soup from heat, and working in batches, purée in a blender. Return puréed soup to the pot.

7. Ladle 1½ cups soup into each of 4 bowls, top with 1 tablespoon Greek yogurt mixture, and serve.

CULINARY KNOW-HOW

Be careful when puréeing a hot mixture in a blender. Only fill the container half full, and be sure the steam can escape as you blend by cracking the lid a bit. Also cover the top with a kitchen towel to avoid hot spatters.

Vegetarian Chili

A garden of ingredients, from vegetables to fiber-rich beans, produces a robust and flavorful chili that's enhanced with smoky paprika.

Yield:	Prep time:	Cook time:	Serving size:
10 cups	10 to 15 minutes	50 to 60 minutes	2 cups

Each serving has:			
168 calories	8 g protein	34 g carbohydrates	10 g fiber
	1 g total fat	0 g saturated fat	460 mg sodium

1 large yellow onion, diced	1 small sweet potato, peeled and diced
2 medium celery stalks, diced	3 TB. chili powder
2 small carrots, peeled and diced	1 TB. smoked paprika
3 cloves garlic, chopped	1 tsp. ground cumin
1 medium jalapeño pepper, seeded and diced	1 tsp. ground coriander
1 cup canned black beans, drained and rinsed	6 cups low-sodium vegetable broth
1 cup canned kidney beans, drained and rinsed	½ tsp. kosher salt
1 cup canned cannellini beans, drained and rinsed	¼ tsp. black pepper

1. Heat a large pot over medium heat, and lightly coat with nonstick cooking spray. Add yellow onion, celery, carrots, garlic, and jalapeño pepper. Cover, and cook for 10 minutes.

2. Add black beans, kidney beans, cannellini beans, sweet potato, chili powder, smoked paprika, cumin, coriander, low-sodium vegetable broth, kosher salt, and black pepper. Cover, and cook for 40 to 45 minutes.

3. Spoon 2 cups chili into each of 5 bowls, and serve.

MAKE IT A MEAL

Serve a piece of cornbread or some crackers alongside a bowl of this chili for a satisfying dinner.

South American Squash Stew

Hearty and satisfying, this South American stew gets a slightly sweet spin from the squashes, *plantains*, and raisins.

Yield:	Prep time:	Cook time:	Serving size:
10 cups	10 to 15 minutes	30 to 35 minutes	2 cups

Each serving has:			
236 calories	4 g protein 1 g total fat	55 g carbohydrates 0 g saturated fat	8 g fiber 403 mg sodium

1 medium yellow onion, diced

1 small carrot, peeled and diced

1 medium celery stalk, diced

3 cloves garlic, minced

1 small butternut squash, diced

1 small sweet potato, peeled and diced

1 small ripe plantain, peeled and diced

1 small buttercup squash, diced

½ cup short-grain brown rice

½ cup raisins

6 cups low-sodium vegetable broth

2 TB. fresh oregano or 1 tsp. dried

2 tsp. ground allspice

½ tsp. kosher salt

¼ tsp. black pepper

1. Heat a large, heavy pot over medium heat, and lightly coat with nonstick cooking spray. Add yellow onion, carrot, celery, and garlic. Cover, and cook for 10 minutes.

2. Add butternut squash, sweet potatoes, plantain, buttercup squash, short-grain brown rice, raisins, low-sodium vegetable broth, oregano, allspice, kosher salt, and black pepper. Cover, and simmer for 20 to 25 minutes or until squash and rice are cooked.

3. Spoon 2 cups stew into each of 5 bowls, and serve.

DEFINITION

Plantains are a cooking banana popular in South America, where they're used like potatoes are in the United States. As the fruit ripens, the skin blackens and the fruit gets sweeter.

Clam, Kale, and Lentil Soup

Calcium-rich kale stands out in this lentil soup with the briny taste of the sea, thanks to the clams.

Yield:	Prep time:	Cook time:	Serving size:
12 cups	15 to 20 minutes	60 minutes	2 cups

Each serving has:			
238 calories	21 g protein 4 g total fat	31 g carbohydrates 1 g saturated fat	10 g fiber 600 mg sodium

1 TB. canola oil

1 medium yellow onion, diced

2 cloves garlic, sliced

1 lb. kale, thick stems and ribs trimmed off, and cut into 1-in. pieces

1 (15-oz.) can diced tomatoes, with juice

8 cups low-sodium chicken broth

1 cup dried lentils, picked over and rinsed

12 littleneck clams, scrubbed and rinsed

1/4 tsp. black pepper

1. Heat a large heavy pot over low heat. Add canola oil, yellow onion, and garlic. Cover, and cook, stirring occasionally, for 10 minutes.

2. Stir in kale, cover, and cook for 4 minutes.

3. Add tomatoes, low-sodium chicken broth, and lentils. Cover, and simmer for 40 minutes.

4. Add littleneck clams, cover, and cook for 5 to 10 more minutes or until clams open. (Discard any unopened clams.) Season with black pepper.

5. Spoon 2 cups soup into each of 6 bowls, top with 2 clams, and serve.

MAKE IT A MEAL

A simple sandwich or some whole-grain crackers and fresh fruit turn a bowl of this soup into a hearty lunch.

Ribollita (Italian Bread Soup)

An Italian take on leftovers, this full-bodied vegetable soup is thickened with crusty bread and rich Parmesan cheese.

Yield:	Prep time:	Cook time:	Serving size:
10 cups	15 to 20 minutes	40 minutes	2 cups

Each serving has:			
260 calories	17 g protein	39 g carbohydrates	9 g fiber
	5 g total fat	2 g saturated fat	574 mg sodium

4 cloves garlic, chopped

1 large red onion, chopped

3 medium celery stalks, chopped

3 small carrots, peeled and chopped

1 (28-oz.) can peeled, whole, unsalted tomatoes, with juice, chopped

¾ to 1 lb. kale, thick stems and ribs trimmed off, and cut into 1-in. pieces

½ cup chopped fresh parsley

2 TB. fresh thyme or 2 tsp. dried

2 TB. chopped fresh rosemary or 2 tsp. dried

2 TB. fresh marjoram or 2 tsp. dried

6 cups low-sodium chicken broth

1 (15-oz.) can cannellini beans, drained and rinsed

4½ slices French or Italian bread, cut into ½-in. cubes

5 TB. grated Parmesan cheese

1. Heat a large pot over medium heat, and lightly coat with nonstick cooking spray. Add garlic, red onion, celery, and carrots. Cover, and cook for 10 minutes.

2. Add canned tomatoes, kale, parsley, thyme, rosemary, marjoram, low-sodium chicken broth, and cannellini beans. Cover, and simmer for 30 minutes.

3. Ladle 2 cups soup into each of 5 bowls. Add ¼ cup cubed French bread and 1 tablespoon grated Parmesan cheese, and serve.

TASTY TIDBIT

Ribollita means "reboiled" in Italian. Leftover minestrone or vegetable soups were reboiled, and the bread from the previous day was added to make a heartier dish.

Moroccan Chicken Medley

Beautifully fragrant spices enrich the flavor of the chicken and blend with the orange and almonds deliciously.

Yield:	Prep time:	Cook time:	Serving size:
8 cups	10 to 15 minutes	40 minutes	1 cup

Each serving has:			
284 calories	15 g protein	36 g carbohydrates	7 g fiber
	9 g total fat	2 g saturated fat	327 mg sodium

¾ lb. boneless, skinless chicken thighs

1 large yellow onion, diced

1 tsp. ground cinnamon

½ tsp. ground coriander

¼ tsp. ground ginger

¼ tsp. kosher salt

⅛ tsp. black pepper

2 cups low-sodium chicken broth

1 (15-oz.) can chickpeas, drained and rinsed

2 medium tomatoes, diced

1 cup couscous

2 TB. extra-virgin olive oil

3 small carrots, peeled and grated

2 medium oranges, peeled and segmented

½ cup toasted slivered almonds

1. Heat a large, heavy pot over medium heat, and lightly coat with nonstick cooking spray. Add chicken thighs and yellow onion, cover, and cook for 10 minutes.

2. Stir in cinnamon, coriander, ginger, kosher salt, and black pepper, and cook for 1 or 2 more minutes.

3. Add low-sodium chicken broth, chickpeas, and tomatoes. Cover, and simmer for 20 minutes.

4. Stir in couscous, cover, remove from heat, and allow to rest for 10 minutes.

5. Uncover couscous, and fold in extra-virgin olive oil and carrots.

6. Spoon 1 cup couscous-chicken mixture into each of 8 bowls, top with 2 orange segments and 1 tablespoon slivered almonds, and serve.

TASTY TIDBIT

In Morocco, a main dish is a *tagine*, which is also the name of the cooking vessel. The cooking vessel is ceramic with a base and a coned lid. The lid promotes condensation.

Texas Chili

Sweet, hot, and smoky flavors all meld with the savory beef in this spicy chili.

Yield:	Prep time:	Cook time:	Serving size:
10 cups	10 to 15 minutes	3½ hours	2 cups

Each serving has:			
293 calories	42 g protein	9 g carbohydrates	2 g fiber
	7 g total fat	3 g saturated fat	317 mg sodium

2 lb. sirloin steak, cut into 1-in. cubes	1 tsp. ground cumin
1 medium yellow onion, chopped	2 tsp. smoked paprika
1 medium red bell pepper, ribs and seeds removed, and chopped	1 tsp. sweet paprika
	1 chipotle pepper in adobo sauce, diced
2 cloves garlic, chopped	1 small jalapeño pepper, seeded and chopped
3 TB. tomato paste	
½ cup red wine	1½ cups low-sodium beef broth
1 TB. dried oregano	¼ tsp. black pepper

1. Heat a large pot over medium heat, and lightly coat with nonstick cooking spray. Add sirloin steak, in batches, and cook for about 10 minutes or until brown on all sides. Remove cooked steak, cover, and keep warm.

2. Add yellow onion, red bell pepper, and garlic to the pot, and cook for 10 to 15 minutes or until vegetables are tender.

3. Stir in tomato paste and red wine, and cook for about 5 minutes or until reduced by half.

4. Add reserved sirloin steak, oregano, cumin, smoked paprika, sweet paprika, chipotle pepper in adobo sauce, and jalapeño pepper, and cook for 2 minutes.

5. Add low-sodium beef broth, water, and black pepper. Cover, and simmer for 3 hours.

6. Spoon 2 cups chili into each of 5 bowls, and serve.

TASTY TIDBIT

In Texas, chili has no beans and often no other vegetables except for chile peppers.

Red Lentil Soup with Chicken

As you taste this lentil dish, first you'll taste the curry and coconut, then heat from the jalapeño, and finally the cooling cilantro.

Yield:	Prep time:	Cook time:	Serving size:
8 cups	25 to 30 minutes	50 minutes	1½ cups

Each serving has:			
354 calories	29 g protein 12 g total fat	32 g carbohydrates 6 g saturated fat	8 g fiber 450 mg sodium

1 large yellow onion, diced

1 medium red bell pepper, ribs and seeds removed, and diced

2 cloves garlic, diced

1 small jalapeño pepper, seeded and diced

4 cups low-sodium chicken broth

1 (15-oz.) can diced tomatoes, drained

¾ (15-oz.) can lite coconut milk

1 TB. curry powder

1 TB. peeled and grated fresh ginger

1 bay leaf

½ tsp. ground cumin

1 lb. boneless, skinless chicken thighs, cut into ½-in. pieces

1 cup red lentils

¼ tsp. kosher salt

⅛ tsp. black pepper

5 TB. chopped fresh cilantro

1. Heat a large, heavy pot over medium heat, and lightly coat with nonstick cooking spray. Add yellow onion, red bell pepper, garlic, and jalapeño pepper. Cover, and cook for 10 minutes.

2. Add low-sodium chicken broth, diced tomatoes, lite coconut milk, curry powder, ginger, bay leaf, cumin, chicken thighs, red lentils, kosher salt, and black pepper. Cover, and simmer for 40 minutes.

3. Remove bay leaf. Ladle approximately 1½ cups soup into each of 5 bowls, garnish with 1 tablespoon cilantro, and serve.

TASTY TIDBIT

Coconut milk is not the liquid inside the coconut. It's made by grating the coconut meat, processing it with water or milk, and squeezing the coconut to extract the milk.

Split Pea and Smoked Turkey Soup

A meaty turkey leg imparts a delicious smoky flavor in this creamy split pea soup.

Yield:	Prep time:	Cook time:	Serving size:
10 cups	10 to 15 minutes	1 hour, 45 minutes	2 cups

Each serving has:			
354 calories	30 g protein	53 g carbohydrates	19 g fiber
	3 g total fat	1 g saturated fat	512 mg sodium

1 medium yellow onion, diced	1 bay leaf
1 small carrot, peeled and diced	1 TB. fresh thyme or 1 tsp. dried
1 medium celery stalk, diced	¼ cup chopped fresh parsley
1 clove garlic, minced	1 (1½- to 2-lb.) smoked turkey leg
8 cups low-sodium chicken broth	¼ tsp. kosher salt
1 lb. split peas, picked over and rinsed	¼ tsp. black pepper

1. Heat a large, heavy pot over medium heat, and lightly coat with nonstick cooking spray. Add yellow onion, carrot, celery, and garlic. Cover, and cook, stirring occasionally, for 10 to 15 minutes.

2. Add low-sodium chicken broth, split peas, bay leaf, thyme, parsley, smoked turkey leg, kosher salt, and black pepper. Cover, and simmer for 1½ hours.

3. Remove smoked turkey leg from soup. Pick off meat, and discard skin, bones, and tendons. Dice meat, and return to soup. Remove bay leaf.

4. Spoon 2 cups soup into each of 5 bowls, and serve.

 TASTY TIDBIT

The split peas pack a lot of fiber into this hearty soup.

Chicken Paprika

Sweet and hot paprikas provide a rich pepper flavor throughout this stew, while sour cream and comforting egg noodles cool the heat a bit.

Yield:	Prep time:	Cook time:	Serving size:
4 cups	15 to 20 minutes	55 minutes	1 cup

Each serving has:			
371 calories	29 g protein 12 g total fat	36 g carbohydrates 4 g saturated fat	2 g fiber 284 mg sodium

1 large yellow onion, diced	¼ tsp. kosher salt
1 lb. boneless, skinless chicken thighs, cut into large pieces	⅛ tsp. black pepper
1 TB. sweet paprika	2 qt. water
1 TB. hot paprika	6 oz. dried egg noodles
2 cups low-sodium chicken broth	¼ cup reduced-fat sour cream

1. Heat a large, heavy pot over medium heat, and lightly coat with nonstick cooking spray. Add yellow onion, cover, and cook for 10 minutes.

2. Add chicken thighs and cook, turning occasionally, for 5 minutes.

3. Stir in sweet paprika, hot paprika, low-sodium chicken broth, kosher salt, and black pepper. Cover, and simmer for 30 minutes.

4. In a large pot over medium-high heat, bring water to a boil. Add egg noodles, and cook according to the package instructions.

5. Place ¾ cup cooked egg noodles into each of 4 bowls. Add 1 cup chicken paprika, top with 1 tablespoon sour cream each, and serve.

TASTY TIDBIT

Chicken paprika, also called paprikash, is one of the famous stews in Hungary.

Goulash

This is a deep, rich, and beefy tomato stew, with the robust taste and fragrance of garlic and caraway seed.

Yield:	Prep time:	Cook time:	Serving size:
8 cups	15 to 20 minutes	3 hours	1½ cups

Each serving has:			
379 calories	30 g protein	50 g carbohydrates	4 g fiber
	6 g total fat	2 g saturated fat	397 mg sodium

2 lb. round steaks, cut into ½-in. cubes

1 large yellow onion, diced

3 cloves garlic, diced

2 medium celery stalks, diced

2 small carrots, peeled and diced

1 medium red bell pepper, ribs and seeds removed, diced

1 tsp. ground caraway

1 TB. fresh marjoram or 1 tsp. dried

2 TB. paprika

2 cups low-sodium beef broth

2 TB. tomato paste

¼ tsp. kosher salt

¼ tsp. black pepper

3 qt. water

10 oz. dried egg noodles

1. Heat a large, heavy pot over medium heat, and lightly coat with nonstick cooking spray. Add round steak, in batches, and cook for about 10 minutes per batch until brown on all sides. Remove cooked beef, cover, and keep warm.

2. Add yellow onion, garlic, celery, carrots, red bell pepper, and caraway. Cover, and cook for 10 minutes.

3. Stir in marjoram, paprika, low-sodium beef broth, tomato paste, kosher salt, and black pepper. Cover, and simmer for 2 hours.

4. In a large pot over medium-high heat, bring water to a boil. Add egg noodles, and cook according to the package instructions.

5. Spoon ¾ cup cooked egg noodles into each of 5 bowls, add approximately 1½ cups goulash, and serve.

TASTY TIDBIT

One of Hungary's national dishes, goulash is a thick stew of meat, vegetables, and paprika traditionally made by cattle herders.

Chicken Stew with Dumplings

Here, comforting, cheesy dumplings soak up the rich, herbed broth created by the garden of vegetables and luscious chicken thighs.

Yield:	Prep time:	Cook time:	Serving size:
6 cups	10 to 15 minutes	35 to 40 minutes	1½ cups

Each serving has:			
383 calories	25 g protein	39 g carbohydrates	1 g fiber
	15 g total fat	4 g saturated fat	788 mg sodium

1 medium yellow onion, diced

1 medium celery stalk, diced

1 medium carrot, peeled and diced

½ cup sliced button mushrooms

1 lb. boneless, skinless chicken thighs, cut into 1-in. cubes

2 cups low-sodium chicken broth

2 TB. fresh thyme or 2 tsp. dried

2 TB. chopped fresh parsley

⅛ tsp. black pepper

1 TB. all-purpose flour

2¼ cups dry biscuit mix

⅔ cup skim milk

2 TB. grated Pecorino Romano cheese

1. Heat a large, heavy pot over medium heat, and lightly coat with nonstick cooking spray. Add yellow onion, celery, carrot, and mushrooms, cover, and cook for 10 minutes.

2. Add chicken and cook for 5 minutes, turning occasionally.

3. Add 1½ cups low-sodium chicken broth, 1 tablespoon thyme, 1 tablespoon parsley, and black pepper. Cover, bring to a simmer, and cook for 15 minutes.

4. In a 1-cup container with a tight-fitting lid, combine remaining ½ cup low-sodium chicken broth and all-purpose flour. Shake vigorously. Stir flour mixture into the pot, and cook for 2 minutes or until mixture begins to thicken.

5. In a medium bowl, combine biscuit mix and skim milk. Drop batter by tablespoonfuls on top of chicken stew. Cover, and cook according to the package instructions.

6. Sprinkle with remaining 1 tablespoon thyme, remaining 1 tablespoon parsley, and Pecorino Romano cheese.

7. Spoon 1½ cups stew into each of 4 bowls, top with 2 dumplings, and serve.

TASTY TIDBIT

Pecorino is the name given to cheeses made with sheep's milk.

Tantalizing Slow Cooker Meals

Chapter 18

In This Chapter

- Plan now for dinner later
- Hearty beef bowls
- Tender chicken dishes
- Fresh veggies by the bowlful

After a long day, isn't it nice to come home to the aroma of something delicious cooking? Cue the slow cooker. A slow cooker allows you to do all the prep work for dinner in the morning and pop it all into the refrigerator. When it's time to start cooking, simply put it into your slow cooker, turn it on, and relax or run some errands for a few hours and return to a delicious hot meal, ready and waiting for you.

Even if your mornings are hectic, don't shun this fantastic invention. Most recipes can be prepared the night before, placed in the slow cooker's removable crockery insert, and refrigerated overnight. When you're ready the next day, all you have to do is put the crockery insert in the cooker, turn it on, and go!

Many of the recipes in this chapter make a good number of servings. That's because slow cookers are a simple way to cook for a crowd. But even if you don't have a crowd to feed, go ahead and make these meals. You can eat the leftovers during the next couple days, or freeze them for dinners a few weeks from now.

Mushroom Beef Barley Soup

This full-bodied soup is rich with the flavors of beef, mushrooms, and garlic with a hint of lemon.

Yield:	Prep time:	Cook time:	Serving size:
10 cups	15 to 20 minutes	4 hours	1¼ cups

Each serving has:			
183 calories	22 g protein 3 g total fat	15 g carbohydrates 1 g saturated fat	3 g fiber 563 mg sodium

1½ lb. top round roast, cut into ¼-in. cubes

1 large yellow onion, diced

1 medium celery stalk, diced

2 cloves garlic, diced

8 oz. button mushrooms, diced

1 (8-oz.) can diced tomatoes, drained

6 cups low-sodium beef broth

1 TB. fresh thyme or 1 tsp. dried

¼ cup fresh parsley, chopped

½ cup pearl barley

2 (½-in.) pieces lemon rind

½ tsp. kosher salt

¼ tsp. black pepper

1. In an 8-quart slow cooker, combine top round roast, yellow onion, celery, garlic, button mushrooms, tomatoes, low-sodium beef broth, thyme, parsley, pearl barley, lemon rind, kosher salt, and black pepper.

2. Cover, and cook on low for 4 hours.

3. Spoon 1¼ cups soup into each of 8 bowls, and serve.

TASTY TIDBIT

Pearl barley has the outer, hard shell removed and is steamed and polished. It's a terrific source of fiber.

Braised Chicken with Apples and Sweet Potatoes

The rich, savory chicken and fragrant herbs are balanced with a touch of balsamic vinegar.

Yield:	Prep time:	Cook time:	Serving size:
8 cups	10 to 15 minutes	4 hours	1½ cups

Each serving has:			
198 calories	17 g protein	20 g carbohydrates	3 g fiber
	6 g total fat	2 g saturated fat	175 mg sodium

5 medium yellow onions, sliced

2½ lb. skinless chicken thighs

1 TB. chopped fresh rosemary or 1 tsp. dried

1 TB. chopped fresh sage or 1 tsp. dried

½ tsp. kosher salt

¼ tsp. black pepper

1 lb. sweet potatoes, skin on and sliced into ½ rings

2 medium Golden Delicious apples, cored and sliced into rings

2 TB. balsamic vinegar

¼ cup low-sodium chicken broth

1. In a slow cooker, place yellow onions.

2. Rub chicken thighs with rosemary, sage, kosher salt, and black pepper, and place on top of onions.

3. Arrange sweet potatoes and Golden Delicious apples around pork. Pour in balsamic vinegar and low-sodium chicken broth.

4. Cover, and cook on high for 4 hours.

5. Spoon approximately 1½ cups stew into each of 5 bowls, and serve.

TASTY TIDBIT

Golden Delicious apples work great in slow cooker dishes. They retain some firmness when cooked.

Layered Beef Stew

This delicious layered dish features buttery Yukon Gold potatoes, tasty fresh vegetables, and hearty Swiss chard.

Yield:	Prep time:	Cook time:	Serving size:
8 cups	15 to 20 minutes	4 hours	1½ cups

Each serving has:			
203 calories	26 g protein 3 g total fat	13 g carbohydrates 2 g saturated fat	2 g fiber 296 mg sodium

1 large Yukon Gold potato, sliced into ¼-in. slices

2 lb. top round roast, cut into ½-in. cubes

1 large yellow onion, sliced into ¼-in. slices

10 cloves garlic, peeled

1 medium carrot, peeled and sliced into ¼-in. slices

1 (15-oz.) can whole plum tomatoes, drained

2 large Swiss chard leaves, chopped

¼ cup chopped fresh parsley

1 TB. chopped fresh rosemary or 1 tsp. dried

¼ cup red wine

¼ cup low-sodium beef broth

½ tsp. kosher salt

¼ tsp. black pepper

1. In an 8-quart slow cooker, layer Yukon Gold potato slices, ¼ of top round roast, yellow onion slices, and garlic. Follow with ¼ of top round roast, carrot slices, ¼ of top round roast, plum tomatoes, and Swiss chard. Top with remaining ¼ top round roast, parsley, and rosemary. Pour in red wine and low-sodium beef broth, and season with kosher salt and black pepper.

2. Cover, and cook on high for 4 hours.

3. Spoon approximately 1½ cups stew into each of 5 bowls, and serve.

CULINARY KNOW-HOW

The Yukon Gold potato is a good variety for a stew. It has less starch than a russet and holds up better during cooking.

Roasted Beef and Peppers

In each bite is the subtle taste of slow cooked garlic mingling with the red wine beef broth.

Yield:	Prep time:	Cook time:	Serving size:
2 pounds roast and 4 cups vegetables	10 to 15 minutes	3 hours	3 ounces sliced roast and $\frac{1}{2}$ cup vegetables

Each serving has:			
249 calories	34 g protein 5 g total fat	11 g carbohydrates 2 g saturated fat	3 g fiber 270 mg sodium

2 lb. top round roast

5 cloves garlic, cut into slivers

1 TB. fresh thyme or 1 tsp. dried

1 TB. fresh rosemary or 1 tsp. dried

$\frac{1}{4}$ cup fresh parsley

$\frac{1}{2}$ tsp. kosher salt

$\frac{1}{4}$ tsp. black pepper

2 medium yellow onions, sliced

5 medium red bell peppers, ribs and seeds removed, and quartered lengthwise

$\frac{1}{2}$ cup red wine

$\frac{1}{2}$ cup low-sodium beef broth

1 bay leaf

1. Place top round roast on a cutting board. Using a paring knife, cut small slits into roast. Insert slivered garlic into the slits. Rub roast with thyme, rosemary, parsley, kosher salt, and black pepper.

2. In a slow cooker, layer yellow onions, roast, red bell peppers, red wine, low-sodium beef broth, and bay leaf.

3. Cover, and cook on high for 1 hour or on low for 3 hours. Remove bay leaf.

4. Slice beef and serve 3 thin slices beef with $\frac{1}{2}$ cup onions, peppers, and broth.

TASTY TIDBIT

The long cooking time allows most of the alcohol in this dish to burn off.

Italian Chicken Stew

This robust stew, lively with the flavors of bell peppers and artichokes, is heightened with a trinity of herbs.

Yield:	Prep time:	Cook time:	Serving size:
8 cups	10 to 15 minutes	4 hours	1½ cups

Each serving has:			
258 calories	29 g protein 11 g total fat	11 g carbohydrates 3 g saturated fat	3 g fiber 592 mg sodium

2 lb. boneless, skinless chicken thighs, trimmed

1 large yellow onion, chopped

1 large red bell pepper, ribs and seeds removed, and chopped

2 cloves garlic, chopped

1 (15-oz.) can artichoke hearts in water, drained and rinsed

2 tsp. fresh oregano or ½ tsp. dried

2 tsp. chopped fresh rosemary or ½ tsp. dried

2 tsp. fresh thyme or ½ tsp. dried

2 cups low-sodium chicken broth

¼ tsp. kosher salt

⅛ tsp. black pepper

1. In a slow cooker, combine chicken thighs, yellow onion, red bell pepper, garlic, artichoke hearts, oregano, rosemary, thyme, low-sodium chicken broth, kosher salt, and black pepper.

2. Cover, and cook on high for 4 hours.

3. Spoon approximately 1½ cups stew into each of 5 bowls, and serve.

CULINARY KNOW-HOW

If you prefer to use chicken breasts, add them in the last hour of cooking. That way, they won't be overcooked.

Chipotle Chicken

Smoky chipotle chiles impart a delicious smoky flavor that mingles with the juices from the chicken and the sweetness of the corn and sweet potatoes.

Yield:	Prep time:	Cook time:	Serving size:
8 cups	10 to 15 minutes	4 hours	1½ cups

Each serving has:			
266 calories	28 g protein	18 g carbohydrates	4 g fiber
	9 g total fat	2 g saturated fat	355 mg sodium

2 lb. boneless, skinless chicken thighs, cut into 1-in. cubes

1 medium yellow onion, sliced

1 medium red bell pepper, ribs and seeds removed, and diced

1 clove garlic, minced

1 cup canned black beans, rinsed and drained

1 medium sweet potato, peeled and diced

1 cup frozen corn

1 chipotle pepper in adobo sauce, diced

¼ tsp. kosher salt

⅛ tsp. black pepper

½ cup low-sodium chicken broth

1. Heat a 12-inch, nonstick sauté pan over medium heat, and lightly coat with nonstick cooking spray. Add chicken thighs, and cook for 5 minutes per side.

2. In a slow cooker, combine yellow onion, red bell pepper, garlic, black beans, sweet potato, corn, chipotle pepper, kosher salt, black pepper, and low-sodium chicken broth. Top with chicken thighs.

3. Cover, and cook on high for 4 hours.

4. Spoon approximately 1½ cups stew into each of 5 bowls, and serve.

CULINARY KNOW-HOW

For a slightly different flavor, replace the sweet potato with 1 cup butternut squash.

Beef Stew with Dumplings

Savory beef and wine broth are accompanied by sweet turnips and parsnips in this hearty stew.

Yield:	Prep time:	Cook time:	Serving size:
8 cups	10 to 15 minutes	4½ hours	1 cup

Each serving has:			
326 calories	27 g protein 10 g total fat	25 g carbohydrates 3 g saturated fat	2 g fiber 591 mg sodium

2 lb. beef stew meat, trimmed	1 medium celery stalk, chopped
1 large yellow onion, chopped	1 cup red wine
2 cloves garlic, diced	1 bay leaf
1 medium carrot, peeled and chopped	1 TB. fresh thyme or 1 tsp. dried
1 medium parsnip, peeled and chopped	1½ cups low-sodium beef broth
1 small white turnip, peeled and chopped	¼ tsp. black pepper
	1 (7.5-oz.) can refrigerated buttermilk biscuits

1. Heat a large, heavy pot over medium heat, and lightly coat with nonstick cooking spray. Add beef stew meat, in batches, and cook for about 10 minutes or until brown on all sides. Remove cooked beef to a slow cooker.

2. Add yellow onion, garlic, carrot, parsnip, white turnip, and celery to the pot, and cook for 10 minutes. Add to the slow cooker.

3. Pour red wine into the pot, increase heat to high, and cook for 10 minutes or until wine is reduced by half. Add to the slow cooker.

4. Add bay leaf, thyme, low-sodium beef broth, and black pepper to the slow cooker.

5. Cover and cook on high for 1 hour and on low for 3 hours.

6. Uncover, and arrange uncooked buttermilk biscuits on top. Cover and cook for 20 to 25 more minutes. Remove bay leaf.

7. Spoon 1½ cups stew into each of 4 bowls, top with dumplings, and serve.

TASTY TIDBIT

Browning the meat on the stovetop first caramelizes its sugars, which creates a wonderful depth of flavor in the finished dish.

Brunswick Stew

Bacon adds a bit of a smoky flavor to this chicken stew.

Yield:	Prep time:	Cook time:	Serving size:
12 cups	25 to 30 minutes	4 hours	1½ cups

Each serving has:			
337 calories	30 g protein 11 g total fat	28 g carbohydrates 3 g saturated fat	5 g fiber 532 mg sodium

2¼ lb. boneless, skinless chicken thighs

½ tsp. kosher salt

¼ tsp. black pepper

1 bay leaf

⅛ tsp. crushed red pepper flakes

3 cups low-sodium chicken broth

4 strips center-cut bacon, diced

2 medium yellow onions, diced

4 medium celery stalks, diced

3 medium red potatoes, cut into ½-in. cubes

1 (15-oz.) can whole tomatoes, drained, seeded, and chopped

1 (10-oz.) pkg. frozen lima beans

1½ cups fresh corn kernels (about 2 or 3 ears)

1. In a slow cooker, combine chicken thighs, kosher salt, black pepper, bay leaf, crushed red pepper flakes, low-sodium chicken broth, center-cut bacon, yellow onions, celery, red potatoes, tomatoes, lima beans, and corn.

2. Cover, and cook on high for 4 hours. Remove bay leaf.

3. Spoon 1½ cups stew into each of 8 bowls, and serve.

CULINARY KNOW-HOW

Chicken thighs work well in a slow cooked stew like this one because they stay moist and tender.

Chicken, Mushrooms, and Wild Rice

This hearty and rich stew has a hint of nuttiness from the wild rice and a slight sharpness from Parmesan cheese.

Yield:	Prep time:	Cook time:	Serving size:
10 cups	10 to 15 minutes	4 hours	1¼ cups

Each serving has:			
339 calories	27 g protein 13 g total fat	27 g carbohydrates 4 g saturated fat	2 g fiber 598 mg sodium

⅓ cup wild rice

1 large yellow onion, diced

1 medium celery stalk, diced

2 medium carrots, diced

1 cup sliced button mushrooms

2¼ lb. boneless, skinless chicken thighs, cut into 1-in. cubes

1 TB. fresh thyme or 1 tsp. dried

¼ cup chopped fresh parsley

¼ tsp. black pepper

1½ cups low-sodium chicken broth

1 (7.5-oz.) can refrigerated buttermilk biscuits

1 TB. chopped fresh sage or 1 tsp. dried

2 TB. grated Parmesan cheese

1. In a slow cooker, layer wild rice, yellow onion, celery, carrots, button mushrooms, chicken thighs, thyme, parsley, black pepper, and chicken broth.

2. Cover, and cook on high for 4 hours.

3. Uncover, and arrange uncooked buttermilk biscuits on top of chicken. Sprinkle with sage and Parmesan cheese, cover, and cook for 20 to 25 more minutes.

4. Spoon 1¼ cups stew into each of 8 bowls, top with dumplings, and serve.

TASTY TIDBIT

Wild rice is not rice. It's actually a grass that's native to the Great Lakes region. It counts as a whole grain.

Part
5

Sassy Snacks

A lot of people feel snacks are just for kids and certainly not something anyone desiring to lose weight should be eating. Boy, is that thinking off the mark! Snacks are a healthy eater's secret weapon. They help quench a sweet or savory craving, offering pleasure while preventing an all-out binge. But they do so much more.

Snacks help fill that food lull between meals. You know, that time of day when you start to get hungry but there are still a few hours until your next meal. A properly created snack can help tide you over until mealtime, preventing overeating at the next meal—not a successful weight-loss strategy.

In Part 5, we give you dozens of recipes for sweet bites to satisfy an evening craving, or savory snacks when the midday munchies hit. If you're on the go a lot, check out the portable recipes in Chapter 21 for ideas you can make ahead so they're ready to grab when you need to go.

Savory Bites

In This Chapter

- Super snacks to keep your waistline in check
- Perfect potluck pleasers
- Party-starting appetizers

In this chapter, we give you an array of snacks for when you have a bit more time on your hands and are looking for something savory and a bit more extravagant than chips and salsa.

But these recipes can be much more than just snacks. They make great appetizers before a light dinner or when you're having company. Plus, next time you're headed out to a potluck, you can double or triple one of these recipes and feel good that you're bringing something yummy and healthy to the party.

Silky Deviled Eggs

Relish adds a touch of sweetness to these rich deviled eggs.

Yield:	Prep time:	Cook time:	Serving size:
8 deviled eggs	5 minutes	12 minutes	2 deviled eggs

Each serving has:			
108 calories	6 g protein 8 g total fat	2 g carbohydrates 2 g saturated fat	0 g fiber 386 mg sodium

2 qt. water	½ tsp. kosher salt
4 large eggs	¼ tsp. black pepper
2 TB. low-fat mayonnaise	Pinch paprika
1 TB. sweet pickle relish	

1. In a large pot over medium-high heat, bring water to a boil. Add eggs, and cook for 12 minutes.

2. Remove eggs from water, and run under cold water to stop the cooking process. Peel eggs under running water.

3. Cut eggs in half lengthwise, remove yolk, and place yolks in a small bowl. Add low-fat mayonnaise, sweet pickle relish, kosher salt, and black pepper.

4. Spoon yolk mixture into egg whites, sprinkle with paprika, and serve.

MAKE IT A MEAL

These pair deliciously with a few whole-grain crackers to give you a protein-packed, fiber-rich snack that will keep you feeling full until mealtime.

Velvety Edamame Hummus

A pop of garlic and hint of red pepper enhance this protein-packed dip.

Yield:	Prep time:	Serving size:	
2 cups	5 to 10 minutes	¼ cup	
Each serving has:			
112 calories	6 g protein 8 g total fat	6 g carbohydrates 1 g saturated fat	2 g fiber 119 mg sodium

1½ cups frozen shelled edamame

3 TB. tahini

2 TB. lemon juice

¼ tsp. kosher salt

2 cloves garlic

½ tsp. ground red pepper

1 TB. extra-virgin olive oil

1. In a microwave-safe dish, heat edamame on high, covered, for 2 or 3 minutes.

2. In a food processor fitted with a chopping blade, process edamame, tahini, lemon juice, kosher salt, garlic, red pepper, and extra-virgin olive oil until smooth.

3. Spoon into a serving bowl, and serve.

TASTY TIDBIT

Soybeans are a fantastic source of protein. Research has shown including them regularly in your diet may help prevent certain cancers.

Spicy Sweet Potato Chips

These crunchy sweet potato chips have a touch of heat.

Yield:	Prep time:	Cook time:	Serving size:
48 chips	5 to 10 minutes	20 to 25 minutes	24 chips

Each serving has:			
115 calories	2 g protein	27 g carbohydrates	4 g fiber
	0 g total fat	0 g saturated fat	281 mg sodium

2 medium sweet potatoes, peeled and sliced ⅛-in. thick	¼ tsp. ground cinnamon
Nonstick cooking spray	¼ tsp. cayenne
½ tsp. ground cumin	¼ tsp. kosher salt

1. Preheat the oven to 400°F. Line a baking sheet with parchment paper.

2. In a large bowl, place sweet potato slices and lightly coat with nonstick cooking spray. Sprinkle with cumin, cinnamon, and cayenne, and arrange in a single layer on the prepared baking sheet.

3. Bake for 20 to 25 minutes, turning after 10 to 12 minutes, or until edges begin to brown.

4. Remove from the oven, and sprinkle with kosher salt before serving.

 MAKE IT A MEAL

Serve these chips with a yummy dip made by mixing a bit of cinnamon with plain fat-free Greek yogurt.

Classic Hummus

Warm garlic and cumin add flavor to mild chickpeas.

Yield:	Prep time:	Serving size:
2 cups	5 to 10 minutes	¼ cup

Each serving has:			
167 calories	5 g protein 13 g total fat	13 g carbohydrates 1 g saturated fat	3 g fiber 245 mg sodium

2 cloves garlic

1 (15-oz.) can chickpeas, drained and rinsed

¼ cup tahini

¼ tsp. ground coriander

½ tsp. ground cumin

2 TB. fresh lemon juice

½ tsp. kosher salt

¼ tsp. black pepper

2 TB. extra-virgin olive oil

2 TB. finely chopped fresh parsley

1. In a food processor fitted with a chopping blade, pulse garlic until minced.

2. Add chickpeas, tahini, coriander, cumin, lemon juice, kosher salt, and black pepper, and blend. With the machine running, gradually add extra-virgin olive oil and blend until mixture is smooth.

3. Spread hummus onto a plate using the back of a spoon, sprinkle with parsley, and serve.

Variation: For **Spicy Vegetable Hummus,** add 1 small jalapeño pepper to the food processor with the garlic. In a medium bowl, combine hummus; ½ cup diced tomatoes; ¼ cup diced scallions, both white and green parts (about 2 scallions); and ¼ cup diced green bell pepper. Spread onto a plate using the back of a spoon, sprinkle with parsley, and serve. *Each serving has: 174 calories, 6 g protein, 14 g carbohydrates, 4 g fiber, 11 g total fat, 1 g saturated fat, 292 mg sodium.*

TASTY TIDBIT

Hummus is popular in Middle Eastern and Greek cultures. It can be used as a dip as well as a sandwich spread.

Bruschetta Caprese

Fresh basil, creamy mozzarella, and juicy tomato blend together deliciously in this classic Italian snack.

Yield:	Prep time:	Cook time:	Serving size:
4 bruschetta	5 to 10 minutes	5 to 10 minutes	1 bruschetta

Each serving has:			
170 calories	8 g protein	12 g carbohydrates	1 g fiber
	10 g total fat	5 g saturated fat	260 mg sodium

4 medium slices Italian bread

Nonstick olive oil cooking spray

1 clove garlic

$\frac{1}{3}$ lb. fresh mozzarella cheese, sliced into $\frac{1}{4}$-in.-thick rounds

1 medium tomato, sliced

12 fresh basil leaves

$\frac{1}{4}$ tsp. kosher salt

$\frac{1}{8}$ tsp. black pepper

1. Preheat the broiler to 500°F. Position the oven rack 3 inches from the heat source.

2. Lightly coat Italian bread with nonstick olive oil cooking spray. Place bread on the prepared baking sheet, and broil for 2 or 3 minutes, watching carefully so bread doesn't burn.

3. Lay bread slices on a work surface, and gently rub with garlic. Layer on mozzarella cheese, tomato, and basil. Season with kosher salt and black pepper, and serve.

TASTY TIDBIT

Caprese refers to a dish that has mozzarella, tomato, and basil as its three staple ingredients.

Spinach-Stuffed Mushrooms

Creamy and cheesy spinach is what you'll find in every morsel of these stuffed mushrooms.

Yield:	Prep time:	Cook time:	Serving size:
20 mushrooms	10 to 15 minutes	40 minutes	4 mushrooms

Each serving has:			
175 calories	11 g protein	20 g carbohydrates	6 g fiber
	3 g total fat	3 g saturated fat	479 mg sodium

20 large button mushrooms	¼ cup low-fat cream cheese
1 medium yellow onion, diced	¼ cup grated Parmesan cheese
2 cloves garlic, minced	¼ tsp. kosher salt
½ cup fresh breadcrumbs	⅛ tsp. black pepper
1 TB. chopped fresh parsley	1 cup low-sodium chicken broth
1 cup cooked spinach, chopped and squeezed to remove liquid	

1. Preheat the oven to 350°F.

2. Remove button mushroom caps, and set aside. Chop mushroom stems.

3. Heat a 12-inch sauté pan over medium heat, and lightly coat with nonstick cooking spray. Add yellow onion, garlic, and mushroom stems, and sauté for 10 minutes.

4. In a medium bowl, combine sautéed onion and mushroom mixture, breadcrumbs, parsley, spinach, low-fat cream cheese, Parmesan cheese, kosher salt, and black pepper.

5. Stuff mushroom caps with cream cheese mixture, and set in an ovenproof dish. Pour low-sodium chicken broth in the bottom of the dish, cover with aluminum foil, and bake for 20 minutes. Remove foil, and allow to brown for 10 minutes.

6. Transfer mushrooms to a serving dish, and serve warm.

Variations: For **Stuffed Mushroom Caps,** replace spinach with 1 tablespoon chopped fresh marjoram or 1 teaspoon dried, and ¼ cup chopped sun-dried tomatoes. Add to the bowl with the sautéed onion and mushroom mixture, breadcrumbs, parsley, cream cheese, Parmesan cheese, kosher salt, and black pepper. *Each serving has: 174 calories, 11 g protein, 20 g carbohydrates, 3 g fiber, 6 g total fat, 3 g saturated fat, 456 mg sodium.*

For **Stuffed Tomatoes,** substitute 2 medium ripe tomatoes, sliced in half and center spooned out, for all but ¼ cup mushrooms. Follow the cooking instructions, substituting the tomato cups for mushroom caps. *Each serving has: 184 calories, 11 g protein, 22 g carbohydrates, 4 g fiber, 6 g total fat, 3 g saturated fat, 509 mg sodium.*

TASTY TIDBIT

Spinach is a nutrient-packed vegetable, loaded with vitamins A and K as well as minerals like iron and folate.

Shrimp Toast

After the initial garlic, scallions, and ginger flavors, the shrimp will appear with a toasted sesame finish.

Yield:	Prep time:	Cook time:	Serving size:
32 pieces	15 to 20 minutes	5 minutes	4 pieces

Each serving has:			
179 calories	12 g protein	24 g carbohydrates	1 g fiber
	4 g total fat	1 g saturated fat	344 mg sodium

½ lb. raw shrimp (31 to 40 count, about 18)

2 cloves garlic, minced

2 medium scallions, white and green parts, minced

1 TB. peeled and grated fresh ginger

½ tsp. toasted sesame seed oil

¼ tsp. black pepper

8 slices firm white bread, crusts removed

1. Preheat the broiler to 400°F. Position the oven rack 3 inches from the heat source. Line a baking sheet with parchment paper.

2. In a food processor fitted with a chopping blade, pulse together shrimp, garlic, scallions, ginger, toasted sesame seed oil, and black pepper 8 to 10 times or until mixture is smooth.

3. Spread shrimp mixture onto white bread, and cut bread into quarters.

4. Place shrimp toasts on the prepared baking sheet, and broil for 3 to 5 minutes or until shrimp paste turns opaque. Serve immediately.

TASTY TIDBIT

Garlic, scallions, and ginger are a major flavor combination in Chinese cooking, similar to the onion, carrot, and celery combination called *mirepoix* in French cooking.

Creamy Mushroom Bruschetta

Rich mushroom flavor abounds in this twist on the classic.

Yield:	Prep time:	Cook time:	Serving size:
8 bruschetta	5 to 10 minutes	25 minutes	2 bruschetta

Each serving has:			
192 calories	9 g protein	29 g carbohydrates	3 g fiber
	4 g total fat	2 g saturated fat	499 mg sodium

8 medium slices Italian bread

Nonstick olive oil cooking spray

3 cloves garlic

1 lb. button mushrooms

1 medium yellow onion, diced

1 TB. chopped fresh parsley

1 cup cooked spinach, chopped and squeezed to remove liquid

¼ cup grated Parmesan cheese

¼ tsp. kosher salt

⅛ tsp. black pepper

1. Preheat the broiler to 500°F. Position the oven rack 3 inches from the heat source.

2. Lightly coat Italian bread with nonstick olive oil cooking spray. Place bread on the prepared baking sheet, and broil for 2 or 3 minutes, watching carefully so bread doesn't burn.

3. Remove bread from the oven, and gently rub with garlic.

4. Heat a 12-inch nonstick sauté pan over medium heat, and lightly coat with nonstick cooking spray. Add button mushrooms and yellow onion, and sauté for 15 to 20 minutes or until onions are soft.

5. In a medium bowl, combine mushroom mixture, parsley, spinach, Parmesan cheese, kosher salt, and black pepper. Spread mushroom mixture on bread slices, broil for 2 or 3 minutes, and serve.

 TASTY TIDBIT

In Italian, *bruschetta* means "to roast over coals," so don't worry about a little burnt edge on your finished bruschetta.

Baba Ganoush

Lemon juice brightens the smoky, earthy flavors of this dip.

Yield:	Prep time:	Cook time:	Serving size:
1¼ cups	10 to 15 minutes	30 to 35 minutes	¼ cup

Each serving has:			
207 calories	5 g protein 14 g total fat	18 g carbohydrates 2 g saturated fat	5 g fiber 288 mg sodium

1 medium eggplant (about 1 lb.)	½ tsp. kosher salt
3 cloves garlic	¼ tsp. black pepper
Juice of ½ lemon	2 TB. extra-virgin olive oil
5 TB. tahini	¼ cup finely chopped fresh parsley
½ tsp. ground cumin	3 (4-in.) 100 percent whole-wheat
½ tsp. ground coriander	pitas, cut into wedges

1. Preheat the oven to 400°F.

2. Prick eggplant several times with a fork. Place on a baking sheet, and bake for 30 minutes or until very soft. Remove from the oven, and allow to cool.

3. Peel cooled eggplant, remove seeds, and drain in a colander.

4. In a food processor fitted with a chopping blade, pulse garlic until minced. Add eggplant, lemon juice, tahini, cumin, coriander, kosher salt, and black pepper, and process until smooth.

5. Spread mixture onto a plate using the back of a spoon. Drizzle with extra-virgin olive oil, sprinkle with parsley, and serve with pita wedges.

TASTY TIDBIT

Eggplant is actually a fruit; to be more specific, it's a berry. But we don't recommend topping your cereal with it.

Shrimp and Jicama Salad

Crunchy *jicama* and bright cilantro shine in this light salad.

Yield:	Prep time:	Serving size:
2 cups	5 to 10 minutes	¼ cup

Each serving has:			
211 calories	17 g protein	33 g carbohydrates	12 g fiber
	1 g total fat	0 g saturated fat	320 mg sodium

½ lb. cooked shrimp (31 to 40 count, about 18), diced

2 medium jicama, peeled and diced

1 small red bell pepper, ribs and seeds removed, diced

Juice of 1 lime

¼ cup chopped fresh cilantro

⅛ tsp. kosher salt

⅛ tsp. black pepper

8 rye crisp crackers

1. In a medium bowl, combine shrimp, jicama, and red bell pepper. Add lime juice, cilantro, kosher salt, and black pepper, and mix well.

2. Serve with rye crisp crackers.

DEFINITION

Jicama is a sweet, crisp root vegetable delicious raw or cooked. It's popular in Central American cuisine.

Black Beans and Roasted Red Pepper Hummus

Black beans and cumin give a slight Latin taste to traditional hummus.

Yield:	Prep time:	Serving size:	
2 cups	5 to 10 minutes	½ cup	

Each serving has:			
248 calories	12 g protein	22 g carbohydrates	6 g fiber
	16 g total fat	2 g saturated fat	509 mg sodium

2 cloves garlic	¼ tsp. ground coriander
1 cup canned chickpeas, drained and rinsed	¼ tsp. ground cumin
1 cup canned black beans, drained and rinsed	½ tsp. kosher salt
½ cup jarred roasted red peppers, drained and rinsed	¼ tsp. black pepper
	2 TB. extra-virgin olive oil
¼ cup tahini	2 TB. finely chopped fresh parsley

1. In a food processor fitted with a chopping blade, pulse garlic until minced.

2. Add chickpeas, black beans, red peppers, tahini, coriander, cumin, kosher salt, and black pepper, and blend until smooth. With machine running, gradually add extra-virgin olive oil, and blend until mixture is smooth.

3. Spread hummus onto a plate using the back of a spoon, sprinkle with parsley, and serve.

Variation: For **Roasted Red Pepper Hummus,** eliminate the black beans and increase the chickpeas to 2 cups. Add 2 tablespoons fresh lemon juice, and blend until smooth. Slice 1 English cucumber into rings. Spoon hummus into the center of a plate, surround with sliced cucumber, and serve. *Each serving has: 177 calories, 8 g protein, 15 g carbohydrates, 4 g fiber, 11 g total fat, 1 g saturated fat, 288 mg sodium.*

MAKE IT A MEAL

You can serve this hummus with cut vegetables, tortilla chips, or whole-grain crackers, to name just a few suggestions.

Autumnal Fruit Salad

Creamy cheese and crisp fruit with a hint of sweetness are the stars in this fall-inspired salad.

Yield:	Prep time:	Serving size:	
1½ cups	5 to 10 minutes	1½ cups	

Each serving has:			
318 calories	7 g protein	60 g carbohydrates	10 g fiber
	7 g total fat	4 g saturated fat	287 mg sodium

1 small Gala or Honey Crisp apple, cored and sliced thin

1 small Bartlett pear, cored and sliced thin

2 tsp. black currant jam

2 TB. Camembert cheese, sliced

1 rye crisp cracker

1. In a medium bowl, combine Gala apple, Bartlett pear, and black currant jam.

2. Serve salad with Camembert cheese and rye crisp crackers on the side.

TASTY TIDBIT

What's the difference between jam and preserves? The size of the fruit pieces. Jams contain small, less-distinguishable pieces than preserves.

Mini Meals

Chapter 20

In This Chapter

- More-than-a-snack dishes
- Not-quite-a-meal meals
- Hunger-satisfying and taste bud–pleasing recipes

Once in a while, even though you've been doing your best to eat in a balanced manner, you may find yourself super hungry. Maybe you were more active than usual or you've gone a bit longer between meals. You don't have time to prepare and sit down to a whole meal, but a bowl of cut veggies just won't do it.

That's when mini meals come in. These one-dish meals don't take much prep work and can be eaten without much to-do.

Steamed Artichoke with Aioli

The rich garlic creaminess of the *aioli* is a perfect match for an artichoke.

Yield:	Prep time:	Cook time:	Serving size:
2 artichoke halves	5 to 10 minutes	25 to 30 minutes	1 artichoke half

Each serving has:			
144 calories	3 g protein 10 g total fat	12 g carbohydrates 2 g saturated fat	4 g fiber 557 mg sodium

1 large artichoke	1 TB. lemon juice
½ medium lemon	¼ tsp. kosher salt
¼ cup low-fat mayonnaise	⅛ tsp. black pepper
2 cloves garlic, minced	

1. In a 2-quart pot with a steaming rack over medium-high heat, bring 2 inches water to a boil.

2. Cut artichoke in ½, through stem, and rub flesh with lemon. Place artichokes on the steaming rack, cut side down, and steam for 25 to 30 minutes or until easily pierced with a knife.

3. Meanwhile, in a small bowl, combine mayonnaise, garlic, lemon juice, kosher salt, and black pepper.

4. Remove center portion from artichoke with a spoon, and serve with aioli.

DEFINITION

Aioli is a garlic mayonnaise from the Provence region of southern France. It goes well with fish, meat, and vegetables.

Loaded Potato

Tang from the yogurt is balanced by the creamy cheese, the zip from the scallions, and the salty bacon in this loaded potato.

Yield:	Prep time:	Cook time:	Serving size:
2 potato halves	15 to 20 minutes	10 to 15 minutes	1 potato half

Each serving has:			
194 calories	10 g protein 3 g total fat	32 g carbohydrates 2 g saturated fat	3 g fiber 405 mg sodium

1 large russet potato

2 TB. plain fat-free Greek yogurt

2 TB. shredded reduced-fat cheddar cheese

2 TB. jarred bacon bits

1 medium scallion, diced

⅛ tsp. kosher salt

⅛ tsp. black pepper

1. Wash russet potato, and prick with a fork. Place potato in a microwave-safe dish and cook on high for 6 to 8 minutes. Turn over potato halfway through the cook time.

2. Preheat the oven to 350°F.

3. When potato is cool enough to handle, cut in ½ lengthwise and scoop out the center, leaving ¼-inch walls. Place potato halves, bowl side up, on a baking sheet.

4. In a small bowl, combine potato flesh, Greek yogurt, cheddar cheese, bacon bits, scallion, kosher salt, and black pepper.

5. Evenly divide potato mixture among potato halves, and bake for 5 minutes. Serve hot.

CULINARY KNOW-HOW

When microwaving potatoes, flip them halfway through the cook time to avoid a tough skin on the bottom.

Broiled Tomatoes

Parmesan- and rosemary-flavored breadcrumbs top these sweet tomatoes.

Yield:	Prep time:	Cook time:	Serving size:
6 tomato halves	10 minutes	5 to 10 minutes	2 tomato halves

Each serving has:			
208 calories	7 g protein	25 g carbohydrates	2 g fiber
	8 g total fat	3 g saturated fat	349 mg sodium

1 cup panko breadcrumbs	1 TB. extra-virgin olive oil
¼ cup grated Parmesan cheese	¼ tsp. kosher salt
2 cloves garlic, minced	⅛ tsp. black pepper
2 tsp. fresh rosemary or ½ tsp. dried	3 medium tomatoes, cut in ½

1. Preheat the broiler to 400°F. Position the oven rack 3 inches from the heat source.

2. In a medium bowl, combine panko breadcrumbs, Parmesan cheese, garlic, rosemary, extra-virgin olive oil, kosher salt, and black pepper. Spread mixture over cut side of tomatoes.

3. Place tomatoes on a baking sheet, and broil for 5 to 10 minutes or until brown. Serve hot.

CULINARY KNOW-HOW

You can use other breadcrumbs, but panko are coarser and give a better crunch.

Deviled Ham–Stuffed Baked Potato

Creamy deviled ham, with a bang of Dijon mustard and Worcestershire sauce, are loaded into tender, fluffy potatoes.

Yield:	Prep time:	Cook time:	Serving size:
2 potato halves	15 to 20 minutes	10 to 15 minutes	1 potato half

Each serving has:			
209 calories	15 g protein	20 g carbohydrates	2 g fiber
	7 g total fat	2 g saturated fat	723 mg sodium

1 medium russet potato	1 TB. chopped fresh parsley
¼ lb. sliced low-sodium ham	¼ tsp. smoked paprika
1 TB. low-fat mayonnaise	½ tsp. Worcestershire sauce
1½ tsp. Dijon mustard	Pinch celery seed
Pinch powdered mustard	
¾ small yellow onion, chopped (1 TB.)	

1. Wash russet potato, and prick with a fork. Place potato in a microwave-safe dish and cook on high for 6 to 8 minutes. Turn over potato halfway through the cook time.

2. Preheat the oven to 350°F.

3. When potato is cool enough to handle, cut in ½ lengthwise and scoop out the center, leaving ¼-inch walls. Place potato halves, bowl side up, on a baking sheet.

4. In a food processor fitted with a chopping blade, pulse ham, mayonnaise, Dijon mustard, powdered mustard, yellow onion, parsley, smoked paprika, Worcestershire sauce, and celery seed until smooth.

5. Evenly divide deviled ham mixture among potato halves, and bake for 5 minutes. Serve hot.

CULINARY KNOW-HOW

If you have extra time, you can bake the pricked potatoes in a 400°F oven for about 45 to 60 minutes. This gives the potato flesh a dryer, softer texture.

Couscous-Stuffed Peppers

Bright lemon zest and earthy mushrooms fill these sweet and tender red bell peppers.

Yield:	Prep time:	Cook time:	Serving size:
2 stuffed pepper halves	10 to 15 minutes	25 minutes	1 stuffed pepper half

Each serving has:			
252 calories	10 g protein 3 g total fat	45 g carbohydrates 2 g saturated fat	6 g fiber 356 mg sodium

1 large red bell pepper, cut in half and ribs and stems removed

Nonstick cooking spray

1 small yellow onion, diced

1 clove garlic, minced

1 cup chopped shiitake mushroom caps, stems discarded

½ cup water

½ cup *couscous*

2 TB. grated Parmesan cheese

Zest of 1 lemon

¼ tsp. kosher salt

⅛ tsp. black pepper

1. Preheat the oven to 350°F.

2. Place red bell pepper halves on a baking sheet, and lightly coat with nonstick cooking spray. Bake for 15 to 20 minutes or until sides are soft. Remove from the oven, and keep warm.

3. Meanwhile, lightly coat a 1-quart pot with nonstick cooking spray, and set over medium heat. Add yellow onion, garlic, and shiitake mushrooms. Cover and cook for 5 to 10 minutes or until onions are translucent and mushrooms are soft.

4. Add water, and stir in couscous. Cover, remove from heat, and let rest for 5 minutes.

5. Add Parmesan cheese, lemon zest, kosher salt, and black pepper, and fluff couscous with a fork. Spoon couscous into warm red bell pepper halves, and return peppers to the oven for 5 minutes. Serve hot.

DEFINITION

Couscous is a pasta made from semolina, a coarsely ground durum wheat. It's a staple in northern Africa.

Caramelized Onion Pizza

A fiber-rich pizza crust adds to the nutty flavor when combined with Asiago cheese, sweet caramelized onions, and earthy spinach.

Yield:	Prep time:	Cook time:	Serving size:
1 (8-inch) pizza	5 to 10 minutes	25 to 30 minutes	½ pizza

Each serving has:			
268 calories	12 g protein 5 g total fat	48 g carbohydrates 2 g saturated fat	8 g fiber 557 mg sodium

1 large sweet onion, sliced	2 TB. grated Asiago cheese
1 clove garlic, minced	⅛ tsp. kosher salt
1 (8-in.) premade 100 percent whole-wheat pizza crust	⅛ tsp. black pepper
¼ cup cooked spinach, chopped and squeezed to remove liquid	

1. Preheat the oven to 350°F.

2. Lightly coat a 1-quart pot with nonstick cooking spray, and set over low heat. Add sweet onion and garlic, cover, and cook, stirring occasionally, for 30 to 35 minutes.

3. Place whole-wheat pizza crust on a baking sheet.

4. In a small bowl, combine onion, garlic, spinach, Asiago cheese, kosher salt, and black pepper. Spread mixture on top of pizza crust, and bake for 10 minutes. Serve hot.

TASTY TIDBIT

Even if you're not an onion lover, give this recipe a try. Caramelizing onions makes them super sweet, so you might like them as part of this pizza.

Broiled Salmon Pumpernickel Bread

Protein-rich salmon marries with the dark molasses flavor of the pumpernickel and the creaminess of the herbed mayonnaise in this hearty bread.

Yield:	Prep time:	Cook time:	Serving size:
1 open-face sandwich	5 to 10 minutes	5 to 7 minutes	1 open-face sandwich

Each serving has:			
289 calories	22 g protein 15 g total fat	14 g carbohydrates 3 g saturated fat	2 g fiber 583 mg sodium

1 (3-oz.) salmon fillet	¼ tsp. chopped fresh parsley
1 TB. low-fat mayonnaise	⅛ tsp. kosher salt
1 TB. plain fat-free Greek yogurt	Pinch black pepper
⅛ tsp. chopped fresh rosemary	1 slice pumpernickel bread
⅛ tsp. chopped fresh thyme	

1. Preheat the broiler to 500°F. Position the oven rack 3 inches from the heat source. Line a baking sheet with aluminum foil.

2. Place salmon on the prepared baking sheet, and broil for 5 to 7 minutes.

3. Meanwhile, in a small bowl, combine mayonnaise, Greek yogurt, rosemary, thyme, parsley, kosher salt, and black pepper.

4. Spread mayonnaise mixture on pumpernickel bread, top with salmon, and serve.

CULINARY KNOW-HOW

When broiling salmon or any fish, the white liquid that appears on top is albumin, the protein from the fish. Its appearance tells you the fish is done.

Pear, Walnut, and Cheddar Cheese Salad

The classic flavor combo of sweet, salty, and sharp is all nestled with the peppery arugula in this delightful salad.

Yield:	Prep time:	Serving size:
1½ cups	5 minutes	1½ cups

Each serving has:			
353 calories	11 g protein	44 g carbohydrates	5 g fiber
	18 g total fat	5 g saturated fat	186 mg sodium

1 medium Bartlett pear, cored and chopped

2 TB. chopped walnuts, toasted

1¼ cups shredded reduced-fat cheddar cheese

1 TB. lemon juice

1 TB. honey

½ cup arugula

1. In a small bowl, combine Bartlett pear, walnuts, cheddar cheese, lemon juice, and honey.

2. Place arugula on a plate, spoon salad on top, and serve.

CULINARY KNOW-HOW

The walnuts contribute half the fat to this fruit dish, but it's an extremely heart-healthy fat.

Grab-and-Go Snacks

In This Chapter

- Portable snacks for the road
- Nibbles for when you need to nosh
- A little something extra for your lunch box

These days, it seems like we're always going somewhere. But in the busy-ness we call life, we can't forget or forgo healthy eating. It's crucial to have simple-to-prepare snacks that can be tossed into a lunch bag, brought with you on the way out the door, or packed for a hike or nature walk. We're sure you'll find a few you love in this chapter.

Toasted Pumpkin Seeds

Warming cinnamon, nutmeg, allspice, and cloves encase crunchy pumpkin seeds in this tasty snack.

Yield:	Prep time:	Cook time:	Serving size:
4 cups	5 minutes	40 minutes	¼ cup

Each serving has:			
71 calories	3 g protein 3 g total fat	9 g carbohydrates 1 g saturated fat	3 g fiber 33 mg sodium

4 cups fresh pumpkin seeds, rinsed and dried

Nonstick cooking spray

1 tsp. pumpkin spice blend

¼ tsp. kosher salt

1. Preheat the oven to 300°F. Line a baking sheet with parchment paper.

2. In a small bowl, light spray pumpkin seeds with nonstick cooking spray. Add pumpkin spice blend and kosher salt, and toss to coat.

3. Arrange pumpkin seeds in a single layer on the baking sheet. Bake for 20 minutes.

4. Toss seeds, lightly spray again with nonstick cooking spray, and bake for 20 more minutes. Serve warm.

5. Allow to cool completely, and store in an airtight container for up to 2 weeks.

Variation: To make a spicier version, use 1 teaspoon ground white pepper in place of the pumpkin spice.

Spicy Sweet Potato Chips

These are a sweet and spicy alternative to plain potato chips.

Yield:	Prep time:	Cook time:	Serving size:
30 to 35 chips	5 to 10 minutes	30 to 35 minutes	about 15 chips

Each serving has:			
132 calories	2 g protein 0 g total fat	32 g carbohydrates 0 g saturated fat	5 g fiber 281 mg sodium

2 medium sweet potatoes, peeled
 and sliced into ⅛-in. rounds

Nonstick cooking spray

2 tsp. chili powder

1 tsp. ground cumin

1 tsp. brown sugar

Pinch cayenne

¼ tsp. kosher salt

1 small lime, sliced into wedges

1. Preheat the oven to 300°F. Line 2 baking sheets with parchment paper.

2. Arrange sweet potato rounds in a single layer on the prepared baking sheets. Lightly spray with nonstick cooking spray. Turn over, and spray again. Bake for 30 to 35 minutes or until edges begin to curl.

3. Meanwhile, in a small bowl, combine chili powder, cumin, brown sugar, cayenne, and kosher salt.

4. In a large bowl, toss together sweet potato chips and spice mixture. Serve with lime wedges.

5. Allow to cool completely, and store in an airtight container for up to a week.

CULINARY KNOW-HOW

Adding the spice mixture after cooking prevents the spices from burning.

Nuts and Fruit

Crunchy and salty nuts combine with chewy and sweet dried fruit with just the right hint of spice.

Yield:	Prep time:	Cook time:	Serving size:
2½ cups	5 minutes	7 minutes	¼ cup

Each serving has:			
154 calories	3 g protein	14 g carbohydrates	3 g fiber
	11 g total fat	1 g saturated fat	27 mg sodium

½ cup chopped walnuts
½ cup slivered almonds
½ cup pecan halves
½ tsp. ground cinnamon
¼ tsp. ground allspice

⅛ tsp. kosher salt
¼ cup dried cranberries
¼ cup chopped dried apricots
½ cup raisins

1. Preheat the oven to 350°F. Line a baking sheet with parchment paper.

2. Arrange walnuts, almonds, and pecans on the prepared baking sheet, and bake for 7 minutes.

3. In a medium bowl, combine roasted nuts, cinnamon, allspice, kosher salt, cranberries, apricots, and raisins.

4. Store in an airtight container.

CULINARY KNOW-HOW

Nuts cook at different rates, depending on their size and if they're whole or chopped. You can roast several varieties at the same time as long as they're physically separated on the baking sheet and can be removed when they're finished roasting.

Pumpkin-Spiced Popcorn

You'll love this sweetly spiced version of the traditional.

Yield:	Prep time:	Serving size:	
3 cups	5 minutes	3 cups	
Each serving has:			
161 calories	3 g protein 9 g total fat	19 g carbohydrates 5 g saturated fat	3 g fiber 70 mg sodium

3 cups freshly popped plain
    air-popped or light microwave
    popcorn

2 tsp. melted butter

¾ to 1 tsp. pumpkin pie spice

1. In a large bowl, combine warm popcorn, butter, and pumpkin pie spice.

2. Serve warm.

TASTY TIDBIT

Popcorn is a deliciously easy source of whole grains. To ensure you get the largest popped kernels, it's best to store unpopped popcorn in an airtight container in the refrigerator.

Fiery Popcorn

Hot and smoky, this popcorn is a nice change to a classic version.

Yield:	Prep time:	Cook time:	Serving size:
16 cups	15 to 20 minutes	10 minutes	4 cups

Each serving has:			
178 calories	3 g protein	21 g carbohydrates	4 g fiber
	12 g total fat	1 g saturated fat	120 mg sodium

3 TB. canola oil

½ cup unpopped popcorn

1 TB. smoked paprika

1 TB. hot paprika

¼ tsp. kosher salt

1. In a 4-quart pot with a lid over medium heat, heat canola oil. Add a few kernels of popcorn, cover, and wait for kernels to pop.

2. After they pop, add remaining popcorn, cover, and cook, carefully shaking the pot back and forth on the burner for 5 to 10 minutes or until the popping begins to slow. Remove the pot from heat.

3. In a large bowl, combine popcorn, smoked paprika, hot paprika, and kosher salt.

4. Serve warm.

TASTY TIDBIT

Smoked paprika is made by drying the pepper over wood smoke. Paprika is also used to color henna.

Peanut Butter Banana Roll-Ups

Creamy peanut butter and a sweet banana are encased in a warm, cinnamon-y tortilla in this tasty snack.

Yield:	Prep time:	Cook time:	Serving size:
2 wraps	15 to 20 minutes	5 minutes	½ wrap

Each serving has:			
192 calories	6 g protein 10 g total fat	23 g carbohydrates 2 g saturated fat	3 g fiber 235 mg sodium

2 (8-in.) 100 percent whole-wheat tortillas	½ tsp. ground cinnamon
Nonstick cooking spray	4 TB. creamy peanut butter
1½ tsp. sugar	1 medium banana, peeled and sliced

1. Preheat the oven to 350°F. Line a baking sheet with parchment paper.

2. Place 2 whole-wheat tortillas on the prepared baking sheet, lightly spray with nonstick cooking spray, sprinkle with sugar and cinnamon, and bake for 5 minutes.

3. Spread 2 tablespoons peanut butter on each tortilla, top each with ½ sliced banana. Roll, cut in half, and serve.

TASTY TIDBIT

The combination of peanut butter and banana is associated with Elvis Presley, but the one ingredient missing from The King's version is crispy bacon. (While a nice treat once in a while, due to its high sodium and fat content, the bacon version shouldn't be an everyday treat.)

Granola Bars

These chewy bars are packed with flavor and nutrition—and chocolate in every bite.

Yield:	Prep time:	Cook time:	Serving size:
16 bars	10 minutes	18 to 22 minutes	1 bar

Each serving has:			
278 calories	5 g protein 11 g total fat	42 g carbohydrates 4 g saturated fat	3 g fiber 99 mg sodium

4 cups rolled oats

½ cup all-purpose flour

½ cup whole-wheat flour

1 tsp. baking soda

1 tsp. vanilla extract

3 TB. butter, melted

¼ cup canola oil

½ cup honey

⅓ cup light brown sugar, firmly packed

1 cup miniature semisweet chocolate chips

1. Preheat the oven to 325°F. Lightly spray a 9×13-inch pan with nonstick cooking spray.

2. In a large bowl, combine rolled oats, all-purpose flour, whole-wheat flour, baking soda, vanilla extract, melted butter, canola oil, honey, and light brown sugar.

3. Stir in semisweet chocolate chips.

4. Lightly press mixture into the prepared pan, and bake for 18 to 22 minutes or until golden brown.

5. Let cool for 10 minutes, and cut into 16 bars. Let bars cool completely in the pan before removing or serving.

6. Store in an airtight container for up to 2 weeks or in the freezer for up to 2 months.

CULINARY KNOW-HOW

If you happen to be eating one of these at home, zap it in the microwave for a few seconds. It's extra yummy warm.

Cape Cod Trail Mix

Dried cranberries, nuts, raisins, and pretzels come together to provide the perfect balance of sweet and salty in this on-the-go snack.

Yield:	Prep time:	Serving size:	
5½ cups	2 minutes	½ cup	

Each serving has:			
286 calories	7 g protein	33 g carbohydrates	3 g fiber
	17 g total fat	3 g saturated fat	135 mg sodium

1½ cups dried cranberries

1 cup peanuts

1 cup chopped walnuts

1 cup yogurt-covered raisins

1 cup mini pretzels

1. In a large bowl, combine cranberries, peanuts, walnuts, yogurt-covered raisins, and pretzels.

2. Store in an airtight container.

CULINARY KNOW-HOW

You can mix and match this trail mix to suit your taste. Add more of one ingredient, less of another, switch nuts, or whatever you like.

S'mores Trail Mix

You're sure to love this sweet snack with flavors reminiscent of sitting by the campfire.

Yield:	Prep time:	Serving size:
5 cups	2 minutes	½ cup

Each serving has:			
292 calories	7 g protein	39 g carbohydrates	2 g fiber
	14 g total fat	5 g saturated fat	131 mg sodium

1½ cups honey graham cereal

1 cup peanuts

1 cup mini marshmallows

1 cup raisins

1 cup milk chocolate chips

1. In a large bowl, combine honey graham cereal, peanuts, mini marshmallows, raisins, and milk chocolate chips.

2. Store in an airtight container.

TASTY TIDBIT

The combination of protein, fat, and carbohydrates is the reason trail mixes like this are ideal snacks for hiking and other activities.

Sweet Nothings

Chapter 22

In This Chapter

- Fantastic fondues
- Sweet cakes and custard
- Fruity favorites
- New twists on classic treats

You'll notice we didn't call this chapter "Desserts." We have a couple reasons for that. First, when you're trying to eat healthy or lose weight, it's important to get out of the mind-set of always needing a dessert after a meal. By not labeling any of our dishes as desserts, we're helping get you started on that way of thinking.

Also, who says a sweet treat can only be enjoyed as dessert? When you're looking for a mid-afternoon snack and feel like something a bit on the sweet side, a couple pieces of Sweet Bruschetta or some fruit dipped into Caramel Fondue or Chocolate Fondue might just hit the spot.

Caramel Fondue

Sweet, warm, gooey caramel is delicious paired with crisp fall fruit.

Yield:	Prep time:	Cook time:	Serving size:
4 cups	5 minutes	10 minutes	¼ cup

Each serving has:			
137 calories	4 g protein 1 g total fat	29 g carbohydrates 0 g saturated fat	2 g fiber 78 mg sodium

1 (14-oz.) bag caramels

1 (12-oz.) can fat-free evaporated milk

2 medium Golden Delicious apples, cored and sliced

2 medium Bartlett pears, cored and sliced

1. In a 1-quart pot over medium heat, combine caramels and fat-free evaporated milk. Bring to a simmer, stirring occasionally.

2. Serve with long forks to make dipping Golden Delicious apples and Bartlett pears easy.

TASTY TIDBIT

Evaporated milk is milk from which 60 percent of the water has been evaporated. When canned, it's a shelf-stable product.

Chocolate Fondue

This rich, creamy, and velvety chocolate is delightful paired with sweet dippers.

Yield:	Prep time:	Cook time:	Serving size:
4 cups	5 minutes	15 minutes	¼ cup

Each serving has:			
139 calories	2 g protein	21 g carbohydrates	1 g fiber
	6 g total fat	4 g saturated fat	79 mg sodium

2½ cups water

1½ cups semisweet chocolate morsels

⅛ tsp. ground cinnamon

1 tsp. cornstarch

½ lb. fresh strawberries, washed and hulled

½ (9-in.) angel food cake, cut into cubes

1. In a 2-quart pot over medium heat, bring 2 cups water to a simmer. Stir in semisweet chocolate morsels and cinnamon until cinnamon dissolves.

2. In a small bowl, combine cornstarch and remaining ½ cup water. Whisk into chocolate.

3. Bring mixture to a boil, whisking continuously. Remove from heat. When it stops boiling, return to heat.

4. Repeat step 3, three times in total, whisking constantly each time.

5. Serve with long forks to make dipping strawberries and angel food cake cubes into fondue easy.

CULINARY KNOW-HOW

Bringing the fondue to a boil three times helps make it deliciously thick.

Sweet Bruschetta

Creamy *mascarpone* and crunchy graham crackers are the cornerstones in this sweet take on an Italian classic.

Yield:	Prep time:	Serving size:	
8 bruschetta	10 minutes	2 bruschetta	

Each serving has:			
172 calories	3 g protein	19 g carbohydrates	1 g fiber
	10 g total fat	5 g saturated fat	77 mg sodium

2 TB. plus 2 tsp. mascarpone cheese

4 (2½×5-in.) pieces graham crackers, each broken in ½ to form squares

8 medium fresh strawberries, hulled and chopped

4 tsp. honey

1. Spread an equal amount of mascarpone cheese onto each graham cracker square.

2. Sprinkle strawberries onto crackers, drizzle with honey, and serve.

DEFINITION

Mascarpone is an Italian cheese made from cream. If you can't find it, you can use softened reduced-fat cream cheese in its place.

Pumpkin Custard

This custard has all the creamy and spicy goodness of pumpkin pie without the crust.

Yield:	Prep time:	Cook time:	Serving size:
6 custards	5 to 10 minutes	30 to 35 minutes	1 custard

Each serving has:			
177 calories	4 g protein	40 g carbohydrates	3 g fiber
	2 g total fat	1 g saturated fat	30 mg sodium

1 (15-oz.) can pumpkin purée	1 tsp. ground cinnamon
1 (12-oz.) can fat-free evaporated milk	½ tsp. ground ginger
¾ cup honey	¼ tsp. ground cloves
	2 large eggs, beaten

1. Preheat the oven to 350°F. Lightly spray 6 (½-cup) ramekins with nonstick cooking spray.

2. In a large bowl, combine pumpkin purée, fat-free evaporated milk, honey, cinnamon, ginger, cloves, and eggs.

3. Place ramekins in a casserole dish, and fill each with pumpkin purée. Fill casserole dish with hot water, halfway up the sides of the ramekins. Bake for 30 to 35 minutes or until a cake tester inserted into center of custard comes out clean.

CULINARY KNOW-HOW

When measuring honey, molasses, or any other sticky ingredient, lightly spray the measuring cup with nonstick cooking spray first to help the sticky ingredient pour out easily and leave a cleaner cup. This also helps ensure you also get all of your ingredient without leaving some in the cup.

Peach Shortcake

A touch of cinnamon warms up this peachy take on shortcake.

Yield:	Prep time:	Cook time:	Serving size:
6 shortcakes	15 minutes	15 minutes	1 shortcake

Each serving has:			
193 calories	3 g protein	38 g carbohydrates	2 g fiber
	5 g total fat	2 g saturated fat	280 mg sodium

1 cup baking mix	1 TB. butter, softened
2 TB. plus ¼ cup sugar	2 (12-oz.) bags frozen peach slices, thawed
¼ cup skim milk	½ tsp. ground cinnamon
2 TB. liquid egg substitute	

1. Preheat the oven to 400°F. Line a 6-cup muffin pan with paper liners.

2. In a medium bowl, combine baking mix, 2 tablespoons sugar, skim milk, liquid egg substitute, and butter until well combined. Do not overmix.

3. Fill prepared muffin cups ⅔ full. Bake for 15 minutes. Remove shortcakes from the pan immediately, and place on a wire rack to cool slightly.

4. Meanwhile, in a medium saucepan over medium-high heat, combine peaches, remaining ¼ cup sugar, and cinnamon. Bring to a boil, reduce heat to low, and simmer, stirring occasionally, for 10 minutes or until juices thicken a bit.

5. To serve, split shortcakes in half, place bottoms on plates, spoon ½ cup peaches on top, add shortcake tops on peaches, top with another ½ cup peaches, and serve.

CULINARY KNOW-HOW

If peaches are in season, feel free to replace the frozen peaches with 2 pounds fresh peaches, peeled, pitted, and sliced. Simmer peach sauce until they reach desired softness.

Angel Food Cake Trifle

Sweet strawberries, creamy pudding, and delicate cake combine here—be sure to get some of each in every bite!

Yield:	Prep time:	Cook time:	Serving size:
6 cups	40 to 45 minutes	10 minutes	1 cup

Each serving has:			
198 calories	5 g protein	44 g carbohydrates	2 g fiber
	0 g total fat	0 g saturated fat	318 mg sodium

2 cups chopped and hulled fresh strawberries

¼ cup sugar

½ (9-in.) angel food cake, sliced

1 (3.8-oz.) box vanilla instant pudding, prepared

1 cup fat-free plain Greek yogurt

1. In a medium bowl, combine 1 cup strawberries and sugar, and mash strawberries with a fork or potato masher.

2. Mix in remaining 1 cup strawberries, cover, and refrigerate for 30 minutes.

3. In a decorative glass bowl, put down a layer of angel food cake slices. Top with a layer of vanilla instant pudding, follow with chilled strawberry mixture, and finish with Greek yogurt.

Variation: For **Chocolate-Covered-Strawberry Trifle,** substitute chocolate instant pudding for the vanilla. Omit the sugar. In place of the yogurt, use 1 cup nondairy whipped topping. Slice strawberries and cube the angel food cake. Layer ½ of cake, ½ of pudding, ½ of strawberries, and ½ of whipped topping. Repeat layers. *Each serving has: 183 calories, 2 g protein, 38 g carbohydrates, 2 g fiber, 3 g total fat, 2 g saturated fat, 269 mg sodium.*

TASTY TIDBIT

Angel food cake is a low-fat dessert because it's made primarily with egg whites, which are virtually fat free.

Mint-Poached Pears

Here, mild pears are enhanced by a sweet mint sauce with a hint of licorice.

Yield:	Prep time:	Cook time:	Serving size:
4 pears	5 to 10 minutes	15 minutes	1 pear

Each serving has:			
198 calories	1 g protein 1 g total fat	50 g carbohydrates 0 g saturated fat	4 g fiber 0 mg sodium

1 qt. strong mint tea	6 cardamom pods
½ cup sugar	Zest of 1 lemon
1 (2-in.) cinnamon stick	4 medium Bosc pears, peeled, cut
3 star anise pods	in ½ lengthwise, and cored

1. In a shallow 2-quart saucepan, combine mint tea, sugar, cinnamon stick, star anise pods, cardamom pods, and lemon zest. Bring to a boil, and reduce heat to low.

2. Add Bosc pears and enough water to cover pears. Cover with a piece of parchment paper, and cook for about 15 minutes or until pears are easily pierced with a knife. Remove pears, and strain solids from liquid. Return liquid to the pan, and cook for 10 minutes or until liquid is reduced to a syrup consistency.

3. Place 1 pear on each of 4 plates, spoon sauce over top, and serve.

Variation: For **Port-Poached Pears,** substitute ½ (750-milliliter) bottle port wine for the mint tea, reduce the sugar to ⅓ cup, and swap out the lemon zest for orange zest. *Each serving has: 315 calories, 1 g protein, 55 g carbohydrates, 4 g fiber, 1 g total fat, 0 g saturated fat, 9 mg sodium.*

CULINARY KNOW-HOW

For this recipe, you don't want to use commercially bottled teas. They're full of sugar. Instead, buy mint-flavored tea bags and brew your own tea.

Peach Cobbler

Sweet peaches combine with a crunchy topping in this comfort food dish.

Yield:	Prep time:	Cook time:	Serving size:
5 cups	5 to 10 minutes	30 minutes	1 cup

Each serving has:			
233 calories	4 g protein 0 g total fat	54 g carbohydrates 0 g saturated fat	1 g fiber 253 mg sodium

½ cup sugar	1 cup skim milk
1 cup all-purpose flour	1 (15-oz.) can sliced peaches in
1 to ½ tsp. baking powder	juice, with juice
⅛ tsp. kosher salt	

1. Preheat the oven to 400°F. Lightly coat a 6-cup baking dish with nonstick cooking spray.

2. In a medium bowl, combine sugar, all-purpose flour, baking powder, and kosher salt. Blend in skim milk. Batter will be lumpy. Pour batter into the baking dish. Do not stir.

3. Add peaches and juice all at once. Do not stir.

4. Bake for 30 minutes or until golden brown. Cobbler will rise up the sides of the pan.

Variation: For **Apple Cobbler,** substitute 2 cups chunky applesauce for the canned peaches. *Each serving has: 220 calories, 4 g protein, 52 g carbohydrates, 1 g fiber, 0 g total fat, 0 g saturated fat, 241 mg sodium.*

CULINARY KNOW-HOW

Be sure to select peaches canned in juice. Syrup-packed fruit contains far more sugar and unnecessary calories.

Rice Pudding

This creamy, warm rice pudding features a light, tropical flavor.

Yield:	Prep time:	Cook time:	Serving size:
6 cups	5 minutes	2 hours	1 cup

Each serving has:			
245 calories	6 g protein 8 g total fat	38 g carbohydrates 6 g saturated fat	1 g fiber 90 mg sodium

¾ cup medium- or long-grain rice	2 large eggs, beaten
1½ cups water	½ cup brown sugar
2 cups skim milk	¼ cup shredded coconut
1 (15-oz.) can lite coconut milk	

1. In a 2-quart pot with a tight-fitting lid over medium-high heat, combine medium- or long-grain rice and water. Cover, bring to a boil, reduce heat to low, and cook for 12 minutes. Do not uncover. Remove the pot from heat, and allow to rest for 5 minutes.

2. Preheat the oven to 300°F. Lightly coat a 2-quart casserole dish with nonstick cooking spray.

3. In a large bowl, combine skim milk, lite coconut milk, eggs, brown sugar, and shredded coconut.

4. Add cooked rice, and stir to blend. Pour mixture into the prepared casserole dish, and bake for 1 hour, 40 minutes or until golden brown on top.

Variation: For **Raisin and Rice Pudding,** substitute 2 cups skim milk for lite coconut milk, ½ cup honey for the brown sugar, and ½ cup raisins for the coconut. *Each serving has: 278 calories, 10 g protein, 56 g carbohydrates, 1 g fiber, 2 g total fat, 1 g saturated fat, 114 mg sodium.*

TASTY TIDBIT

If you omit the sugar, you can enjoy rice pudding as a savory dish. You could add lemon zest or your favorite herbs.

Apple Crisp

Brown sugar, cinnamon, and nutmeg combine with the natural sweetness of dates, raisins, and apples to create a treat that's both yummy and full of fiber.

Yield:	Prep time:	Cook time:	Serving size:
4 cups	10 to 15 minutes	40 to 45 minutes	½ cup

Each serving has:			
267 calories	3 g protein 1 g total fat	66 g carbohydrates 0 g saturated fat	8 g fiber 3 mg sodium

1 cup pitted dates	¼ cup raisins
2 cups hot water	3 TB. brown sugar
1 cup rolled oats	¼ cup all-purpose flour
½ tsp. ground cinnamon	
¼ tsp. ground nutmeg	
8 medium Gala, Honey Crisp, or Golden Delicious apples, peeled, cored, and cut into wedges	

1. Preheat the oven to 325°F.

2. In a small bowl, combine dates and hot water. Set aside to soak for 10 minutes. Remove dates and reserve liquid.

3. In a food processor fitted with a chopping blade, combine rolled oats, cinnamon, and nutmeg. With the machine running, add soaked dates one at a time. Mixture will resemble a coarse meal.

4. In a medium bowl, toss together Gala apple slices, raisins, brown sugar, and all-purpose flour.

5. Place apple slices in a shallow baking dish, add reserved liquid from dates, and top with date crumbs. Cover with aluminum foil, and bake for 40 to 45 minutes or until apples are soft and bubbling.

TASTY TIDBIT

The largest date-producing countries are located in the Middle East and North Africa. In their markets, you can find as many as 30 to 40 different varieties. Two popular varieties are Medjool and Deglet; both are grown in California.

S'mores Pie

Crispy toasted marshmallows top a creamy chocolate filling in this fun spin on the classic campfire treat.

Yield:	Prep time:	Cook time:	Serving size:
1 (9-inch) pie	20 minutes, plus 3 or 4 hours chill time	13 minutes	1/8 of pie

Each serving has:

310 calories	4 g protein	52 g carbohydrates	2 g fiber
	10 g total fat	5 g saturated fat	284 mg sodium

20 (2½-in. square) graham crackers, finely crushed (1½ cups)	2 (3.9-oz.) boxes chocolate instant pudding mix
⅓ cup butter, melted	2 cups skim milk
3 TB. sugar	1½ cups mini marshmallows

1. Preheat the oven to 350°F.

2. In a medium bowl, combine graham cracker crumbs, butter, and sugar. Press mixture into the bottom and up the sides of a 9-inch pie pan to form a crust. Bake for 10 minutes, and allow crust to cool.

3. In a medium bowl, whisk chocolate instant pudding with skim milk for 2 minutes. Spoon into cooled crust, and chill 3 or 4 hours.

4. When ready to serve, preheat the broiler.

5. Sprinkle mini marshmallows evenly over pie, and broil for 2 or 3 minutes or until marshmallows begin to puff and turn light brown.

6. Serve immediately. Store leftovers in the refrigerator.

CULINARY KNOW-HOW

For a nonchocolate version, try a vanilla wafer crust and vanilla pudding, and top with mandarin oranges. Skip the broiling.

Chapter 23

Thirst Quenchers

In This Chapter

- Cool and refreshing drinks
- Warm and comforting mugfuls
- All-natural sippers

Often we get in drink ruts. A glass of ice-cold water or a soda on a hot day. A mug of steaming hot tea or coffee on a chilly afternoon. But why not treat yourself to something a little more interesting—and a lot more flavorful?

There's nothing like a tall, cold glass of homemade lemonade on a muggy afternoon. Sure, you could always mix up an instant powder with some water. But when you do that, you often end up with preservatives and artificial flavorings. For just a few minutes more, you could be sipping a glass of limeade made with real, honest-to-goodness limes or enjoying a mug of hot chocolate that actually has *real chocolate* in it.

Plus, these recipes make multiple servings, and most can be made ahead up to a point. So take a few minutes on one day to do all the prep work, and stick the syrup mixture in the fridge. The next time you want an all-natural thirst quencher, all you need to do is add water, mix, and enjoy.

Ginger Spritzer

The warming, slight spiciness of ginger balances with the perfect amount of sweetness in this fun spritzer.

Yield:	Prep time:	Cook time:	Serving size:
8 cups syrup	1 hour	5 minutes	1 (1½-cup) drink
Each serving has:			

14 calories	0 g protein	4 g carbohydrates	0 g fiber
	0 g total fat	0 g saturated fat	0 mg sodium

¼ lb. fresh ginger, washed and unpeeled

1 qt. water

¾ cup sugar

1 cup soda water per serving

1. In a food processor fitted with a chopping blade, pulse ginger 3 times for 2 seconds each time.

2. In a large saucepan over medium-high heat, bring water to a boil. Add sugar, and stir until sugar dissolves. Remove from heat.

3. Add ginger to the saucepan, and allow to steep for 1 hour.

4. Strain and refrigerate.

5. Serve ½ cup ginger syrup with 1 cup soda water in a tall glass with crushed ice.

Variation: For **Hot Ginger Tea,** replace 1 cup soda water with ½ cup hot water. *Each serving has: 14 calories, 0 g protein, 4 g carbohydrates, 0 g fiber, 0 g total fat, 0 g saturated fat, 0 mg sodium.*

TASTY TIDBIT

Soda water, also called carbonated water or seltzer, is plain water with carbonation added to make it fizzy. It's sodium and calorie free. Club soda, while also calorie free, contains about 50 milligrams sodium per 8-ounce serving.

Lemonade

This refreshing summertime favorite combines the perfect amount of tart and sweet.

Yield:	Prep time:	Cook time:	Serving size:
8 cups syrup	20 minutes	5 minutes	1 (1½-cup) drink

Each serving has:			
18 calories	0 g protein 0 g total fat	5 g carbohydrates 0 g saturated fat	0 g fiber 8 mg sodium

9 medium lemons	⅛ tsp. kosher salt
7 cups water	Lemon slices (optional)
1 cup sugar	1 cup cold water per serving

1. Roll 8 lemons on a cutting board to loosen juice inside. Slice 8 lemons in half, squeeze out juice, and reserve juice and rinds.

2. In a large saucepan over medium-high heat, bring 7 cups water to a boil. Add sugar, and stir until sugar dissolves.

3. Remove from heat, add reserved lemon rinds, and allow to steep, stirring occasionally, for 15 minutes.

4. Strain into a pitcher, add reserved lemon juice, and stir. Taste and add kosher salt. Refrigerate until needed.

5. Serve ½ cup lemon syrup with 1 cup cold water in a tall glass with crushed ice and garnished with lemon slices (if using).

Variations: For a **Lemonade Spritzer,** substitute 1 cup soda water for 1 cup water. *Each serving has: 18 calories, 0 g protein, 5 g carbohydrates, 0 g fiber, 0 g total fat, 0 g saturated fat, 8 mg sodium.*

For **Limeade,** substitute limes for the lemons. *Each serving has: 18 calories, 0 g protein, 6 g carbohydrates, 0 g fiber, 0 g total fat, 0 g saturated fat, 8 mg sodium.*

For a **Limeade Spritzer,** substitute 1 cup water for 1 cup soda water. *Each serving has: 18 calories, 0 g protein, 6 g carbohydrates, 0 g fiber, 0 g total fat, 0 g saturated fat, 8 mg sodium.*

CULINARY KNOW-HOW

Rolling lemons and limes on a hard surface before squeezing helps loosen the juice inside so you extract more juice.

Cherry Fizzy

A bright cherry flavor enhances this homemade and healthy version of soda.

Yield:	Prep time:	Serving size:	
2 cups	5 minutes	1 (1-cup) drink	
Each serving has:			
70 calories	0 g protein 0 g total fat	17 g carbohydrates 0 g saturated fat	0 g fiber 8 mg sodium

1 cup mineral or seltzer water   1 cup cherry juice

1. In a tall glass, combine mineral water and cherry juice.

2. Chill until ready to drink.

Variations: For a **Blueberry Fizzy,** replace cherry juice with blueberry juice. *Each serving has: 65 calories, 0 g protein, 16 g carbohydrates, 0 g fiber, 0 g total fat, 0 g saturated fat, 8 mg sodium.*

For a **Peach Fizzy,** replace cherry juice with peach nectar. *Each serving has: 67 calories, 0 g protein, 17 g carbohydrates, 0 g fiber, 0 g total fat, 0 g saturated fat, 9 mg sodium.*

TASTY TIDBIT

Next time you're craving a carbonated drink, skip the soda and use this recipe to turn any of your favorite juices or nectars into a healthy alternative.

Mulled Cider

Allspice, nutmeg, cloves, and more blend with warm cider to create a virtual apple pie in a glass.

Yield:	Prep time:	Cook time:	Serving size:
4 cups	5 minutes	30 minutes	1 cup

Each serving has:			
130 calories	0 g protein 0 g total fat	32 g carbohydrates 0 g saturated fat	0 g fiber 25 mg sodium

1 (2-in.) cinnamon stick	4 whole cloves
1 star anise	1 qt. apple cider
3 allspice berries	Zest of 1 medium orange
¼ grated nutmeg seed	Juice of 1 medium orange

1. In a 6-inch square of cheesecloth, wrap cinnamon stick, star anise, allspice berries, nutmeg seed, and cloves. Secure with a string.

2. In a large saucepan over medium heat, combine spices, apple cider, orange zest, and orange juice. Cover, bring to a simmer, and simmer for 30 minutes.

3. Strain and serve.

Variation: For **Pomegranate Cider,** decrease the apple cider to 3 cups and add 1 cup pomegranate juice. *Each serving has: 135 calories, 0 g protein, 33 g carbohydrates, 0 g fiber, 0 g total fat, 0 g saturated fat, 26 mg sodium.*

CULINARY KNOW-HOW

To save you the step of straining, put all the spices in a tea ball or wrap in cheesecloth. Then, when you're ready to serve, all you have to do is lift out the tea ball or spice sack.

Hot Cocoa

You'll love the hint of cinnamon in this thick, rich chocolate drink inspired by Mexican hot cocoa.

Yield:	Prep time:	Cook time:	Serving size:
3½ to 4 cups	5 minutes	15 minutes	½ cup

Each serving has:			
200 calories	3 g protein 14 g total fat	23 g carbohydrates 10 g saturated fat	3 g fiber 0 mg sodium

2½ cups water

12 to 14 oz. semisweet chocolate

⅛ tsp. ground cinnamon

1 tsp. cornstarch

1. In a 2-quart pot over medium-high heat, bring 2 cups water to a boil. Reduce heat to low, and stir in semisweet chocolate and cinnamon until melted and well combined.

2. In a small bowl, combine cornstarch and remaining ½ cup water. Whisk into chocolate mixture, and bring to a boil, whisking continuously. Remove from heat. When mixture stops bubbling, return to heat.

3. Repeat previous step 2 more times, whisking constantly.

4. Serve hot in small cups.

TASTY TIDBIT

To give this drink a boost of calcium and protein, use skim or 1 percent milk in place of the water.

Glossary

aioli A garlic mayonnaise from the Provence region of southern France that goes well with fish, meat, and vegetables.

agave nectar A sweetener derived from the sap of the agave plant. Its flavor is a cross between honey and maple syrup.

al dente Italian for "against the teeth," this term refers to pasta or rice that's neither soft nor hard but just slightly firm against the teeth.

all-purpose flour Flour that contains only the inner part of the wheat grain. It's suitable for everything from cakes to gravies.

allspice A spice named for its flavor echoes of several spices (cinnamon, cloves, nutmeg) used in many desserts and in rich marinades and stews.

andouille sausage A sausage made with highly seasoned pork chitterlings and tripe. It's a standard component of many Cajun dishes.

antipasto A classic Italian-style appetizer that includes an assortment of meats, cheeses, and vegetables such as prosciutto, capicolla, mozzarella, mushrooms, and olives.

arborio rice A plump Italian rice used for, among other purposes, risotto.

artichoke heart The center part of the artichoke flower, often found canned in grocery stores.

arugula A spicy-peppery green with leaves that resemble a dandelion and have a distinctive and very sharp flavor.

Asian rice noodle A long, thin, translucent white noodle. They're sold dry in cellophane packages, cook very quickly, and can simply be added to very hot broth or soaked and cooked briefly in boiling water.

bake   To cook in a dry oven. Dry-heat cooking often results in a crisping of the exterior of the food being cooked. Moist-heat cooking, through methods such as steaming, poaching, etc., brings a much different, moist quality to the food.

baking powder   A dry ingredient used to increase volume and lighten or leaven baked goods.

balsamic vinegar   Vinegar produced primarily in Italy from a specific type of grape and aged in wood barrels. It's heavier, darker, and sweeter than most vinegars.

basil   A flavorful, almost sweet, resinous herb delicious with tomatoes and used in all kinds of Italian- and Mediterranean-style dishes.

basmati rice   Fragrant, white or brown, long-grained rice from India.

baste   To keep foods moist during cooking by spooning, brushing, or drizzling with a liquid.

bay leaf   Bay leaves add a distinctive flavor to braises, soups, and stews. They're usually sold dried. They should be removed before serving because they are bitter and chewy and can be a potential choking hazard.

beat   To quickly mix substances.

Belgian endive   *See* endive.

blacken   To cook something quickly in a very hot skillet over high heat, usually with a seasoning mixture.

blanch   To place a food in boiling water for about 1 minute or less to partially cook the exterior and then submerge in or rinse with cool water to halt the cooking.

blend   To completely mix something, usually with a blender or food processor, slower than beating.

boil   To heat a liquid to the point where water is forced to turn into steam, causing the liquid to bubble. To boil something is to insert it into boiling water or bring it to a boil with the water. A rapid boil is when a lot of bubbles form on the surface of the liquid.

bok choy   A member of the cabbage family with thick stems, crisp texture, and fresh flavor. It's perfect for stir-frying. Also called napa cabbage.

bouillon   Dried essence of stock from chicken, beef, vegetables, or other ingredients. It's a popular starting ingredient for soups because it adds flavor (and often a lot of salt).

braise   To cook with the introduction of some liquid, usually over an extended period of time.

brine   A highly salted, often seasoned, liquid used to flavor and preserve foods. To brine a food is to soak, or preserve, it by submerging it in brine. When soaking meat, the salt in the brine penetrates the fibers of the meat and makes it moist and tender.

broil   To cook in a dry oven under the overhead high-heat element.

broth   *See* stock.

brown   To cook in a skillet, turning, until the food's surface is seared and brown in color, to lock in the juices.

brown rice   A whole-grain rice, including the germ, with a characteristic pale brown or tan color. It's more nutritious and flavorful than white rice.

bruschetta (or **crostini**)   Slices of toasted or grilled bread with garlic and olive oil, often with other toppings.

bulgur   A wheat kernel that's been steamed, dried, and crushed and is sold in fine and coarse textures.

cake flour   A high-starch, soft, and fine flour used primarily for cakes.

canapé   A bite-size hors d'oeuvre usually served on a small piece of bread or toast.

caper   The flavorful buds of a Mediterranean plant, ranging in size from *nonpareil* (about the size of a small pea) to larger, grape-size caper berries produced in Spain.

caramelize   To cook sugar over low heat until it develops a sweet caramel flavor, or to cook vegetables (especially onions) or meat in butter or oil over low heat until they soften, sweeten, and develop a caramel color.

caraway   A distinctive spicy seed used for bread, pork, cheese, and cabbage dishes. It's known to reduce stomach upset, which is why it's often paired with foods like sauerkraut.

cardamom   An intense, sweet-smelling spice used in baking and coffee and common in Indian cooking.

carob   A tropical tree that produces long pods from which the dried, baked, and powdered flesh—carob powder—is used in baking. The flavor is sweet and reminiscent of chocolate.

cayenne   A fiery spice made from hot chile peppers, especially the cayenne chile, a slender, red, and very hot pepper.

ceviche   A seafood dish in which fresh fish or seafood is marinated for several hours in highly acidic lemon or lime juice, tomato, onion, and cilantro. The acid "cooks" the seafood.

chevre   A creamy-salty soft goat cheese. Chevres vary in style from mild and creamy to aged, firm, and flavorful.

chickpea (or **garbanzo bean**)   A roundish yellow-gold bean used as the base ingredient in hummus. Chickpeas are high in fiber and low in fat.

chiffonade   Finely shredded leafy vegetables (basil, spinach, sage, and lettuce, for example) sometimes used as a garnish for soup. The leaves are stacked and sliced delicately to produce long, thin, uniform strips.

chile (or **chili**)   Any one of many different "hot" peppers, ranging in intensity from the relatively mild ancho pepper to the blisteringly hot habanero.

chili powder   A warm, rich seasoning blend that includes chile pepper, cumin, garlic, and oregano.

Chinese five-spice powder   A pungent mixture of equal parts cinnamon, cloves, fennel seed, anise, and Szechuan peppercorns.

chipotle peppers in adobo   Jalapeño peppers that have been smoked until they're brown and shriveled. Their flavor loses its intense heat in the process and becomes somewhat chocolaty. The adobo sauce they're sometimes canned in is dark red and made of marinated ground red peppers and herbs.

chive   A member of the onion family, chives grow in bunches of long leaves that resemble tall grass or the green tops of onions and offer a light onion flavor.

chop   To cut into pieces, usually qualified by an adverb such as "*coarsely* chopped" or by a size measurement such as "chopped into $1/_2$-inch pieces." "Finely chopped" is much closer to minced.

chorizo   A spiced pork sausage that can be eaten alone or as a component in many recipes, usually Mexican.

chutney   A thick condiment often served with Indian curries made with fruits and/or vegetables with vinegar, sugar, and spices.

cider vinegar   A vinegar produced from apple cider, popular in North America.

cilantro   A member of the parsley family used in Mexican dishes (especially salsa) and some Asian dishes. Use in moderation because the flavor can overwhelm. The seed of the cilantro plant is the spice coriander.

cinnamon   A rich, aromatic spice commonly used in baking or desserts. Cinnamon can also be used for delicious and interesting entrées.

clove   A sweet, strong, almost wintergreen-flavor spice used in baking.

coconut milk   Popular in Thai dishes, coconut milk is made by simmering equal parts water and shredded coconut until it foams and then straining the liquid through cheesecloth. The pulp can be discarded, and the "milk" used in a variety of dishes.

compote   Fruit that has been cooked slowly in a simple syrup so it retains its shape and then chilled.

coriander   A rich, warm, spicy seed used in all types of recipes, from African to South American, from entrées to desserts.

cornstarch   A thickener used in baking and food processing. It's the refined starch of the endosperm of the corn kernel. To avoid clumps, it's often mixed with cold liquid to make into a paste before adding to a recipe.

count   In terms of seafood or other foods that come in small sizes, the number of that item that compose 1 pound. For example, 31 to 40 count shrimp are large appetizer shrimp often served with cocktail sauce; 51 to 60 count are much smaller.

couscous   Granular semolina (durum wheat) that's cooked and used in many Mediterranean and North African dishes.

cream   To beat a fat such as butter, often with another ingredient such as sugar, to soften and aerate a batter.

crème fraîche   A smooth, creamy dairy product similar to sour cream but richer and less acidic. It can be heated in sauces and stews without curdling or used in place of whipped cream on desserts or fruit.

crimini mushroom   A relative of the white button mushroom that's brown in color and has a richer flavor. The larger, fully grown version is the portobello. *See also* portobello mushroom.

crudité   Fresh vegetables served as an appetizer, often all together on one tray.

cumin   A fiery, smoky-tasting spice popular in Middle Eastern and Indian dishes. Cumin is a seed; ground cumin seed is the most common form used in cooking.

cure   To preserve uncooked foods, usually meats or fish, by either salting and smoking or pickling.

curry   Rich, spicy, Indian-style sauces and the dishes prepared with them. A curry uses curry powder as its base seasoning.

curry powder   A ground blend of rich and flavorful spices used as a basis for curry and many other Indian-influenced dishes. Common ingredients include hot pepper, nutmeg, cumin, cinnamon, pepper, and turmeric. Some curry can also be found in paste form.

custard   A cooked mixture of eggs and milk popular as a base for desserts.

daikon radish   Large, sweet, and firm Japanese radish. Daikons are shaped more like a parsnip or large carrot than the root vegetable most Americans recognize as the radish. They can be cream colored or black on the outside and crispy and white on the inside. They're good raw, such as in salads, or cooked.

dash   A few drops, usually of a liquid, released by a quick shake.

deglaze   To scrape up bits of meat and seasoning left in a pan or skillet after cooking. Usually this is done by adding a liquid such as wine or broth and creating a flavorful stock that can be used to create sauces.

delicata squash   An oval winter squash with a delicate green and white skin; sometimes they're yellow-orange on the outside, like their flesh, without many noticeable markings. Look for dense, firm squashes. The easiest way to prepare the delicata is to bake it, although it can be cooked in a variety of ways.

devein   To remove the dark vein from the back of shrimp with a sharp knife.

dice   To cut into small cubes about $\frac{1}{4}$-inch square.

Dijon mustard   A hearty, spicy mustard made in the style of the Dijon region of France.

dill   An herb perfect for eggs, salmon, cheese dishes, and, of course, vegetables (pickles!).

dollop   A spoonful of something creamy and thick, like sour cream or whipped cream.

double boiler   A set of two pots designed to nest together, one inside the other, and provide consistent, moist heat for foods that need delicate treatment. The bottom pot holds water (not quite touching the bottom of the top pot); the top pot holds the food you want to heat.

dredge   To coat a piece of food on all sides with a dry substance such as flour or cornmeal.

drizzle   To lightly sprinkle drops of a liquid over food, often as the finishing touch to a dish.

edamame   Fresh, plump, immature soybeans, similar in color to lima beans, often served steamed and either shelled or still in their protective pods.

emulsion   A combination of liquid ingredients that don't normally mix well (such as a fat or oil with water) that are beaten together to create a thick liquid. Creating emulsions must be done carefully and rapidly to ensure the particles of one ingredient are suspended in the other.

endive   A green that resembles a small, elongated, tightly packed head of romaine lettuce. The thick, crunchy leaves can be broken off and used with dips and spreads.

entrée   The main dish in a meal.

extra-virgin olive oil   *See* olive oil.

extract   A concentrated flavoring derived from foods or plants through evaporation or distillation that imparts a powerful flavor without altering the volume or texture of a dish.

falafel   A Middle Eastern food made of seasoned, ground chickpeas formed into balls, fried, and often used as a filling in pitas.

fennel   In seed form, a fragrant, licorice-tasting herb. The bulbs have a mild flavor and a celery-like crunch and are used as a vegetable in salads or cooked recipes.

flour   Grains ground into a meal. Wheat is perhaps the most common flour, but oats, rye, buckwheat, soybeans, chickpeas, etc., can also be used. *See also* all-purpose flour; cake flour; whole-wheat flour.

fold   To combine a dense and a light mixture with a circular action from the middle of the bowl.

frittata   A skillet-cooked mixture of eggs and other ingredients that's not stirred but is cooked slowly and then either flipped or finished under the broiler.

fry   *See* sauté.

garlic   A member of the onion family, a pungent and flavorful vegetable used in many savory dishes. A garlic bulb contains multiple cloves. Each clove, when chopped, provides about 1 teaspoon garlic.

ginger   A flavorful root available fresh or dried and ground that adds a pungent, sweet, and spicy quality to a dish.

Greek yogurt   A strained yogurt that's a good natural source of protein, calcium, and probiotics. Greek yogurt averages 40 percent more protein per ounce than traditional yogurt.

handful   An inexact measurement, it's the amount of an ingredient you can hold in your hand.

hearts of palm   Firm, elongated, off-white cylinders from the inside of a palm tree stem tip.

herbes de Provence   A seasoning mix of basil, fennel, marjoram, rosemary, sage, and thyme common in the south of France.

hoisin sauce   A sweet Asian condiment similar to ketchup made with soybeans, sesame, chile peppers, and sugar.

hors d'oeuvre   French for "outside of work" (the "work" being the main meal), an hors d'oeuvre can be any dish served as a starter before a meal.

horseradish   A sharp, spicy root that forms the flavor base in condiments such as cocktail sauce and sharp mustards. Prepared horseradish contains vinegar and oil, among other ingredients. Use pure horseradish much more sparingly than the prepared version, or try cutting it with sour cream.

hulled   The process of removing the hull, the outside of a grain, fruit, or nut. With a strawberry, the hull is the green end.

hummus   A thick, Middle Eastern spread made of puréed chickpeas, lemon juice, olive oil, garlic, and tahini.

infusion   A liquid in which flavorful ingredients such as herbs have been soaked or steeped to extract their flavor into the liquid.

Italian seasoning   A blend of dried herbs, including basil, oregano, rosemary, and thyme.

Jasmine rice   An aromatic, white or brown, long-grained rice native to Thailand.

jicama   A juicy, crunchy, sweet, large, round Central American vegetable. If you can't find jicama, try substituting sliced water chestnuts.

julienne   A French word meaning "to slice into very thin pieces."

Kaffir lime leaf   Used in Thai food, Kaffir lime leaves are shiny and dark green on the top and softer green on the underside. They look like two ovals attached tip to tip. Their aroma and flavor are citrusy.

kalamata olive   Traditionally from Greece, a medium-small, long, black olive with a rich, smoky flavor.

Key lime   A very small lime grown primarily in Florida and known for its tart taste.

knead   To work dough to make it pliable so it holds gas bubbles as it bakes. Kneading is fundamental in the process of making yeast breads.

kosher salt   A coarse-grained salt made without any additives or iodine.

lemongrass   This tropical grass is largely used in Asian cooking. Lemongrass looks somewhat like scallions but, as the name suggests, has a lemony fragrance and flavor.

lentil   A tiny lens-shape pulse used in European, Middle Eastern, and Indian cuisines.

marinate   To soak meat, seafood, or another food in a seasoned sauce (a marinade) that's high in acid content. The acids break down the muscle of the meat, making it tender and adding flavor.

marjoram   A sweet herb, cousin of and similar to oregano, popular in Greek, Spanish, and Italian dishes.

meld   To allow flavors to blend and spread over time. Melding is often why recipes call for overnight refrigeration and is also why some dishes taste better as leftovers.

meringue   A baked mixture of sugar and beaten egg whites, often used as a dessert topping.

mesclun   Mixed salad greens, usually containing lettuce and other assorted greens such as arugula, cress, and endive.

millet   A tiny, round, yellow-colored, nutty-flavored grain often used as a replacement for couscous.

mince   To cut into very small pieces, smaller than diced, about $\frac{1}{8}$ inch or smaller.

mirepoix   A mixture of diced aromatic vegetables (onions, carrots, celery) and herbs, usually sautéed in butter, that's added to a variety of foods such as stews or braises.

mirin   Sweet, mild rice wine used in Japanese cooking.

miso   A fermented, flavorful soybean paste, key in many Japanese dishes.

mouthfeel   The overall sensation in the mouth resulting from a combination of a food's temperature, taste, smell, and texture.

mung bean sprout   Common bean sprouts used in all types of cooking, notably in Asian cooking and salads. The bean itself is tiny, usually with a pale green exterior and a yellow inside.

nutmeg   A sweet, fragrant, musky spice used primarily in baking.

olive   The fruit of the olive tree commonly grown on all sides of the Mediterranean. Black olives are also called ripe olives. Green olives are immature, although they're also widely eaten. *See also* kalamata olive.

olive oil   A fragrant liquid produced by crushing or pressing olives. Extra-virgin olive oil—the most flavorful and highest quality—is produced from the first pressing of a batch of olives; oil is also produced from later pressings.

oregano   A fragrant, slightly astringent herb used in Greek, Spanish, and Italian dishes.

orzo   A rice-shape pasta used in Greek cooking.

oxidation   The browning of fruit flesh that happens over time and with exposure to air. Minimize oxidation by rubbing the cut surfaces with lemon juice.

paella   A Spanish dish of rice, shellfish, onion, meats, rich broth, and herbs.

palm sugar   Granular brown sweetener made from the sap of the coconut palm. Like agave syrup, this sweetener is lower on the glycemic index than cane sugar.

panko   A unique variety of breadcrumbs used primarily in Japanese cooking for frying that results in a light, crispy texture.

paprika   A rich, red, warm, earthy spice that lends a rich red color to many dishes.

parboil   To partially cook in boiling water or broth.

parsley   A fresh-tasting green leafy herb, often used as a garnish.

pâté   A savory loaf that contains meats, poultry, or seafood; spices; and often a lot of fat. It's served cold and spread or sliced on crusty bread or crackers.

Pecorino Romano   A hard, sharp Italian cheese made from sheep's milk.

pesto   A thick spread or sauce made with fresh basil leaves, garlic, olive oil, pine nuts, and Parmesan cheese.

pilaf   A rice dish in which the rice is browned in butter or oil and then cooked in a flavorful liquid such as a broth, often with the addition of meats or vegetables. The rice absorbs the broth, resulting in a savory dish.

pinch   An unscientific measurement for the amount of an ingredient—typically, a dry, granular substance such as an herb or seasoning—you can hold between your finger and thumb.

pine nut   A nut that's rich (high in fat), flavorful, and a bit pine-y. Pine nuts are a traditional ingredient in pesto and add a hearty crunch to many other recipes.

pita bread   A flat, hollow wheat bread often used for sandwiches or sliced pizza style. They're terrific soft with dips or baked or broiled as a vehicle for other ingredients.

pizza stone   A flat stone that, when preheated with the oven, cooks crusts to a crispy, pizza-parlor texture.

poach   To cook a food in simmering liquid such as water, wine, or broth.

polenta   A mush made from cornmeal that can be eaten hot with butter or cooked until firm and cut into squares.

porcini mushroom   A rich and flavorful mushroom used in rice and Italian-style dishes.

portobello mushroom   A mature and larger form of the smaller crimini mushroom. Brown, chewy, and flavorful, portobellos are often served as whole caps, grilled, or as thin sautéed slices. *See also* crimini mushroom.

preheat   To turn on an oven, broiler, or other cooking appliance in advance of cooking so the temperature will be at the desired level when the assembled dish is ready for cooking.

prosciutto   A dry, salt-cured ham that originated in Italy.

purée   To reduce a food to a thick, creamy texture, typically using a blender or food processor.

quinoa   A nutty-flavored seed that's extremely high in protein and calcium.

reduce   To boil or simmer a broth or sauce to remove some of the water content, resulting in more concentrated flavor and color.

render   To cook a meat to the point where its fat melts and can be removed.

reserve   To hold a specified ingredient for another use later in the recipe.

rice vinegar   Vinegar produced from fermented rice or rice wine, popular in Asian-style dishes. (It's not the same thing as rice wine vinegar.)

rice wrapper   Rice wrappers, or rice papers, are made of rice flour and often look like very thin, silvery, translucent discs, although they come in a variety of shapes and sizes. They're used for wrapping fresh spring rolls, among other things. They must be soaked in very hot water before using until they're pliable and sticky.

risotto   A popular Italian rice dish made by browning arborio rice in butter or oil and then slowly adding liquid to cook the rice, resulting in a creamy texture.

roast   To cook something uncovered in an oven, usually without additional liquid.

rosemary   A pungent, sweet herb used with chicken, pork, fish, and especially lamb. A little goes a long way.

roux   A mixture of butter or another fat and flour used to thicken sauces and soups.

saffron   An expensive spice made from the stamens of crocus flowers. Saffron lends a dramatic yellow color and distinctive flavor to a dish. Use only tiny amounts.

sage   An herb with a musty yet fruity, lemon-rind scent and "sunny" flavor.

sake   A sweet rice wine from Japan that's brewed rather than fermented.

sauté   To pan-cook over lower heat than what's used for frying.

savory   A popular herb with a fresh, woody taste. Can also describe the flavor of food.

scald   To heat milk just until it's about to boil and then remove it from heat. Scalding milk helps prevent it from souring.

scant   An ingredient measurement directive not to add any extra, perhaps even leaving the measurement a tad short.

sear   To quickly brown the exterior of a food, especially meat, over high heat.

serrano pepper   Hotter than the jalapeño, but not quite as hot as the cayenne, unripe serrano peppers are green but also can be red, orange, or yellow. They can be eaten raw or chopped and cooked to give a zing to soups and stews.

sesame oil   An oil made from pressing sesame seeds. It's tasteless if clear and aromatic and flavorful if brown.

shallot   A member of the onion family that grows in a bulb somewhat like garlic but has a milder onion flavor. When a recipe calls for shallot, use the entire bulb.

shellfish   A broad range of seafood, including clams, mussels, oysters, crabs, shrimp, and lobster.

shiitake mushroom   A large, dark brown mushroom with a hearty, meaty flavor. It can be used fresh or dried, grilled, as a component in recipes, or as a flavoring source for broth.

short-grain rice   A starchy rice popular in Asian-style dishes because it readily clumps, making it perfect for eating with chopsticks.

simmer   To boil a liquid gently so it barely bubbles.

skillet (also **frying pan**)   A generally heavy, flat-bottomed, metal pan with a handle designed to cook food over heat on a stovetop or campfire.

skim   To remove fat or other material from the top of liquid.

slurry   The result of adding water to flour to reach a pancake batter–like consistency. It is whisked into stews or sauces to thicken them.

soft peak   The consistency of egg whites when they're beaten for a period of time. At soft peak stage, the whites harden enough to form little waves or peaks that barely hold their shape, as opposed to stiff peaks, which would be used for meringue.

sport peppers   Small, green, spicy peppers that are packed, whole, in jars and used in Southern cooking. They're similar in hotness to the tobacco pepper.

sprig   A small stem with leaves, as in parsley or another fresh herb, used as a garnish.

star anise   The seedpod of an Asian evergreen that looks like a brown eight-point star and has a sharp licorice flavor. It's one of the ingredients in Chinese five-spice powder and is used in baked goods and teas.

steam   To suspend a food over boiling water and allow the heat of the steam (water vapor) to cook the food. This quick-cooking method preserves a food's flavor and texture.

steep   To let sit in hot water, as in steeping tea in hot water for 10 minutes.

stew   To slowly cook pieces of food submerged in a liquid. Also, a dish prepared by this method.

sticky rice   *See* short-grain rice.

stir-fry   To cook small pieces of food in a wok or skillet over high heat, moving and turning the food quickly to cook all sides.

stock   A flavorful broth made by cooking meats and/or vegetables with seasonings until the liquid absorbs these flavors. The liquid is strained, and the solids are discarded. Stock can be eaten alone or used as a base for soups, stews, etc.

strata   A savory bread pudding made with eggs and cheese.

Swiss chard   One of the most vitamin- and mineral-packed vegetables, chard comes in several varieties, but all are green and leafy with defined stalks. Swiss chard has white stalks and large, dark green leaves. It can be steamed, sautéed, or braised.

tahini   A paste made from sesame seeds used to flavor many Middle Eastern recipes.

tamarind   A sweet, pungent, flavorful fruit used in Indian-style sauces and curries.

tapas   A Spanish term meaning "small plate" that describes individual-size appetizers and snacks served cold or warm.

tapenade   A thick, chunky spread made from savory ingredients such as olives, lemon juice, and anchovies.

tarragon   A sweet, rich-smelling herb perfect with seafood, vegetables (especially asparagus), chicken, and pork.

tempeh   An Indonesian food made by culturing and fermenting soybeans into a cake, sometimes mixed with grains or vegetables. It's high in protein and fiber.

teriyaki   A Japanese-style sauce composed of soy sauce, rice wine, ginger, and sugar that works well with seafood as well as most meats.

thyme   A minty, zesty herb.

tofu   A cheeselike substance made from soybeans and soy milk.

trimmed   Cut to uniform size. Or removed of unwanted fat in the case of meat, or of unsavory parts, as in vegetable or fruit trimming.

turmeric   A spicy, pungent, yellow root used in many dishes, especially Indian cuisine, for color and flavor. Turmeric is the source of the yellow color in many prepared mustards.

tzatziki   A Greek dip traditionally made with Greek yogurt, cucumbers, garlic, and mint.

veal   Meat from a calf, generally characterized by its mild flavor and tenderness.

vegetable steamer   An insert with tiny holes in the bottom designed to fit on or in another pot to hold food to be steamed above boiling water. *See also* steam.

venison   Deer meat.

vinegar   An acidic liquid widely used as a dressing or seasoning, often made from fermented grapes, apples, or rice. *See also* balsamic vinegar; cider vinegar; rice vinegar; white vinegar; wine vinegar.

wasabi   Japanese horseradish, a fiery, pungent condiment used with many Japanese-style dishes. It's most often sold as a powder to which you add water to create a paste.

water chestnut   A white, crunchy, and juicy tuber popular in many Asian dishes. It holds its texture whether cool or hot.

whisk   To rapidly mix, introducing air to the mixture.

white mushroom   A button mushroom. When fresh, white mushrooms have an earthy smell and an appealing soft crunch.

white vinegar   The most common type of vinegar, produced from grain.

whole grain   A grain derived from the seeds of grasses, including rice, oats, rye, wheat, wild rice, quinoa, barley, buckwheat, bulgur, corn, millet, amaranth, and sorghum.

whole-wheat flour   Wheat flour that contains the entire grain.

wild rice   Not a rice at all, this grass has a rich, nutty flavor and serves as a nutritious side dish.

wine vinegar   Vinegar produced from red or white wine.

yeast   Tiny fungi that, when mixed with water, sugar, flour, and heat, release carbon dioxide bubbles, which, in turn, cause the bread to rise.

zest   Small slivers of peel, usually from a citrus fruit such as a lemon, lime, or orange.

Resources

Whenever you're trying something new, it's great to have additional resources to turn to for more information. You never know when you'll find an idea that can change your life. In this appendix, we've included additional books and websites that can provide you with the latest information, new recipes, and more.

Books

Blatner, Dawn Jackson. *The Flexitarian Diet: The Mostly Vegetarian Way to Lose Weight, Be Healthier, Prevent Disease, and Add Years to Your Life.* Columbus, OH: McGraw-Hill, 2010.

Clark, Nancy. *Nancy Clark's Sports Nutrition Guidebook.* Champaign, IL: Human Kinetics, 2008.

Duyff, Roberta Larsen. *The American Dietetic Association's Complete Food and Nutrition Guide, Third Edition.* New York, NY: John Wiley & Sons, 2006.

Gans, Keri. *The Small Change Diet: 10 Steps to a Thinner, Healthier You.* New York, NY: Gallery, 2011.

Grotto, David. *101 Foods That Could Save Your Life.* New York, NY: Bantam, 2010.

Institute of Medicine. *Dietary Reference Intakes: The Essential Guide to Nutrient Requirements.* Washington, DC: The National Academies Press, 2006.

McIndoo, Heidi Reichenberger. *The Pocket Idiot's Guide to Superfoods.* Indianapolis, IN: Alpha Books, 2007.

———. *When to Eat What.* Avon, MA: Adams Media, 2011.

Taub-Dix, Bonnie. *Read It Before You Eat It: How to Decode Food Labels and Make the Healthiest Choice Every Time.* New York, NY: Plume, 2010.

Tessmer, Kimberly, and Stephanie Green. *The Complete Idiot's Guide to the Mediterranean Diet.* Indianapolis, IN: Alpha Books, 2010.

Ward, Elizabeth. *MyPlate for Moms, How to Feed Yourself and Your Family Better: Decoding the Dietary Guidelines for Your Real Life.* Reading, MA: Loughlin Press, 2011.

Zied, Elisa. *Nutrition at Your Fingertips.* Indianapolis, IN: Alpha Books, 2009.

Websites

Academy of Nutrition and Dietetics
eatright.org

Around the Plate
aroundtheplate.org

Choose My Plate (U.S. Department of Agriculture)
choosemyplate.gov

Nutrition Babes
NutritionBabes.com

The Nutrition Experts
thenutritionexperts.com

U.S. Department of Health and Human Services
healthierus.gov/dietaryguidelines

The Zied Guide
elisazied.com

Index

Numbers

A

B

H

I

J–K

L

M

P

Q

R

W–X–Y–Z